THE CARTOGRAPHIC

THE CARTOGRAPHIC EYE
How Explorers Saw Australia

SIMON RYAN

Arts and Sciences
Australian Catholic University

CAMBRIDGE
UNIVERSITY PRESS

Published by the Press Syndicate of the University of Cambridge
The Pitt Building, Trumpington Street, Cambridge CB2 1RP, UK
40 West 20th Street, New York, NY 10011–4211, USA
10 Stamford Road, Oakleigh, Melbourne 3166, Australia

Printed in Hong Kong by Colorcraft

National Library of Australia cataloguing-in-publication data
Ryan, Simon, 1964– .
The cartographic eye: how explorers saw Australia.
Bibliography.
Includes index.
1. Explorers – Australia – Diaries. 2. Geographical
perception – Australia. 3. Landscape assessment –
Australia. 4. Cognition and culture. 5. Australia –
Discovery and exploration. I. Title.
304.23

Library of Congress cataloguing-in-publication data
Ryan, Simon, 1964–
The cartographic eye: how explorers saw Australia / Simon Ryan.
p.   cm.
Includes bibliographical references and index.
1. Australia – Discovery and exploration – Historiography.
2. Australia – History – 1788–1900 – Historiography. 3. Explorers –
Australia – Historiography. I. Title.
DU97.R94 1996
994.01–dc20   96–20910

A catalogue record for this book is available from the British Library.

ISBN 0 521 57112 X Hardback
ISBN 0 521 57791 8 Paperback

Cover illustrations:
Country NW of tableland, Aug. 22 (detail); by S. T. Gill, ca. 1846.
Courtesy National Library of Australia.
Bultje (detail); drawing by Mitchell. From Thomas Mitchell,
Journal of an Expedition into the Interior of Tropical Australia.
Courtesy Mitchell Library, State Library of New South Wales.

For my parents

Contents

Illustrations

Acknowledgments

Much of the research for this book was completed while I was a doctoral student in the Department of English, University of Queensland, from 1989 to 1992. I owe the department a debt of gratitude for the support, intellectual and material, it offered me. In particular, Chris Tiffin's seemingly infinite patience, and his unwillingness to allow the passage of glib evasions, has conferred a valuable rigour upon this work. Robert Dixon's kind advice, and the example of his writing, has inspired my interest in nineteenth century Australian culture. To Helen Tiffin I owe my thanks for her efforts in establishing and maintaining postcolonial studies. Alan Lawson, Elizabeth Gee, Laurie Hergenhan, Martin Duwell, Leigh Dale, Chris Lee, Dorothy Seaton, Antoinette Bauer, Susie O'Brien and Delyse Anthony all offered helpful suggestions. Graeme Turner's advice in the early stages of this project, and Bronwy Levy's in its later formation were most valuable.

The later development of this book has taken place at the Australian Catholic University. Its research office has been particularly generous with funds that have made possible much of the research undertaken in the Mitchell Library and the National Library. I am grateful for the assistance of Maureen Strugnell and Mary De Jabrun, and particularly for the optimistic insistence of Louise Edwards.

An early form of part of chapter 3 appeared as 'Exploring Aesthetics: Appropriative Gazing in Journals of Australian Exploration', in *Australian Literary Studies* 15.4 (October) 1992. A section of chapter 2 appeared as 'Discovering Myths: The Creation of the Explorer in Journals of Exploration', in *Australian-Canadian Studies* 12.2 (March) 1994. A version of chapter 4 was published as 'Inscribing the Emptiness: Cartography, exploration and the construction of Australia', in Chris Tiffin and Alan Lawson (eds), *De-Scribing Empire: Post-colonialism and textuality* (London: Routledge, 1994). Parts of chapters 5 and 6 appeared as 'A Word with the Natives: Dialogic Encounters in Journals of Australian Exploration', in *Australian and New Zealand Studies in Canada* (8) March 1993, and 'The Aborigines in Journals of Australian Exploration', in *ARIEL* 25.3 (July) 1994. Sections of chapters 4 and 7 were published as '"Like a map at our feet": visually commanding the land in journals of Australian exploration', in *Southern Review* 27.2 (July) 1994, and 'Voyeurs in Space: The Gendered Scopic Regime of Exploration', in *Southerly* July 1994. The Mitchell Library, State Library of New South Wales, has kindly permitted the reproduction of illustrations.

1

Introduction

Space – the final frontier

One of my favourite books when a child was *The Children's Encyclopedia*. A British periodical, it was compiled and published as an encyclopaedia in several popular editions through the 1930s. *The Children's Encyclopedia* was content to exist within the genre of children's instructional writing of the time. The adult world possessed a collection of facts which could be transmitted to the young reader in discrete parts through maps, pictures, essays and a series of question and answer passages. This last section, entitled 'Plain Answers to the Questions of the Children of the World' included such queries as: 'What is the Great Pitch Lake of Trinidad?', 'What is a Mirage?' and 'Why is a White Man More Civilised than a Black Man?'. If at times the world the encyclopaedia presented seemed to be an accumulation of discrete things, a powerful and unified world view was maintained through the religious and moral instruction that could be found in almost every section. History was essentially a moral struggle; conflict and death, largely the products of moral infirmity. Fortunately, the universe was ordered for progressive improvement under Britain's benevolent tutelage.

One crucial element in this interpellation of the reader into a progressivist ideology was the narrative of the spread of this benign empire. And central to this narrative were voyages of discovery and travels of exploration. *The Children's Encyclopedia* mobilises many of the tropes and rhetorical strategies discussed in this work in order to construct exploration as an heroic practice furthering the frontier of empire, penetrating and conquering unknown and unowned lands. This mythologisation of exploration and individual explorers allows them to be used as a focus for imperial discourses of vigorous, manly expansion

1

and occupation of land. When juxtaposed against the active and courageous individual explorer, an indigenous population, which is usually treated as an undifferentiated mass, is easily portrayed as being composed of lazy wastrels. Farmers and other settlers may also serve this function of contrast, but explorers can carry the ideological burden of the pure motivation. Mythologically, they are driven, not by prospects of material reward, but solely by the quest for knowledge.

The danger of books like *The Children's Encyclopedia* is that they do not spontaneously combust when their ideology is no longer compatible with the culture in which they are produced. A child reader has little basis of comparison and is constructed by the book to unreservedly accept its 'facts'. Thus, as a child I read this about the relationship between the settler and indigenous cultures in Australia:

> The people who lived there when white man arrived, the aborigines, were of such a primitive type, so few and scattered and migratory from place to place, that they could not have been a difficulty. No one could say they really occupied the land. They do not number 100,000, scattered over a continent larger than the United States of America. They were, and are, too backwards either to help or be in the way of progress. As a remnant of very early mankind they are interesting to the student of human progress, but they are not a serious problem.[1]

The excess in the dismissal of the Aborigines ('could not have been a difficulty', 'are not a serious problem'), and the change in tense between these two formulae, points to a continuing guilt about the treatment of the rightful owners of the land. The 'problem' of the Aborigines was not solved by frequent massacres, nor by patriarchal dislocation and placement within missions.

In fact, by the 1980s Aborigines and Torres Strait Islanders had organised themselves to be a very serious 'problem' for non-Aboriginal Australia. In 1982 three Murray Islanders instituted proceedings against the State of Queensland in the High Court of Australia. Eddie Mabo, David Passi and James Rice asserted that the Meriam people had continuously occupied and enjoyed the Murray Islands from time immemorial and had been granted by the State of Queensland traditional native title. They sought a declaration to that effect. The State of Queensland responded by passing the Queensland Coast Islands Declaratory Act 1985, which stated that, upon annexation, all previous rights were removed and that the islands were considered waste lands of the Crown of Queensland, and that no compensation was payable for any rights pre-existing annexation. The High Court found in 1988 that such a statute contravened the 1975 Racial Discrimination Act and therefore failed: unilateral State legislation could not remove native title if it existed. In

1992 the High Court ruled that native title did exist in common law, its source being the traditional occupation of land. It also ruled that, because of the obligations imposed by the Racial Discrimination Act, native title could only be extinguished with compensation.

In positing that such a ruling was applicable to the mainland the High Court unleashed the 'Mabo debate', which continued through the passing of what is commonly known as the 'Mabo legislation'. Henry Reynolds has thoroughly covered the nineteenth century legal background to the colonial appropriation of land in *Law of the Land* (1987). *The Cartographic Eye* is not about legal definitions of land and property, but about the ideologies that underlie the very possibility of land as property. In particular, it focuses on the colonial moment when there is widespread appropriation of land. And even more specifically it interrogates the writings of those figures – the explorers – who are icons of the discovery of 'new' lands to be occupied.

This interrogation is far from being an isolated intellectual exercise, nor is it simply an autopsy of a deceased genre. Ongoing land rights debates force European Australia to reconsider foundation myths, including the mythologies of exploration. A report in the Brisbane *Courier-Mail* illustrates some of the difficulties in reforming an area which is created by its own lexicon: words such as 'discover', 'conquer' and 'possess', while not unique to exploration, form a large part of the vocabulary used to discuss it as a practice. The *Courier-Mail* reported on the rewriting of a Year Five social studies textbook, which occurred on the ground that it was demeaning to Aborigines.[2] Part of the problem with the source book was that it reproduced William Dampier's description of west coast Aborigines as the 'miserablest people in the world'. 'His observations', the textbook continues, 'remained the most detailed description of the Western Australian Aborigines for well over a century'. The textbook fails to offer a critique of Dampier's attitude, and indeed produces him as a credible authority.

This case opens many questions about how the history of exploration should be taught. Excising Dampier from the record entirely is un-satisfactory, as his description is an early example of the hierarchisation of the Aboriginal race and its culture according to perceived material and technological poverty. But an uncritical inclusion of Dampier as an authority is just as destructive, as it implies his vision is accurate. A letter to the *Courier-Mail* responding to its report argued that 'the careful observations of William Dampier in 1688 concerning the desolate West Australia and the people he saw there' should not be ignored.[3] Dampier's observations were undoubtedly 'careful'; but, as this work will show, the writing of these observations is, and must always be, intractably caught up in pre-existent tropes and stereotypes. There can be no question that any particular description possesses 'accuracy'; rather, descriptions are produced as accurate by the genre in which they are found, and by the way in which they articulate with other discourses.

As well as the proto-ethnography of the journals this book discusses the ways in which they create space. In discussing the 'creation' of space I am taking an anti-essentialist point of view. I do not seek to deny that space exists or that the Australian desert is very big. Rather, I argue that once one begins to describe land, to talk about space, one is involved in a cultural and linguistic activity that cannot refer outside itself to an unmediated reality.

Space has usually been categorised in one of two ways. There is the absolute space of geometry, cartography and physics, and there is the relative space of individual cognitive mapping and landscape appreciation. This categorisation of space into the objective and the personal constructs a duality which ignores how space is socially produced. Edward Soja has argued that space is produced mentally, physically and *socially*, and that this three-part schema allows a more complex theorisation of the relationship between these elements.[4] Both ideational and physical space must be seen as in part socially produced: the individual's notion of space is determined by his or her socialisation, and the theorisation of an absolute space (or the architectural construction of spaces) takes place through institutions of society.[5] This book discusses space as it is socially produced in the context of the colonial enterprise.

The space of empire is universal, Euclidean and Cartesian, a measurable mathematical web constructed and maintained by positivism. This space is understood as objectively being 'out there', a natural state, alternatives to which are difficult to imagine. This commonsense view of space does not have to be accepted as objective 'fact' however; it can be seen to be a belief naturalised by a certain social arrangement in such a way that this works in its favour. Soja remarks that time and space 'like the commodity form, the competitive market, and the structure of social classes, are represented as a natural relation between things, and are explainable objectively in terms of the substantive physical properties and attributes of these things in themselves'.[6] The imperial endeavour encourages the construction of space as a universal, mensurable and divisible entity, for this is a self-legitimising view of the world. If it were admitted that different cultures produced different spaces, then negotiating these would be difficult, if not impossible. Constructing a monolithic space, on the other hand, allows imperialism to hierarchise the use of space to its own advantage. In imperial ideology the Aborigines do not have a different space to that of the explorers; rather, they under-utilise the space imperialism understands as absolute. The construction of a universal space also allows a homogeneous mapping practice to be applied to all parts of the world: maps become an imperial technology used to facilitate and celebrate the further advances of explorers, and display worldwide imperial possessions.

The explorers are ostensibly at the vanguard of the establishment of a colonial space. They measure the course of rivers, the coastline, a range of mountains – inserting all objects into the coordinates of Cartesian space. The mythology of exploration constructs explorers as the 'first' to see 'new' continents, but I shall argue that their production is merely a rewriting of a space which already exists in early cultural constructs of an austral continent.

The explorers' own spatial construction (or re-construction) takes place primarily through specular means. John Coetzee's *Dusklands*, the fictional journal of the explorer Jacobus Coetzee, best explains the dynamic of this specular method.

> In the wild I lose my sense of boundaries. This is a consequence of space and solitude. The operation of space is thus the five senses stretched out from the body they inhabit, but four stretch into a vacuum. The ear cannot hear, the nose cannot smell, the tongue cannot taste, the skin cannot feel ... Only the eyes have power. The eyes are free, they reach out to the horizon all around. Nothing is hidden from the eyes. As the other senses grow numb or dumb my eyes flex and extend themselves. I become a spherical reflecting eye moving through the wilderness, and ingesting it. Destroyer of the wilderness, I move through the land cutting a devouring path from horizon to horizon. There is nothing from which my eye turns, I am all that I see ... What is there that is not me ? I am a transparent sac with a black core full of images ...[7]

In *Dusklands* John Coetzee presents the explorer as someone who finds self-identification only through distinguishing (and killing) the other. Killing is a way of controlling the 'other', the wilderness – 'every wild creature I kill crosses the boundary between wilderness and number', writes Jacobus Coetzee. Self-identification, then, proceeds from this understanding of oneself as being in the world, yet separate from it. In the case of the explorer this setting up of boundaries between self and other takes place through a fundamentally specular axis. Exploration is primarily a visual activity, aimed at determining through mensuration the dimensions of the outside via an act that simultaneously determines the self as objective observer. Yet, there is, clearly, a confusion of boundaries for the explorer. Jacobus Coetzee asks 'what is there that is not me?'. I will suggest that this is the question that exploration never asks itself. Many of the descriptions, judgements and reactions of the explorers are born in European anxieties; they work through an archive of pre-existent images and tropes, in which the journals (and the authors themselves) have their existence. Explorers often carry the 'outside' with them.

That what they see is somehow part of them must be denied to preserve 'objectivity'. The attitude of the explorers in the journals towards the outside is Cartesian. Space, fixed and Newtonian, may be mathematically proscribed and described by the central observer. Michel de Certeau writes that:

> a Cartesian attitude ... is an effort to delimit one's own place in a world bewitched by the invisible powers of the Other ... It is also a mastery of places through sight. The division of space makes possible a panoptic practice proceeding from a place whence the eye can transform foreign forces into objects that can be observed and measured, and thus control and 'include' them within its scope of vision.[8]

The explorative gaze is a mastery of space. This book is about this gaze, about its discursive construction in the journals and its meaning within the context of the colonial enterprise. Once again Michel de Certeau, describing the Cartesian system's positioning of the observer, describes exactly the explorer's 'point of view':

> His elevation transforms him into a voyeur. It puts him at a distance. It transforms the bewitching world by which one was 'possessed' into a text that lies before one's eyes. It allows one to read it, to be a solar Eye, looking down like a god. The exaltation of a scopic and gnostic drive; the fiction of knowledge is related to this lust to be a viewpoint and nothing more.[9]

This work tracks how the Cartesian stance informs exploration descriptions, and how this outlook is instrumental in discursively constructing itself as the most authoritative viewpoint. Everything which de Certeau mentions as indicative of a Cartesian observer is true of the explorer: he is at times the voyeur 'unveiling' a feminised landscape; a reader of his construction of the land as text; an elevated eye, with a viewpoint regarded as privileged. This privileged 'point of view' is external to the system. Looking down like a god absolves one of complicity with the scene: it is objectively 'there' and the spectator is merely a passive witness, a 'viewpoint and nothing more'. The example *par excellence* of this distanced viewpoint can be found in Henry Morton Stanley's *Through the Dark Continent*.

> From my lofty eyrie I can see herds upon herds of cattle, and many minute specks, white and black, which can be nothing but flocks of sheep and goats. I can also see pale blue columns of ascending smoke from the fires, and upright thin figures moving about. Secure on my lofty throne, I can view their movements, and laugh at the ferocity of the savage hearts which beat in those thin dark figures; for I am a part of Nature now, and for the present as invulnerable as itself. As little do they know that human eyes survey their forms from the summit of this lake-girt isle as that the eyes of the Supreme in heaven are upon them.[10]

This description does not simply construct the explorer's voyeuristic vision; rather, this vision is celebrated. The god-like point of view ascribed to the explorer is instrumental in establishing his view of things as the most accurate, the most complete. The creation of knowledge here through vision – the joining of the scopic and gnostic drives – is celebrated as a moment of power. The explorer is 'secure' on his 'throne' and replete with the knowledge his vision gives him, while the ignorant natives below are objects of vision, and cannot return the gaze. Significantly, the construction of the land as female is disallowed here because Stanley himself is 'part of Nature', a phrase which removes him from the 'scene'. Height takes over as the way in which value is attributed; the vertical hierarchy stands for the hierarchy in the imagined 'chain of being' – the European 'naturally' being stationed higher than the African.

Stanley's vision is an exercise and celebration of visual power; like many 'visions' within explorers' journals, it is also a prospect which looks temporally forward as well as out into space. Stanley muses on the possibility that the hour will come 'when a band of philanthropic capitalists shall vow to rescue these beautiful lands'; he sees the future as one of steamers on the lakes, great trading ports and 'all the countries round about permeated with the nobler ethics of a higher humanity'.[11] The vision as power, then, is also a vision of future power, the exercise of which did not in reality embody the 'nobler ethics of a higher humanity'.

One can align the subject position in Stanley's description with that of de Certeau's formulation of the voyeuristic observer's 'lust to be a viewpoint and nothing more'. Stanley says that he is 'a part of Nature now', effacing his status as alien, European and invader. The Cartesian system attempts to provide a place for the perceiver which is, paradoxically, at once privileged and non-existent; the viewer is 'outside' or 'above' what is viewed, but simultaneously is unimportant, a cypher. What is seen is objectively there, and the veracious discursive transmission of the 'seen' as objective reality depends upon the negation of the particular observer in favour of assertions about scientific or objective writing.

The codification of scientific or objective description must be denied or dismissed in favour of the notion of the text as transparent. This is 'necessarily accompanied by the occultation of the enunciating subject as discursive activity ... Galileo's I becomes Descartes' we'.[12] The 'we' Reiss identifies is a function of the depersonalised style of scientific writing; the individuality of the point of view is hidden in descriptions which begin 'we can see ...'. The institutional theorisation of what a scientific document should be encourages the effacement of the narrator and the related production of textual 'transparency' at the expense of a certain narrative style. This strategy helps deny that scientific documents are in any way perspectival. But this approach breaks down somewhat in the exploration journals, where the explorer himself is an object in the body of knowledge gained. If the explorer is a roving eye like Jacobus Coetzee, then he is transparent to himself. Jonathan Culler argues that:

> the Cartesian cogito, in which self is immediately present to itself, is taken as the basic proof of existence, and things directly perceived are apodictically privileged. Notions of truth and reality are based on a longing for an unfallen world in which there would be no need for the mediating systems of language and perception, but everything would be itself with no gap between form and meaning.[13]

Exploration epistemology, then, depends on the explorer's transparency to himself. That which sees but is not seen is always deferred: this can be traced by looking for the 'outermost' narrative level, where the narrator has a point of view from which he can describe both the land and the explorers within it from a privileged position (an analysis which is undertaken at the end of chapter 2 of this work). A tension is generated between the effacement of the observer and the generic construction of the explorer as a centre of interest. Ultimately, the journal genre itself prevents the establishment of a unified central observer.

Journals of exploration work through generic conventions which assure the reader that what is reported is accurate. But the journals are not dispassionate records with declarative statements such as 'that can be seen', or 'this river turns east here'. Rather, they are personal records, and the descriptions work through first-person statements such as 'I saw this' or 'I followed the river'. The construction of vision in the journals depends intimately on the figure of the explorer: he is at the centre of what he sees, and is at the centre of the narrative (and, in Australia at least, the explorer usually is male, too). The genre of the exploration journal requires the construction of this central voice. It is through this central voice, indeed, that the exploration journal may be differentiated from the travel guide: exploration journals never slip into the travel guide's second-person address of 'on your way to the desert you must see this'. Rather, journals create the heroic explorer, and he is the vehicle for the production of a centralised visual discourse. The genre itself makes this individual vision inevitable; for the explorer/narrator tells the story, and the story in the journals is what is seen during the exploration. It is important for the journals to have this central point of view, as their authority relies on a monolithic and non-contradictory discourse. The problem with polyphonic narration, of course, is that it is exactly this author/ity which is undone. The heroic explorer as created in the journal is more than just self-promotion of the individual involved; it is an essential part of the way in which the journals produce their claim to truth.

Chapter 2 of this book takes up questions of the construction of the explorer; how it is that he is accorded this especially privileged position as truth-teller, and how this is a 'point of view' from which truth is established. In part, the building of this mythology is to give the explorer privileged access to a penetrative vision: 'discovery' itself means an 'unveiling' of the land, where the feminised continent is rendered open to the explorer's gaze. This point of view is the prerogative of the explorer alone. The sealer or the settler may be the first European to view the land, but even if their reactions are recorded they do not have the institutionally granted positions to enter into the mythology of the 'discovering' gaze. Explorers are accorded this position to see because of institutional support.

Discursively, they construct themselves through the canon of explorers, comparing themselves to earlier discoverers, but in their specific historical milieu they are institutionally created as quite different to previous explorers. No longer are they fearfully negotiating the unknown, nor are they (openly) plundering the land for easy riches; now, under the guidance of the Royal Geographic Society, exploration as a practice is recreated as newly scientific venture. I have said that the discourse of vision depends upon the journal's 'heroic explorer', and that this figure is created by the genre of the exploration journal. The genre in turn is partly determined by the institutional pressures which can be applied to it, and its role within the practice of exploration. Chapter 2 examines those institutional strictures applied to journals, and the reward system which ensured journals remain within specific generic guidelines. Finally, chapter 2 shows how examination of the role of the narrator results in a collapse of the unity of the narrator/explorer, and thus of the logic of the journals' production of truth. Explorative epistemology is dependent on the self being immediately present to self, but the journal form disallows the unity of the writer and explorer or of the past and present self. Writing the self becomes an exercise in deferring the final authoritative voice.

The critique of the production of accuracy is continued in chapter 3. It begins by analysing how codes of accuracy and picturesqueness inevitably collide in verbal descriptions and illustrations. The picturesque aesthetic itself is then subject to a critique which, following Ann Bermingham's and Malcolm Andrew's work in particular, identifies an ideological agenda residing in the picturesque. It is, firstly, a European notion belonging to certain class interests; secondly, it constructs vision as a possessive force. Seeing is understood as a mode of appropriation. Hence, the way in which Australian areas are seen as resembling gentleman's parks can be understood, not merely as an attempt to contain the unfamiliar via a comparison with the familiar, but as a way of establishing the land as 'naturally' suited to a reproduction of Britain's land-owning and, therefore, social system.

This work attempts to assign a locus to many different modalities of vision. In this vein, chapter 3 follows the way that constructions of 'the seen' attribute to the viewer a particular privileged location. In pictur-esque illustrations the scene is arranged for the visual pleasure of the spectator – trees being moved to provide a framing device, Aborigines conveniently present to provide an interesting and varied foreground. In the panorama the viewer is positioned at the centre of the world. In cartography, the founding assumption is that the viewer is above the earth and the land, recumbent, is revealed to the viewer.

Chapter 4 investigates the relationship between cartography and viewer-position, and interrogates the way in which the map acts as a semiotic space. Once again the implicit claims to accuracy that maps present can be undermined through an analysis of how they are ideological tools, rather than simply being reflections of a given reality. Examining them as ideological constructs, rather than 'accurate' repre-sentations, enables the tracing of their particular geographies of centre and margin, plenitude and emptiness through time, as a way of showing their effectiveness as constructions. The continuities of maps, and map-inspired notions of the world are displayed by this trans-historical analysis to allow an analysis of the connectivity between medieval and Victorian world-pictures.

This book proceeds from the assumption that there is no rupture between reality and representation, but that representations form reality. 'Discovery' may produce initial disturbance to a particular set of expecta-tions, but what is found through an examination of explorers' journals is how seldom a discovery genuinely surprises. Almost everything seen for the first time has already been, in some way, anticipated. It is as if there is a particular Australian myth that creates an expectaton of the unex-pected. This is the myth of antipodality, where Australia is positioned as a repository of all that is perverse, odd, unexpected. Thus, when something unexpected is found – the kangaroo, for example – it is immediately contained within this field of the expected unexpected. Chapter 4 argues that maps have played a significant role in the pro-duction of the southern continent as a place for projection of European fears and hopes. It is expected that there will be oddities and perversities in the fauna and flora, and that the inhabitants will be likewise perverse, and, of course, uncivilised. Chapter 4 claims that this notion of anti-podality was one map-inspired trope used to explain the Australian inhabitants, and to produce the colonial enterprise as a natural and normalising mission. Another cartographic trope was the southern continent as blank, awaiting colonial inscription; this is also a semiotic construction of a continent, which justifies, indeed urges, European intervention. It is also another way of rendering indigenes as spurious, by ignoring their presence.

Description of the indigenous population was one aim of some of the expeditions. The letter of instructions given to Sturt break up the indigene into a number of discrete characteristics which are to be recorded.

> You will note the description of the several people whom you may meet, the extent of the population, their means of subsistence, their genius and disposition, the nature of their amusements, their diseases and remedies, their objects of worship, religious ceremonies, and a vocabulary of their language. (*Two Expeditions into . . . Southern Australia* 1: 187–88)

The construction of the ethnographic object began with the nineteenth century's newly scientific approach to other populations. There is the continuing pretence in the journals that the new objectivity given by scientific investigation uncouples the explorers' texts from previous tropological constructions of the indigene. But the old tropes remain, and scientific discourse adds a patina of 'accuracy' to the racist judgements of the journals. The native as 'black devil' still remains into the late nineteenth century as an acceptable description, but is accompanied by scientific and pseudo-scientific discourses such as evolutionism and phrenology, which work to position the Aborigine as undeniably inferior. Chapter 4 interrogates ways in which the exploration journals semiotically construct the indigene, and the legal notions of land and possession are examined in chapter 5.

My work on the semiotic formation of the indigene is influenced by Terry Goldie's *Fear and Temptation: The Image of the Indigene in Canadian, Australian and New Zealand Literatures* (1989) but, unlike Goldie, I do not see the construction of the indigene as a system impervious to outside influence. Richard Terdiman's *Discourse/Counter-Discourse: The Theory and Practice of Symbolic Resistance in Nineteenth-Century France* (1985) supplies a way in which the journals' formation of the Aborigine can be seen to deconstruct itself, yet this too sees discourse as a self-sufficient and impervious system. The work of Homi Bhabha has been a significant influence on the discussion of the construction of the indigene in colonial discourses. In a series of articles Bhabha develops the notion of 'hybridity' in colonial discourses. Replacing a simplistic notion of colonial textuality as a system which entirely dominates the indigenes, or which without question constructs the indigene through Western discourses, Bhabha draws attention to the disturbance to European knowledges in the colonial field. Positing colonialism as a complex psychic/textual event, Bhabha relieves analysis of a sterile binarism, and his theories have productively underwritten the section of this work on relations between explorer and Aborigine.

What emerges in the journals is that the formation of the Aborigine fragments at the two points of dialogue and sight. Dialogic encounters display Aborigines as subversive of the place made for them – instead of being humble and childish native interlocutors, the Aborigines emerge as possessors of informational power, the transmission of which is at their discretion. Sight is also a battlefield between explorer and indigene. Here, there is a real struggle for the power that sight confers, and an Aboriginal challenge to the discourse of sight in the journals which creates the explorer as its sole possessor. These are not sentimentalist readings which, by inversion of the usually understood power relationship, attempt to recuperate the journals or make fun of the explorers. Rather they are ways of conceiving of the journals as records of cultural contact, displaying all the racial biases of their authors, but also showing indigenous resistance to imperial interpellatory strategies. Ultimately the indigenes deconstruct the central specular epistemology of exploration by looking back; they destroy the monolithic vision of empire by demonstrating the multiplicity of viewing positions.

Other spaces: histories of exploration

Other travellers
It is the nature of space that its metaphorical uses span many activities. Thought and writing both have their share of spatial metaphors: one travels through a book, arrives at a conclusion, loses oneself in a story. A scholarly work, by being an original analysis, differentiates itself from cognate works. It is the introduction's purpose to create a space for its particular study, staking out its territory, patrolling boundaries and perhaps taking part in dialogue across them.

In *Dark Side of the Dream: Australian Literature and the Postcolonial Mind* (1990), Bob Hodge and Vijay Mishra argue that the impact of the explorer on the popular imagination has been rather slight. They hypothesise that the public monument has been the only successful transmitter of images of exploration to a later generation.[14] A brief tracing of the mythology of exploration can demonstrate a quite different state of affairs. While explorers, it is true, have not been the subject of as foregrounded a set of mythologies as convicts, swagmen or bushrangers, they nevertheless have formed a touchstone in the constant construction and reconstruction of Australia's national identity. And an essential, though little recognised, part of this construction of nation takes place through the teaching of discovery and exploration in schools. Here, one can see all the classic tropes being reproduced without question: the explorers are heroes; the land is still 'new' – a mysterious box which must be 'unlocked' or an equally mysterious female who must be 'unveiled' and possessed. Few Australians will have proceeded through school without being inculcated with explorers and their red lines of discovery on maps. Most of those educated in Australia have at least some vague notion that Ludwig Leichhardt disappeared, that Aborigines helped and sometimes attacked explorers, and that Burke and Wills did not make it back alive.

Hodge and Mishra's claim that exploration has had only a modest role in the development of Australian culture also ignores representations of discovery which occur outside the school. Before exploration had been completed Ernest Favenc was already writing his *History of Australian Exploration* (1888), which placed exploration at the centre of Australian history. Of course, we may not agree with this construction of national history; nor does Favenc's effort prove that exploration was of great interest. But fiction does respond to public interest. During the 1890s and the first decade of the twentieth century there was an explosion of 'lost race' romances heavily influenced by H. Rider Haggard, and focusing on the activities of their fictional explorer heroes. J. F. Hogan's *The Lost Explorer: An Australian Story* (1890), W. Carlton Dawe's *The Golden Lake, or the marvellous history of a journey through the great lone land of Australia* (1894), Ernest Favenc's *The Secret of the Australian Desert* (1895), and Alexander MacDonald's *The Lost Explorers* (1906) – these were some of the fantastic narratives of exploration into the heart of the continent. They often included the discovery of a Ludwig Leichhardt-like 'lost explorer', a similarly 'lost' race of pseudo-Aborigines more sophisticated than the regular indigene, and the uncovering of a giant volcano, which would provide a convenient, if destructive, end to the story. Exploration, then, did not quickly subside in the public imagination with the end of organised expeditions; it continued with these fantastic journeys, which supplemented the often disappointing results of real expeditions.

The twentieth century has seen a steady stream of interpretations of exploration. The last fifteen years in particular have seen a prodigious biographical effort. Edgar Beale has interrogated the myth of Charles Sturt in *Sturt: The Chipped Idol* (1979) and uncovered new information on the life of Edmund Kennedy in *Kennedy: The Barcoo and Beyond* (1983). Colin Roderick's *Leichhardt: The Dauntless Explorer* (1980) and Elsie Webster's *Whirlwinds in the Plain* (1980) are both serious and detailed attempts to explain the circumstances and motivations behind Leichhardt's explorations. Ray Ericksen's *Ernest Giles: Explorer and Traveller 1835–1897* (1978) and William C. Foster's *Sir Thomas Livingston*

Mitchell and His World 1792–1855 (1985) are scholarly investigations of the explorers and the circumstances under which they worked. Ann Millar's *'I See No End to Travelling': Journals of Australian Explorers 1813–76* (1985), a sophisticated addition to the coffee-table genre, carries voluminous and well-chosen excerpts from exploration journals, including maps and pictures. The Reader's Digest publication, *The Exploration of Australia* (1987), and Robert Clancy and Alan Richardson's *So They Came South* (1988) are well-researched and generously illustrated accounts of the history of exploration. Tim Bonyhady's extraordinary research enlivens his *Burke & Wills: From Melbourne to Myth* (1991), an expedition this book does not discuss. Finally, Ian McLaren's remarkable bibliographical effort, *Australian Explorers by Sea, Land and Air 1788–1988* (1988–) will encourage the production of more research and writing about exploration.

Bill Peach's *The Explorers*, an ABC series of one-hour programmes and the popular book of the series, gives a general history of the exploration of Australia. Peach argues that 'in reaction to nineteenth century heroics, there is a modern tendency to regard the explorers as clownish flag-wavers or mere self-seekers, and to dismiss their journals as exercises in self-promotion'.[15] He seeks to correct this bias by arguing that the explorers were a courageous group, who were 'men of their time' and therefore inevitably shared imperial attitudes towards the land and the inhabitants. Peach is right to warn against easy moral judgements from a smug and self-righteous position of historical privilege. Yet Peach mobilises tropes which one must see as harmful. With the advent of inland exploration, he writes, 'the great blank within the chart of the coastline drawn up by Matthew Flinders gradually came to life'.[16] This is to repeat the notion that Australia really is a lifeless blank until 'discovered' and inhabited by Europeans. The rewriting of exploration, then, cannot simply be a matter of reversing an attitude towards another historical period, changing the image of the 'heroic explorer' to ravenous agent of imperialism. Such a simple inversion does not take sufficient account of how linguistic practices enable exploration and how these same linguistic strategies still survive. The condemnation of exploration, and indeed of the entire imperial enterprise, is justifiable, but it must be carried out through a process of examination of language's ability to shape cultural attitudes and the material conditions and relations that these cultures create.

Colonial discourse studies

Academics have also had a part to play in investigating the texts of exploration. Prominent studies which have examined explorer texts and influenced this work include Robert Dixon's *The Course of Empire: Neo-*

Classical Culture in New South Wales (1986) and Ross Gibson's *The Diminishing Paradise: Changing Literary Perceptions of Australia* (1984). *The Course of Empire* argues persuasively for a hitherto unacknowledged influence of Enlightenment values in the formation of Australian nationalism, and to two chapters in particular, 'An Inferior Branch of the Art' and 'The Continental Empire', this work is indebted.

There have also been important works which have examined exploration texts that describe South America and Africa. *Imperial Eyes: Travel Writing and Transculturation* (1992), Mary Louise Pratt's epic work on the texts of exploration in the Americas and Africa is a sophisticated reading of the language of exploration. Her article, 'Scratches on the Face of the Country; or, What Mr Barrow Saw in the Land of the Bushmen', is one of the most important pieces in the emerging field of study of exploration journals. Another study of travel and exploration writing is Sara Mills's *Discourses of Difference* (1991), an analysis of women's travel and descriptive writing. Because *The Cartographic Eye* examines the 'discipline' of exploration, which rigorously excluded women, *Discourses of Difference* should be read as a companion volume to see how the masculinist construction of viewing and landscape may sometimes be avoided. *Discourses of Difference*, as well as being a feminist text, reads exploration writing from a postcolonial angle. Postcolonial theory not only draws attention to the way that postcolonial writing contests empire, it offers ways in which to read for the density, contradiction and ambiguity in colonial discourses. In the Australian context, Nicholas Thomas's recent *Colonialism's Culture: Anthropology, Travel and Government* (1994) is particularly useful in that it challenges the works of some postcolonial theorists whose ideas threaten to become uncriticised doctrine. Contesting the globalised focus of much contemporary colonial discourse theory, Thomas reminds us that colonial situations and the discourses that arose from them had their historical specificities, their logic and their moments of conflict and confusion.

In rejecting a globalised theory, Thomas also casts doubts upon the psychoanalytic theory that such work employs. By its very nature, psychoanalytic theory has a universalist tendency, and certainly critics such as Homi Bhabha have employed Freud and Lacan to make sometimes sweeping statements about the nature of 'colonial discourse', as if it was a monolithic body of work. Yet, rather than abandoning the psychoanalytic cause altogether, I have tried to ameliorate its universalism by using it as one of a number of ways to read the productions of the explorers of one geographical entity in a roughly sixty-year period. In doing so, I have at least localised the range of texts so that a number of historical and cultural trajectories are similar. The works of African explorers may have some passages concerning sight, for example, which are very similar to those by Australian explorers, but they are placed within journals which record travels with a very different set of logistics, and within a continent, 'Africa', the name itself being redolent with a set of meanings very different to 'Australia'. That there are occasional universalising impulses of psychoanalysis when used in colonial theory does not mean this theoretical nexus should be abandoned. Freud's own description of women as the 'dark continent' underscores the close relationship between nineteenth century and early twentieth century discourses of geography and gender. The land as a female which must be investigated is a trope in the journals which may be productively analysed; this is focused upon in chapter 7.

Any record of the cultural treatment of exploration texts in Australia would be incomplete without Paul Carter. Carter's *The Road to Botany Bay* (1987) received a good deal of critical attention at the time of its publication, much of which involved an attack upon the difficulty of his writing style.[17] It is a difficult book, but has much of value. Its central premise is that history as it has been practised is an 'imperial history', constructing space as a stage where events are played out through the crucial vector of time.[18] Space, then, is relegated to insignificance – 'the Governor erects a tent here rather than there; the soldier blazes a trail in that direction rather than this' (xvi). This creation of a spatial stage is the fault of 'imperial historians', although it is never quite clear in *The Road to Botany Bay* if Carter regards all traditional historians as imperial historians. For imperial history seems in Carter's formulation to be the result of any history (besides his) which seeks to recount events from an historically privileged point of view. If this seems dismissive of historians in general, and anti-imperial historians such as Manning Clark in particular, then Carter's alternative spatial history offers ways of reading which effectively avoid repeating the 'stage' effect of traditional history.

Carter urges that we should 'focus on the intentional world of historical individuals, the world of active, spatial choices' (xvi). *The Road to Botany Bay* is at its best when it examines how the playing out of this intentional world through language reveals that knowledge-generation is always incomplete, hesitant and fragmentary. Carter correctly argues that knowledge comes into being through language and that language does not simply reflect a knowledge somehow directly gained. But Carter's ultimate target is not how language alone forms the frontier of knowledge accumulation, but how individuals' intentions operate. Carter defines the difference between imperial and spatial history thus:

> ... the former tends to regard historical statements as transitive, as verbal glosses on physical actions; but the latter, by contrast, interprets statements as indicative of states of mind, as symbolic representations of intention. (*Road to Botany Bay* p.138)

In eschewing the idea of language as transparent of the 'real', Carter lurches to the other extreme, where the thoughts of the writer may be divined from what he has written. Such an idea seems a remarkably retrograde step towards an even more simplistic history than the traditional one Carter himself criticises – towards a history that describes what the historical personage was thinking when he wrote, as a way of explaining how he acted. The intentional fallacy forms a large part of Carter's exegesis of explorers' journals, and results in his book advocating historically and theoretically disparate and contradictory ways of reading.

The peculiar quality of *The Road to Botany Bay* is that it fails where it most nearly succeeds. Part of Carter's critique of history's staging technique is that it treats space as if it was already there, rather than being created through exploration, and travels (xxi). Carter is fundamentally correct in this evaluation; land cannot exist before it is culturally assimilated. His work on the interrelationship of genres and exploration journals is insightful, but he surely errs in focusing on European discovery as the initiating moment of cultural formation of Australia. The (non-Aboriginal) cultural generation of Australia as a space has been taking place since European geographical speculations began. The idea of discovery as an originary moment for this cultural generation of a continent leads Carter to postulate a transparent response to physical phenomena rather than one which was largely preconstructed by earlier scientific and fantasy discourses.

> Nothing was unpredictable because nothing was predicted. It was a truthful account of the world's appearance, as it appeared in time and space. And it was in this sense that the journal resembled an empirical science: for, however elaborately the explorer might hypothesize (or simply dream) about what lay beyond the horizon, in the foreground, as it were, he gave himself up to the appearance of phenomena. A change of soil, a rise in temperature, an accident with a gun, were hardly facts of interest to science: but the explorer's attitude towards them was itself scientific, laconic. Illness, thirst and human error were treated as natural facts, events that, once classified, required no further interpretation. (*Road to Botany Bay* p.73)

The journey was created as a narrative, Carter correctly argues; but he then describes this supposedly innocent reception of the world of facts (72–73). Explorers were not blank tablets giving themselves up to the moment of perception, but were informed by pre-existent discourses that determined what they wrote. Something *was* predicted for Australia: long before its discovery, there was the determination that this continent was inverted, and representations of this imaginary place hinted that it was a void. The language of the explorers is filled with pre-formed tropes, which ingest and normalise that which is seen on explorations; in this sense there is nothing which is truly surprising to the explorer, as everything is a version of something previously predicted or imagined.

Knowledge-generation may ultimately be fragmentary, as Carter suggests, but its effectiveness is what is at stake in the colonising process. Exploration discourse's prime feature is a demonstration of control over the landscape; this is achieved, not by 'giving oneself up to the appearance of phenomena', but by actively constructing the scene through pre-existent descriptive paradigms. One of these paradigms is a description of the land as an ocean. Carter's analysis of the same trope defines the difference between his work and mine.

> But the likeness in difference felt in contemplating the sea as land-like, the land as sea-like, goes deeper than this. It is rooted phenomenologically in our most primitive sensations of earth and water and of their common heritage in the wind filled sky. (*Road to Botany Bay* p.92)

This work avoids such mystical speculations, in favour of an analysis of this particular trope's incorporation into the general construction of the land. Chapter 4 of this work argues that the classic description of the land as sea is part of an homogenisatory aesthetic, which may be linked to other constructions of the land as blank or empty. This aesthetic response is also a political strategy; it helps to produce Australia as an empty space requiring filling by European colonisation.

In eschewing discussion of already extant tropes, *The Road to Botany Bay* loses much of its potential force as a critique of the imperial project as carried on in 'imperial history'. Carter's work criticises imperial history's tendency to legitimise what happened, but his project offers insufficient grounds for a rebuttal to imperial/empirical logic; for the logic of imperialism works as efficiently along the vector of space as of time. In Carter's book there is an ideological commitment to the idea that imperialism embodies a fundamentally destructive agenda, a commitment Carter puts forward in his attack on imperial history but which disappears in the body of the work.

Australian explorers

True European exploration of Australia was not done by a handful of men called 'explorers', but by women, sealers, travellers, and drovers. I have chosen to concentrate on the celebrated explorers because their journals had the greatest currency during the nineteenth century, and the explorers themselves remain today as heroic figures whose exploits, children are taught, are admirable. An exercise in de-canonisation is certainly overdue, but I have elected here first to analyse 'canonised' explorers. The particular explorers I have chosen to examine, with the

exception of Leichhardt and Eyre, were institutionally financed, either
at the colonial or state level, or by the Royal Geographical Society. These
particular explorers, then, are never simply disinterested individuals, but
agents of various centres of imperial power.

Thomas Livingston Mitchell (1792–1855) was the Surveyor-General of
New South Wales from 1828 until his death. His *Three Expeditions into the
Interior of Eastern Australia* [*3Ex*] (1839) recounts his exploration in search
of a north-flowing river reputed to exist west of the Great Dividing
Range. This river, the product of the imagination of the convict George
'The Barber' Clarke, was not found, and these expeditions (carried out
in 1831–32) were inconclusive. The next expedition (in 1835) was
scarcely more successful. Mitchell had hoped to find evidence to
contradict his rival Charles Sturt's notion that the Darling river met the
Murray. Mitchell followed the river far enough to prove to his own
satisfaction, or dissatisfaction, that Sturt was right. This expedition was
blighted by a conflict in which numerous Aborigines were killed as a
result of Mitchell setting an ambush for them. In 1836 he began yet
another expedition which this time met with success, discovering the
area he called 'Australia Felix', which is now agricultural land in Victoria.
Even here, his achievement was undercut by his meeting with Europeans
who had already settled at Portland, thereby taking the shine off his
claims to discovery. Mitchell's *Journal of an Expedition into the Interior of
Tropical Australia* [*EITA*] (1848), relates his journey through what is now
Queensland. Once again he was searching for a river flowing north and
believed he had found it in the stream now called the Barcoo. He
described it as the river flowing to India, a pathway which would allow
the export of goods from the land he had found; but, owing to being low
on provisions, he did not explore it further. Later it was discovered that
the river turns south-west, joins Cooper Creek, and ultimately flows into
Lake Eyre.

Mitchell's rival, Charles Sturt (1795–1869) was without professional
surveying experience, and so was to Mitchell's mind an amateur; yet, he
managed to outline many of the river systems of south-east Australia. In
1830, in an epic journey recorded in *Two Expeditions into the Interior of
Southern Australia* [*2Ex*] (1833), Sturt and his party rowed down the
Murray river into Lake Alexandrina, and then rowed over 2500
kilometres back in a continuous effort over February, March and April
1830. Sturt's second series of expeditions decribed in *Narrative of an
Expedition into Central Australia* [*ECA*] (1849) resulted in even greater
hardships.[19] Travelling north of Broken Hill, he and his party were
trapped in 1845 for five months at Depot Glen, sheltering from the
effects of summer, and they were never to reach the continent's centre.

George Grey (1812–98) landed with a small party in Hanover Bay on the north-west coast in 1837, hoping to find fertile lands inside the intimidating coastal areas. *Journals of Two Expeditions of Discovery in North-west and Western* Australia (1841) records how on his first day exploring he nearly died through heat exhaustion and then drowning, and after travelling for two weeks was seriously injured by Aboriginal spears. After returning to Perth, he set out on another expedition in 1839, but he and his party were marooned and had to walk back to Perth, surviving with Aboriginal help. If this seems a litany of disaster and the product of ineptitude, then his journals read differently. He was among the most open-minded of explorers, willing to learn Aboriginal languages, and his journal is one of the first records of cave paintings in northern Australia. Edward Eyre (1815–1901) was, likewise, sensitive to Aboriginal culture. His 1841 crossing of the Nullarbor plain with the Aborigine Wylie, after his partner had been shot and his party had deserted, is a remarkable story of endurance and fortune.

The Cartographic Eye also analyses some of the work of John Lort Stokes, Ludwig Leichhardt, John McDouall Stuart, Ernest Giles and Peter Warburton. The task of this book is not to criticise the efforts of these men from some smug position of assumed moral superiority any more than it is to envelop these figures in a miasma of hero worship; it is to scrutinise and undermine the methodology of exploration, and to show that knowledge production is invariably an exercise of power.

2

Exploring Culture: The Formation and Fragmentation of the Explorer

The construction of the author

Confronted by the differences of the 'new' world, colonial authors not only have to construct the land through language but they have to construct themselves anew as well. Whatever genre they work in – exploration journal, personal diary or travel narrative – they have to create themselves as observers of, and participants in, their new world. The official documents of colonial description in particular require the formation of an authoritative and knowledgeable observer. This position of the authoritative observer, in the field of exploration, is built up 'inside' and 'outside' the texts. The authoritative voice is produced in the journals through the controlling 'I' of the narrative. 'Outside' the journals, institutions create 'exploration' as a monocentric endeavour by constructing it as a practice of the heroic individual, by rewarding the leader, and by encouraging the development of a controlling narrative voice in the journal writing. But the unity of the narrative voice, so important to colonial discourses in general, and exploration literature in particular, is ultimately fractured by the nature of narration itself.

Explorer as hero

The mythology of exploration insists that the explorer be pitted against the vicissitudes of nature, hounded by inconsiderate indigenes and worn out by hunger in the service of his country. Above all, the explorer is an heroic *individual*: in exploration hagiographies there is rarely mention of the other members of the party; rather, 'Sturt' travels into the interior, 'Grey' walks down the west coast to Perth, and 'Stuart' crosses the continent from south to north. The monocentric approach to exploration is, in part, a result of the class dynamics of the exploration party. The leader would usually be from a relatively privileged background, whereas the 'men' were convicts or labourers, a situation that enabled the explorer to position himself as superior in knowledge and judgement to the party. In constructing an authoritarian exploration practice, the explorer necessarily positions himself as the hero of the party: Charles Sturt writes that for the sake of discipline he 'deemed it absolutely necessary to arm myself with powers with which I could restrain my men even in the Desert' (*ECA* 2: 142). Here, it is not only with external dangers that the individual explorer is faced but with dissensions within the party, too. Such internal difficulties, however, are often only indirectly referred to in the journals, or are explained in terms of the 'men's' class origin and their resultant moral defects or foolish notions, and one has to turn to unauthorised records, such as that of Daniel Brock in Sturt's second expedition, to find alternative and more informative accounts of internal bickering.

The journals construct the explorer as a man who is subject to extremes but who remains in control. At times there is a desperate search for superlatives; Sturt, in particular, had a habit of combining boast and insult. He notes in regard to his venture into central Australia that Edward Eyre had 'shrank from the task I had undertaken' (*ECA* 1: 51). Peter Warburton writes that 'the country is terrible ... I do not believe men ever traversed so vast an extent of continuous desert' (Warburton 258) – a description which does not offer a portrait of the land but rather which operates to construct Warburton as a member of the order of explorers, a club which requires priority of some kind in the newcomer, whether it be of land discovered or simply endurance. The pre-existent myth of the savage lurking with murderous intent around the explorer is used by John Lort Stokes to emphasise the heroism of his project. In reminding readers of the destiny of other explorers, he is directing them towards the dominant social myth of the savage through which they are to understand his experience; thus, Stokes writes of a narrow escape, 'ours would have been the fate of so many other explorers; – the hand of the savage almost grasped our throats – we should have fallen a sacrifice in the cause of discovery' (Stokes 2: 110). The social myth, it may be argued, operates independently from actuality, relatively few Australian explorers having been choked to death by Aborigines; but more important is the way this myth acts as a generic expectation in journals of exploration. It is surprising if the explorers at some point are not 'threatened' by Aborigines. Even if they are not threatened, it is nevertheless still possible for the journals to present the indigenes as inherently dangerous; in lieu of violence, Thomas Mitchell writes that they were lucky to live through the night (*3Ex* 1: 226), though there seems little reason for suspicion of native intentions. The generic expectations of the exploration here are mixed with the stereotypes the explorers themselves carry with them, stereotypes for which journals of exploration are themselves largely responsible.

'Discovery'

We still commonly speak of explorers having 'discovered' new lands, and most non-Aboriginal Australians would be puzzled at the notion that this is in any way offensive. Some argue that 'discovery' means nothing more than inclusion of the land within a European sphere of knowledge, yet it still carries the implication that the land was not previously known. Certainly, the self-constitution of the explorer depends upon the assumption that during some part of the journey he will be the 'first' to see 'new' land. For discovery to be possible, all knowledge of the land must be denied, including prior Aboriginal knowledge. George Grey speaks of an 'utterly unknown country' (Grey 1: 94), Stokes desires to 'penetrate into the ... unknown and mysterious country' (Stokes 1: 210), and Ernest Giles enjoys the 'pleasure and delight of visiting new and unknown places' (Giles 1: xlviii). The effacement of Aboriginal knowledge is usually an unstated given, 'discovery' being reserved for Europeans. Mitchell is guilty of this, but also offers a moment of resistance when he writes of white settlers who had been forced off their land by Aborigines that they were 'not only not the real discoverer of the country, but not even the occupiers of what they had discovered' (*EITA* 20). Mitchell reserves his attack on the idea of 'discovery' for squatters rather than for explorers, but at least it is an admission of Aboriginal priority. The resistance in the journal to the idea of white priority conflicted with social constructions of 'discovery'. The *Blackwood's Edinburgh Magazine* review of Mitchell's *Three Expeditions into ... Eastern Australia* constructs discovery as directly connected to expanding the territory of the colony; that is, everything that is seen is at once owned. This extraordinary claim is naturalised via a comparison to inheritance, an analogy which especially emphasises the power and pleasure of sight.

> The expedition was through a soil where every portion of their progress was not only new, but an addition to the actual territory of the explorer's country ... It had somewhat of the feeling which an heir must have in taking a view of his inheritance for the first time – all before him new, and all before him his own.[1]

The metaphor of inheritance presents discovery as an individual event, but one which is licensed and, indeed, enabled by society. The nexus between sight and ownership will be further examined in chapter 3 of this work, especially in regard to conventions of viewing encouraged by picturesque estates.

'Discovery' was a process which involved the regulated practice of exploration but which, paradoxically, was described in personal, rather than official terms in the journal. The moments of discovery are presented as episodes of near rapture for the explorer: Stokes writes of the 'feverish enjoyment of discovery' (Stokes 1: 416) and of the 'intense pleasure afforded by traversing water that had never before been divided by any keel' (Stokes 2: 6–7). The personal reward of the discovery is frequently described in terms of specular pleasure – this pleasure resulting from the fact that no European eyes have previously intruded upon the scene. The land is 'new' because it has never been seen by the organ of knowledge-generation, the European eye, and this gaze is construed as an imposition of power. Stokes writes of the pleasure of viewing a 'wide and far-spread landscape then first submitted to the scrutiny of an European' (1: 150). The submission of the land is to a gaze which is constructed according to travelling: the eye 'wanders' across the landscape and the land accrues value precisely because it has never been previously seen. Stokes climbs a high tree and describes a wide but disappointing prospect, which is nothing 'but mangroves and mudbanks; still interesting from the fact that upon them the wandering gaze of the curious European had never been bent' (1: 129).

The importance of sight as an element in the construction of discovery cannot be overlooked. Almost all the discoveries made are constructed as totally visual events, and if that vision of the 'new' land is not available then the claims to discovery are vulnerable to attack. The Burke and Wills expedition attempted to cross the continent from south to north; on reaching the north coast, they were prevented from traversing to the actual shore by dense mangroves, although the presence of salt water and tidal flows indicated that they had, to all intents and purposes, arrived at the edge of the continent. In his introduction to John McDouall Stuart's journal the editor, William Hardman, attempts to demonstrate, by criticising the lack of visual proof from Burke and Wills, why Stuart had a better claim to crossing the continent. 'Other explorers', he argued, referring to Burke and Wills, 'had merely seen the rise and fall of the tide in rivers, boggy ground and swamps intervening and cutting off all chance of ever seeing the sea' (xi). The myth of 'discovery', then, is based upon vision.

Original yet repetitive

Discovery, by definition, is an originary act: one may follow Cook along the east coast, but he is taken as the beginning, the original moment from which point the European narrative of the exploration of the east coast (and often of all Australia) departs. I have argued that discovery is also a personal vision – the individual's pleasure and reward being pre-eminent. But, paradoxically, discovery is framed in terms of explorative predecessors; the construction in Mitchell's journal of his discovery of a river in the north-east quarter of the continent which he hopes will provide a highway to the Orient positions him within a grand history of explorers.

> Ulloa's delight at the first view of the Pacific could not have surpassed mine on this occasion, nor could the fervour with which he was impressed at the moment have exceeded my sense of gratitude, for being allowed to make such a discovery. From that rock, the scene was so extensive as to leave no room for doubt as to the course of the river, which, thus and there revealed to me alone, seemed like a reward direct from Heaven ... (Mitchell *EITA* 309)

The river did not turn out to lead straight to the spice warehouses of India as Mitchell hoped; it was not the 'grand goal ... of explorers by sea and by land from Columbus downwards' (*EITA* 332). Paul Carter is surely right when he points out that the mistaking of Ulloa (the discoverer of the Colorado) for Balboa reveals that, subconsciously, Mitchell desired to be remembered as a great discoverer of rivers; more important than Mitchell's psychology, however, is the dynamic of the description.[2] It is a claim to priority, to originality, yet it must be framed in terms of a historic precedent – the claim to originary status being undermined by its own appeal to history. Discovery is a personal vision, but it is also the same vision belonging to the pantheon of explorers. The description is less effective in placing Mitchell within the honour roll of explorers than it is in constructing a mythology of sight: in this, the explorers are the individual historical agents but sight is the trans-historical power in which discovery resides.

The journals also attempt to place the explorer within the canon of great explorers, in other ways. Most explorers are too modest to compare themselves with predecessors directly; so the introduction and other material external to the actual record of the journey serve this function. In his *Explorations in Australia* (1875) John Forrest includes a report of the speeches of the Perth welcoming committee, which places him in the pantheon of heroic explorers. Forrest's name deserves to 'stand side by side in the page of history':

> with such men as Mungo Park; Bruce, who explored the sources of the Nile; and Campbell, who, labouring in the same cause, traversed the wilds of Africa; and that greatest and noblest of all explorers, the dead but immortal Livingstone! (Forrest 311)

It is curious that all of these precursors are explorers of Africa, and not of Australia. The point being made is that Forrest belongs by parentage to the nation responsible for these explorers, thus it is made clear that the celebration is of imperial rather than national achievements. In his *Australia Twice Traversed: The Romance of Exploration* (1889) Ernest Giles's formation of the canon of explorers that he joins is very different. It does not depend upon the reported congratulations of others but is, rather, a result of the way he constructs himself.

> I have been a delighted student of the narratives of voyages of discoveries, from Robinson Crusoe to Anson and Cook, and the exploits on land in the brilliant accounts given by Sturt, Mitchell, Eyre, Grey, Leichhardt, and Kennedy, constantly exciting my imagination, as my own travels may do that of future rovers, and constantly spurred me on to emulate them in the pursuits they had so eminently graced. (Giles 1: lv)

Giles is not simply joining this prestigious group but has been formed by their writings, an argument which allows Giles to portray his journal as equally important. The construction of the personal through the mythological enables the explorer to present himself on the one hand as original (for, unlike these great explorers, Giles through his historical position has privileged access to these previous explorers' knowledge by means of their journals); yet, at the same time, he is a repetition, for he seeks only to 'emulate' their pursuits.

This tendency to construct the discoverer in terms of previous discoveries merges with the explorers' search for superlative status, to produce claims for being the 'final' explorer the continent requires. Giles writes that 'though I will not attempt to rank myself amongst the first or greatest, yet I think I have reason to call myself, the last of the Australian explorers' (Giles 2: 342). Unfortunately for Giles, the claim to being the 'last of the explorers' had already been made for Forrest, which he included in his journal. Forrest had written a letter to the surveyor-general of Western Australia, Malcolm Fraser, stating that his proposed exploration would be the 'finishing stroke of Australian discovery'. This letter is included in Forrest's journal with a government memorandum which states that, if successful, Forrest's 'name will fitly go down to posterity as that of the man who solved the last remaining problem in the Australian continent; and . . . he will have been the last . . . of the great Australian explorers' (Forrest 152). There is no doubt that the explorers did feel the burden of exploration history.[3] The effect of the strategy of constructing the self through the canon of the explorers, however, is not simply to display this burden, nor does it only work to include the explorer within this canon; rather it leaves the persona of the explorer incomplete – he is explicable only insofar as he is a repetition of others.

The explorer and the discourse of class

Charles Sturt: officer and gentleman

The class attitudes expressed in the journals produce the author as a man who is privileged over the other members of the party; he may look at them, see their faults and foolish beliefs, but his motivations are to them often mysterious. This position of privileged surveillance also allows the explorer to discuss various social classes as he sees them. Charles Sturt's journals are of particular interest for the way they reveal class dynamics within the exploration party, and for their lengthy disquisition on the class composition of the colony of South Australia.

Sturt offers plentiful examples of conservative social ideas, especially in the depiction of the relationship between the leader and his party, and between the officers and the 'men'. Edgar Beale has noted how the pressure of Sturt's presence and his disapproval of trespassing social boundaries prevented the surgeon, Browne, from participating in the digging of wells – the work being left to the 'men'. When Sturt is not present Browne joins the men in manual labour (*ECA* 1: 218, & 2: 32).[4] Sturt unashamedly describes himself as sitting by while one of the men, Morgan, digs the well (*ECA* 1: 182), and this division of labour continues through the journals. Later, the digging seems to be a group effort as 'we' (*ECA* 2: 34, 38) dig another well, although there is no evidence that Sturt actually joins in, and elsewhere the 'men' are depicted as being spontaneously enthusiastic about digging wells (*ECA* 2: 32).

Sturt's condescending attitude towards the members of his party is evidenced by the journals' complete lack of attention to the individuality of the members; not only are they seldom described or even mentioned, but their names and even number are hopelessly confused by Sturt.[5] In his report to the Colonial Secretary, published as Appendix V in *Two Expeditions into ... Southern Australia*, Sturt writes that the members of his party deserve the 'warmest approbation', for they have 'borne their distresses, trifling certainly, but still unusual, with cheerfulness' (*2Ex* 1: 217). The belittling of his party's efforts does not stand well against his continued complaints of personal hardships, especially his lament of his blindness which opens the volume (*2Ex* 1: iii–iv).

The relegation of the exploration party to the background and the dismissal of their sufferings in favour of Sturt's, it may be argued, is merely self-aggrandisement on Sturt's part. This is undoubtedly partly true, but the organised bias against the class identity of the 'men' cannot be ignored or simply dismissed, especially when it occurs within a journal which embodies a particularly vicious view of the natural hierarchy of society. Despite the occasional use of 'we', there is never any doubt in the journal that the narrator is an entirely separate entity from the labourers of the party. It is also clear that, as a class, they are severely defective; the 'men' exist in a different 'sphere of life' to Sturt and, being born without 'moral courage', they cannot be trusted (*ECA* 1: 228). A descending hierarchy organises the introductory list of men in *Expedition into Central Australia*, Sturt writing that the expedition 'mustered in its full force' consisted of 'officers, men and animals' (1: 45).

The exploration party is a microcosm of society. The description of the colony of South Australia is also structured by using a descending order of position: the government officers, the 'leading or upper classes' (including squatters), tradesmen, lower orders, Germans and Aborigines (*ECA* 2: 266–76). The gentlemen who form a 'distinct class' are epitomised by Colonel Robe, the late governor of South Australia, whose house was the 'seat of most unmeasured hospitality', whose 'table was covered with every delicacy' and whose 'wines were of the very best' (267). In congratulating the governor on his material wealth, and praising its consumption, Sturt describes the officer class as an 'irreproachable example to the community who are instrumental in giving it tone' (267). But, as Sturt argues, the bulk of the officer class lack the finances necessary for such ostentation, having been superseded in material terms by the 'leading classes' and the squattocracy. Sturt observes that the tradesmen of South Australia are successful and the lower classes possess a superfluity of mechanical genius (269). The objectification of people for analysis can be seen in these descriptions to work through a comparison in which the unstated norm is Great Britain – the location of both the author and his addressees. The situation of government parties in South Australia differs 'not in the slightest degree from that of similar parties in this country' (267); the 'lower orders' taken as an 'aggregate' are approvingly described as 'thoroughly English, both in their habits and their principles' (269); the Germans are censored for being 'too exclusive', but they live in stereotypically 'picturesque' houses (273). Sturt – all of us are – was a product of the discourses of his time and, though his strict hierarchies seem snobbish and perhaps priggish to us, they are views typical of the officer class of his day. My aims here are not biographical; what is of interest is how the explorer constructs class difference through this voyeuristic discourse.

The production of people as objects to be displayed is most powerful in the description of the class below all others – in other words, the Aborigines. Sturt wishes to 'exhibit' the Aborigines in a 'more favourable light than that in which they are presently regarded' (*ECA* 2: 274). The metaphors of lighting and exhibition reveal Sturt as a showman who displays the Aborigine-as-object for the amazement of the viewer. The mechanics of the production of the Aborigine can be perceived here. First, Sturt is a showman who controls the light and thus the perception of the object: its existence depends on how it is strategically lit, and the explorer completely controls this. Second, to exercise this control, he must exhibit the object: he thus produces it as something that exists only to be seen. The production of the Aborigines as 'seen' is a strategy of description used in his construction of all class strata – only the 'exceedingly retired' officer class have any protection from display. Sturt may wish to improve the Aborigines' status, but he is not interested in the removal of a social hierarchy, merely in its refinement. He inevitably places Aborigines last on his descending list, but benevolently opines that they should not occupy 'so low a place in the scale of human societies, as that which has been assigned to them' (274). The intersection of class and racial discourses, then, leads to the proletarianisation of the Aborigines, their assimilation becoming an immediate relegation.

A classless society?

Not all the explorers shared Sturt's approval of a class-stratified society, but there were few attempts to construct the possibility of alternate forms of social organisation. Stokes lamented that the 'increased number of settlers ... rendered inevitable the formation of circles more or less exclusive, and which, with the forms of European society, promised to introduce many of its defects' (Stokes 2: 519). In accepting the 'inevitability' of class formations, however, he also naturalised this feature of social ordering. That class stratification is a European characteristic establishes the possibility of a culturally relative analysis, where the possibility that no class exists would at least be left open. However, the first structure that Stokes looks for in Aboriginal culture is class division, and he concludes that 'they are very particular about the distinction of classes', but simultaneously admits that 'we could never discover which was the superior and which the inferior class' (Stokes 1: 393).

There was in fact room for the positing of Aboriginal society as classless, because the discourse of Aboriginal social classes emerges at the intersection of the construction of the Rousseauesque Noble Savage, experiential anthropological observations, and European class views. The first – informing judgements such as that of James Cook, who opined that the Aborigines 'live in a Tranquillity which is not disturb'd by the Inequality of Condition'[6] – constructs a paradisal social formation which is in every way the opposite of a degenerate Europe. The Noble Savage trope and the subsidiary discourse on the equal society need not necessarily have been controverted by actual experience of the Aborigines' condition. But the possibility of classless society had a particular political potency, which meant that it was not always welcome.

Thomas Mitchell, one of the few explorers from a working-class background, wrote that an Aboriginal friend was

> a very perfect specimen of the *genus homo*, and such as never is to be seen, except in the precincts of savage life, undegraded by any scale of graduated classes, and the countless bars these present to the free enjoyment of existence. (*EITA* 64–65)

But such an opinion was met with derision when the *Journal of an Expedition into the Interior of Tropical Australia* was reviewed. The reviewer in *Blackwood's Edinburgh Magazine* asked of Mitchell's theory whether:

> this is actually a recommendation that we should throw off our clothes and walk in nudity, for the purposes of recovering the original elegance of our shapes, or whether it is the borrowed rapture of some savage ... we know not; but he has *not* made us converts to the pleasures of cold, hunger, filth and bloodshed, which furnish the realities of savage life ... the savage, in his original state, is simply an animal.[7]

It is interesting that George Grey, product of a far more privileged background than Mitchell's, drew a completely contradictory conclusion about Aboriginal and, indeed, European society. Grey admits that class differentiation does not exist as an actual notion in Aboriginal society but is, rather, an untheorised practice. Grey argued that 'if asked, were all men equal? they would be unable to comprehend the question; but there is no race that imposes more irksome restraints upon certain classes in the community' (Grey 2: 218).

The mobility of the word 'class' is obviously being utilised here: it slides from being a word used to describe socio-economic stratification to one being applied to specific cultural practices. The fact that the Aborigines were seen to own little or nothing made this adaptation necessary, if indeed the notion of 'class' was to be used at all. The transportation of this word is, of course, a violence done to Aboriginal culture; it is an employment of universalist notions, which allows Grey to judge Aboriginal society as essentially similar to that of Europe, only worse. He argues that these Aboriginal restrictions on certain 'classes' 'violate all the holier feelings of our nature, and excite a disgust' (2: 218), and that, while the victims of Aboriginal repression are locked into their social category, those in the lower classes in Britain are free to work their way into the privileged classes. In civilised life, Grey argues, 'we see certain privileges even hereditarily enjoyed; but the weak and strong, the rich and poor, the young and old have paths of honourable ambition laid open to them, by entering on which they can gain like immunities' (2: 218). By ascribing a fanciful mobility to British class divisions, Grey allows a comparison to be made which is detrimental to the Aborigines. At the intersection of race and class discourse, then, occur the two essential strategies of othering. Cook and, later, Mitchell project upon Aboriginal society the Rousseauesque fantasy of innocent class homogeneity; Grey constructs Aboriginal society as similar to European, in that it is structured by class division; but this similarity is only a ground on which the Aboriginal system can be shown to be inherently inferior. The explorer's ethnological gaze is not directed simply towards the indigenous population, nor to the settlers; but the judgement of one is inevitably interwoven with the judgement of the other.

The Royal Geographical Society and the author/ity of the explorer

The explorer and institutions

There is a generic expectation in a journal of exploration that the explorer will be multi-faceted; its varying discourses create a narrator familiar with, if not an expert on, geology, cartography, anthropology, meteorology and biology. Class-based analysis that explorers engage in constructs them as proto-sociologists, but it also constructs the individual author – the 'Sturt' or 'Mitchell' of the journal. Grey's and Mitchell's differing discourses about class may invite biographical investigation into their own class backgrounds, but analyses of this nature tend towards speculative summaries of the 'mind' or 'beliefs' of the individual, and create an individual independent of his organisational position or formation. It is more productive to eschew analysis of Sturt's or Grey's opinions – to treat them as individual foibles – and instead examine how class-based institutions were instrumental in reproducing social formations in the discourse of exploration. The institutions with which explorers were inevitably involved not only regulated the method and reportage of exploration and ensured that explorers reflected institutional ideas of class, science and colonisation, they were also central in creating the unified author/explorer figure. The remainder of this chapter shows how this attempt at authorial unity was made at an institutional as well as a textual level, and ultimately how it unravels in the textual playing out of the journal.

The Royal Society of London

The Royal Society of London is the earliest of these institutions, but was perhaps the least immediately influential in the development of Australian exploration. The Royal Society, from its inception, relied upon the financial contributions of its members and therefore was the preserve of the wealthy, though not necessarily learned. Indeed, during the forty-two-year presidency of Joseph Banks all that was required of its Fellows was that they were interested in 'natural knowledge'; they did not have to be practitioners of any method of scientific investigation.[8] The 'gentlemen's club' character of the Royal Society, however, was unable to withstand the increasing specialisation of scientific investigation and the consequent desire to establish specialised societies. It is tempting to use the word 'professional' to describe those who were employed as scientists – its use is anachronistic, as scientists were usually employed in various government departments or by patronage, rather than possessing the institutional and employment autonomy generally associated with professionalism. Nevertheless, 'professional' is a useful description to highlight the differences between those scientists and the amateurs of the Royal Society. The year 1830 is generally considered to be a watershed in the history of the Royal Society, when the election to the presidency became a contest between John Herschel, the candidate of 'scientists', and the Duke of Sussex, who represented the status quo and the reign of the 'gentlemen'. The amateurs won, 199 to 111, thus preserving much of the aristocratic cohesiveness of the organisation.[9]

The Royal Society left some influential conventions for the construction of scientific reports (to which I shall return), but its most important influence was in institutionalising the process of knowledge-gathering. It was never an institution free of connections with politics, nor concerned with gathering knowledge solely for its own sake, but was always intimately connected with the higher levels of government. Hence, it embodied intimate connections between power and knowledge, on which imperial expansion was fundamentally dependent.[10]

The practice of exploration was only sporadically supported by the Royal Society. Markham has pointed out that, of 5336 papers published under the aegis of the Society in its *Philosophical Transactions*, only 77 were geographical or topographical in content.[11] When the Royal Society did support exploratory expeditions, it was concerned that its particular scientific interests, especially magnetism and magnetic variation, were investigated.[12] Rather than being a directly influential force upon exploration, the Royal Society represents the particularly restricted social fields which cohered to form centralised knowledge-gathering institutions and served as a model for more specifically directed organisations.

The Royal Geographical Society

The monopoly on scientific investigation Banks established had begun to erode in his lifetime with the founding of the Geological Society (1807) and Royal Astronomical Society (1820).[13] The Royal Geographical Society joined these specialist groups in 1830, shortly before the professional scientists received their setback at the Royal Society. The Royal Geographical Society (RGS) was organised with the promotion of exploration in mind: its origin lay in the African Association, founded by Banks in 1788 to advance the cause of African exploration, and the Raleigh Club, dedicated to serious exploration.[14] The Royal Geographical Society reproduced the alliance between scientific institution and aristocracy which characterised the Royal Society. Keltie, in his short work outlining the history of the Royal Geographical Society has noted that 'the first list of the Society numbered 460 and was composed almost entirely of men of high social standing ... it may be regarded as having been to some extent a Society Institution to which everybody who was anybody was expected to belong'.[15] The wealthy and fashionable flocked to its doors; within eight weeks of the Society's formation it had organised a charter, patronage and a roll of 460 members.[16] Stoddart's list showing the social positions of 304 of the original 460 members[17] is worth reproducing as it indicates the relative preponderance of those belonging to a high socio-economic standing, and the continuance of this social exclusivity via shared membership between the Royal Geographical Society, the Royal Society and the Geological Society.

Fellows of the Geological Society	19
Fellows of the Royal Society	124
Army officers	55
Naval officers	32
Baronets, Knights	38
Other peers	24
Earls	9
Dukes	3

The influence of the aristocracy and the officer class of the military in the RGS was (unsurprisingly) disproportional to their numerical presence in British society as a whole.

The Royal Geographical Society embodied one end of the social hierarchy, and also aided explorers' social progress. Exploration was a way by which one could gain entry into the RGS, as well as elevation within it and, by these means, into otherwise restricted levels of society. The explorers often achieved meteoric ascent through the ranks of the military, a new social mobility, the foundation of a career in politics and the possibility of pecuniary reward in related financial or pastoral fields. Grey, Eyre and Forrest were examples of how this process could succeed: they all gained careers in politics after becoming well-known through feats of exploration.[18] The contacts made with the RGS hierarchy undoubtedly helped this process, but the recognition and reward structure for the explorer could operate only while the RGS maintained exploration as a valuable social practice. Exploration needed the validation of a group of exclusive and privileged men, and it was these men who monopolised the right to give exploration the final seal of approval. In creating exploration as a practice, they were at pains to distinguish it from mere adventuring; instead, it was 'professionalised'. The RGS played a role in this, by urging that the explorers' rewards be concomitant with this professional status; winning its support and rewards was essential for one's recognition as an explorer. In R. A. Stafford's words, the RGS was dedicated to the 'delineation of the *tabula rasa* upon which "men on the spot" engraved their careers'.[19] Two revealing quotes from Mitchell show that there was some overlap between personal and imperial motivations.

> I have written the name of Britain deeply into the rocks and mountains of Australia by the roads and passages already made.

> I have written my name on the rocks and on the mountains of the country, so that they will be monuments of my labour.[20]

The construction of Australia as a place to be written on is dealt with later (see chapter 4), but here the emphasis is on Mitchell's ambiguity as to whether the nation or the individual is the beneficiary of his explorations. Of course, the individual and the nation both benefit by exploration, and one of the roles of the RGS was to reward explorers as richly as it was able to.

The RGS and its rewards to explorers

Through its important role in dispensing honours to explorers for their achievements for the empire, the RGS thoroughly welded the interests of the individual to those of empire. One way the RGS officially validated explorations was by presenting the returned explorer with either the Patron's or Founder's Medal. If the awarding of medals 'codified schools of thought, and legitimised scientific paradigms'[21], then the determination by the RGS of who was to be rewarded represented a powerful strategy for deciding what kind of exploration took place and, more importantly, how it was to be reported. The rewards encouraged the expansion of exploration beyond physical prudence – in the words of Clements Markham, an early historian and (subsequently) a president of the RGS, they became, 'goals which aroused the ambition of young explorers, and urged them on to renewed efforts ... they have always been highly prized, and have been strong incentives to brave and even desperate enterprise in the cause of discovery'.[22] The awarding of a medal offered both the explorer and his journal official legitimation and approval. But the mere promise of an award was at least as powerful an influence. The promise of a reward which could be withheld ensured that exploration reports conformed generically as well as in terms of imperial attitudes and RGS expectations. It also helped to ensure that the *Journal of the Royal Geographical Society* was the preferred place of first publication, whether the RGS had been involved in the exploration or not.

Australian explorers were generously rewarded by the RGS: A. C. and F. T. Gregory, John Forrest and John McDouall Stuart received gold medals for their (respectively) 'extensive and important', 'successful', 'numerous successful', and 'remarkable' explorations.[23] Peter Warburton, Ernest Giles and Ludwig Leichhardt also received RGS medals. Count Paul Strzelecki was awarded the Founder's Medal for his explorations in south-east Australia and subsequently became a member of the RGS controlling body, the council – no doubt with the aid of his social position.[24] Edward Eyre received the first RGS medal for Australian exploration, being rewarded for his 'enterprising and extensive explorations in Australia, under circumstances of peculiar difficulty'.[25] When Eyre again found himself in peculiar difficulties after his suppression of an uprising in Jamaica cost 600 lives, Roderick Murchison, four times president of the RGS, helped form the Eyre Defence Committee, and publicly congratulated Eyre on the hanging of the rebellion's leader.[26]

The awarding of medals reinforced the construction of exploration as an individual enterprise. The commendation to Sturt on the presentation of his medal reads 'for explorations in Australia, and especially for his journey fixing the limits of Lake Torrens'.[27] No mention is made of the fifteen people accompanying him. One RGS policy in particular confirmed the status of the explorer as an individual unencumbered by the aid of others. In 1862 Robert O'Hara Burke received posthumously the RGS Founder's Medal. His partner Wills did not receive a medal, as it was the Society's policy to award one medal only to an exploration party. The survivor of the exploration, John King, was supplied with a gold watch, as were McKinlay, Landsborough and Walker, leaders of expeditions searching for Leichhardt.[28]

As Sturt published *Narrative of an Expedition into Central Australia* two years after receiving an RGS medal, he was in a position to allude to his reward. He does not let the opportunity lapse, but in mentioning the medal also brings the authority of the Society to his defence. He validates the decision to turn back from the desert by quoting the president of the RGS, who congratulated Sturt on the 'prudence with which further advance was abandoned, when it could only have risked the loss of those entrusted to my charge' (*ECA* 2: 51). Further, Sturt's recalling the fact that he was awarded the medal at the same time as Leichhardt (whose journal noted that he, Leichhardt, had been awarded an RGS Gold Medal [544]) gives extra significance to Sturt's prudence since, when *Narrative of an Expedition* was published (in 1849), Sturt was unaware that Leichhardt had disappeared on his 1848 expedition. His readers, however, would have been able to compare Sturt's prudence with Leichhardt's lack of it. Later, the RGS again defended Sturt's decision to turn back. Clements Markham remarks in his history, *The Fifty Years' Work of the Royal Geographical Society* (1881), that Sturt's decision to retreat was a result of the illness of one of his party, a conclusion that contradicts the series of events as narrated in Sturt's own journal (Markham 63; *ECA* 2: 49–51).

The RGS, then, was a convenient authority that could be used as a support for explorers' reputations; it also actively defended explorers' decisions. It offered a powerful reward system for those expeditions – as represented through reports and journals – which conformed with RGS expectations of what an explorer, and his journal, should be. The RGS was a socially exclusive group; this meant that a large range of views on the land and geography did not find an official voice, and also ensured that access to RGS support and guidance was open only to those with an appropriate background. Women were totally excluded from fellowship of the RGS: although Mary Somerville had received a gold medal for her *Physical Geography* in 1869, neither she, nor any other women, were admitted as 'fellows' until 1913.[29]

If these were some of the indirect pressures the RGS placed upon the production of exploration journals, then it would be supposed that direct financial involvement was even more influential. Markham records over ninety contributions by the RGS to various expeditions. Most of these are relatively small amounts, however, rarely exceeding £500, and many are directed at funding the purchase of instruments for the expedition rather than at more central costs.[30]

The RGS rarely involved itself in a direct and large-scale way in Australian exploration. Its large financial contributions lay mainly in a series of explorations in Africa, and in the 1840s and 1850s the Society had few excess funds to divert to exploration in an area that was so logistically difficult as Australia. As Ian Cameron has correctly identified, however, lack of direct involvement did not mean that the RGS was not interested in a particular exploration. The RGS was:

> nearly always indirectly involved: offering advice behind the scenes, using its influence to secure government patronage, using its association with the Navy

to obtain ships and crews, oiling the diplomatic wheels by which every
expedition has to be set in motion, and above all ... by publishing their
results.[31]

However, the RGS also more directly supported explorations of Australia.
The first exploration of George Grey was supported by £1000 from the
RGS. Sir John Barrow, Second Secretary of the Admiralty was an
enthusiastic supporter of northern Australian settlement, and a vigorous
enemy of anyone who doubted the suitability of that area for
settlement.[32] He was also the RGS president in 1835–37, when settlement
attempts were being made. Under a facade of gentlemanly science, the
RGS was an organisation with a fundamentally instrumentalist agenda.
And the agenda was expansion of empire.

The rewards to the RGS

What then did members of the RGS receive in return for their support of
exploration? That the explorers almost invariably chose its journal in
which to publish ensured the centrality of that organisation in the
expansion of the empire of knowledge. To the actual scientists in the
RGS it meant that they had early access to new geological, botanical and
mineralogical discoveries. And to the president and secretary it meant
that they would be immortalised through the nomenclatural privilege of
the discoverer. The naming of rivers, mountains and islands provides
opportunities for explorers to reward past support, and to secure it for
the future. Gregory names a river the 'Ashburton, after the noble
President of the Royal Geographical Society' (67) and the Norton plains
after the 'talented Secretary' of the RGS (78); he also names a river
'Murchison' and its tributaries 'Roderick' and 'Impey' after another
president of the RGS. If they had two surnames, then there was an extra
chance for their name to be memorialised. Forrest named 'two remarkable flat-topped hills ... Mount Bartle and Mount Russell, after the
distinguished President [of the RGS] and Foreign Secretary' (175) and
then named a series of mountains the 'Frere ranges, after Sir Bartle
Frere, the distinguished President' of the RGS (179). The opportunity of
naming is used not simply as a reference to the individual's talent but
also to the organisation's importance. Leaving Barrow's Island, Stokes
writes that 'we cannot quit this island without reminding our readers that
it was named after the distinguished Secretary to the Admiralty [who has
been] the promoter of all geographical research, and mainly instrumental in founding a society which is of growing importance to Great
Britain' (Stokes 2: 211). That explorers repay supporters through naming is fairly obvious, but it is seldom recognised that the practice of

naming features after prominent members of an organisation is more than a reward by an individual to an individual; it has institutional resonances.

'A close, naked, natural way of speaking': Writing within the genre

Institutions and writing

Institutions like the RGS, the surveying department and the colonial administration, which ensured that the authority of the explorer was given only to those with the correct attitude, also worked to control the genre of the exploration journal. Explorers were given very specific sets of instructions which prioritised those things to be observed and recorded. The Secretary for the Colonies and the first president of the RGS, Viscount Goderich, wrote to Bourke stressing that the selection process for explorers should be rigorous and careful, and that 'no one should be employed in the service, who may not have shown himself fitted for the prosecution of such an undertaking'. In the same communication he asks that the 'attention of the Head of the Expedition be directed to the importance of keeping an accurate Journal of his progress'.[33] The letter of instruction to Sturt from Governor Darling, which Sturt included as Appendix One in *Two Expeditions into . . . Southern Australia,* amplifies these concerns about detailed observations. Instructions 11–12 state:

> you are to keep a detailed account of your proceedings in a journal, in which all observations and occurrences of every kind, with all their circumstances, however minute, are to be carefully noted down. You are to be particular in describing the general face of the country through which you pass . . . you will note the description of the several people whom you may meet, the extent of the population, their means of subsistence, their genius and disposition, the nature of their amusements, their diseases and remedies, their objects of worship, religious ceremonies, and a vocabulary of their language. (*2Ex* 1: 187–88)

The instructions place a surprising emphasis upon ethnographic observation, but what is more surprising is that they are included in the journal at all. The instructions construct the explorer as a closely supervised government servant whose task is to painstakingly enumerate the objects which fall within his view. He is not independent but merely part of a large, government-controlled information-gathering process. This works against the construction of the explorer the journal attempts to erect. In the journals the explorer is a courageous and heroic individual but, above all, a new breed of scientific entrepreneur. He operates from his own fascination with the detail of the natural world and even when he has no formal credentials he can, like Sturt, admit that he does not pretend to science, but is a lover of it (*ECA* 1: ii). The listing of government regulations undermines the picture of the self-activated explorer and reduces him from heroic individual to public servant.

The instructions given to Sturt carry with them the empiricist's view of the world as a collection of things to be listed. This attitude towards the journal's role influenced its content, but not necessarily its form. The generic conventions of the exploration journal derive from long-standing regulatory pressures rather than from contingent instructions. The Royal Society was one of the first organisations to attempt to regulate the exploration journal genre, emphasising the need for a Baconian clarity of expression. Thomas Sprat's *History of the Royal Society* contains advice that is essentially similar to that given to Sturt. The observer's purpose is to 'make faithful records, of all the works of nature, or art, which can come within their reach ... and to accomplish this, they have endeavoured to separate the knowledge of nature from the colours of rhetoric, the devices of fancy, or the delightful deceit of fables (61–62). Language is to be made as transparent as possible and the method for achieving this is described by Sprat. He excoriates the 'luxury and redundancy of speech' (111) and calls for the rejection of 'all the amplifications, digressions, and swellings of style' (113) that characterise the prose of the day. Sprat nostalgically calls for the return to the 'primitive purity, and shortness, when men delivered so many *things*, almost in equal number of *words*' (113). The objects investigated, then, are not represented but presented for the reader in prose which effaces its own existence for the veracious transmission of information. Sprat refers to the control the Royal Society exerts on the scientific discourse of the day. The Society has exacted from its members:

> a close, naked, natural way of speaking; positive expressions, clear senses; a native easiness: bringing all things as near the Mathematical plainness, as they can: and preferring the language of Artizans, Countrymen, and Merchants, before that, of Wits or Scholars. (113)

It is easy to find examples in the journals of style which strays from what these instructions demand; the point is, however, that the Royal Society's guidelines represent the first level of institutional control of the explorer's journal. The Royal Society established the generic conventions of the exploratory journal and a successful explorer had to adhere to these conventions. At the same time as the Society was recognising the journal's importance, and the labour required in its writing, its recommendations were paradoxically an attempt to efface the writerliness of the journal. It held out the promise that the journal can be an immediate presentation of reality, and a compaction of the signifier/signified/referent relationship into a simpler signifier/referent order, where the signifier is as close to transparency as possible.

The insistence upon the transparency of the text creates the explorer as percipient in a certain way. As noted earlier, the 'Cartesian cogito' gives primacy to the things that are perceived directly, without mediation. The Cartesian system confers upon the subject the privileged status of the unitary: there is a 'subject' which is singular and which is capable of fully knowing itself without the mediation of language. This logocentric construction of the self depends on this faith in the ultimate 'presence' of self to itself, a faith which must deny the opacity of language in the subject's self-construction. The equally logocentric notions of truth and reality, on which explorers' texts depend, rely on this ability of the subject to know itself without mediation; the texts are repetitions of this unmediated knowledge which are based on this faith in the unitary self-knowing subject. This is why the exploration texts struggle to create the self as unitary. It is also why such a significant role is played in the texts by the nostalgia for the 'unfallen' world in which, without the need for language and perception to mediate, there would be 'no gaps between form and meaning' – in other words, the nostalgia for writing texts that are transparent to the point of non-existence.[34]

Prefatorial remarks

The preface often strives to construct the text as transparent, by explaining that the author relies on 'plain language'. These prefatorial defences are a strategy to differentiate the exploratory from the ordinary travel journal, and create the expectation of a serious work unconcerned with the rhetorical fireworks that the travel journal characteristically displays. The preface to Eyre's journal says that where 'a simple statement of occurrences has been more attended to than the language in which they are narrated, plainness and fidelity will, it is hoped, be considered as some compensation for the absence of embellishments of a more finished style, or a studied composition' (Eyre 1: viii). The similar preface in Warburton's journal establishes it as a 'narrative so simply and unaffectedly told that no mere embellishment of language could add to its charm or heighten its effect' (132); but, in simply considering the journal's 'effect', the preface throws a shadow on the journal as an immediate and 'innocent' document, uninterested in the aesthetic requirements of the genre. When not distancing themselves from what they construct as the more rhetorically dense travel narratives, the journals insist on the connections between truth and simplicity of language. Stokes writes of the journal of Abel Tasman that:

such is the account of this distinguished and trustworthy discoverer, upon whose veracity I should be the last to attempt to affix suspicion: his very simplicity of detail, and the entire absence of rhetorical artifice, would convey sufficient internal evidence of his truth, had not the subsequent progress of Australian discovery served to confirm all the material facts of his narrative. (Stokes 1: 87)

The 'close, naked, natural way of speaking' produces its own authority; it is a dialect adapted by a certain class, encouraged by scientific institutions and, when recognised in the writings of others, it immediately produces respect for its veracity. As a code designed to produce acceptance of what it reports, 'plain language' is particularly powerful, and indeed it is constructed in masculine terms.

Manly discourse

If, as Sprat says, this style is 'naked', then its gender is unmistakable. After reading a passage in which Mitchell complains of the extirpation of the kangaroo from certain areas and the hardship this causes for the Aborigine, the reviewer in *Blackwood's Edinburgh Magazine* exhorts Mitchell to return to the 'manly' style which best suits his purpose.

If this had been said or sung in a modern novel, it might have been properly placed; but it has no relationship to the general grace and manly style required in important works, and of which we find so many able instances in the present writer.[35]

Fiction, then, is the refuge of the feminine style, unsuitable in 'important works'. But it is simply not possible for the journals to extricate themselves entirely from their relationship with either non-serious travel narratives or travel fiction. Either they are denying their similarity with these forms (or the reviewers are denying it for them), or they are constructing themselves, sometimes sardonically, through their competitors. Giles notes on one occasion that 'as a novelist would say, we flung ourselves into the saddles as fast as we could, and gave our enemies the slip' (Giles 2: 12). He complains that the journals are not read, and he puts this down to the passion for novels, or, at least, the bias against non-fiction: 'Strange as it may appear, it seems because the tales of Australian travel and self devotion are true, that they attract but little notice, for were the narratives of the explorers *not* true we might become the most renowned novelists the world has ever known' (Giles 1: xxxvi).

A polar dynamic is in operation here: the journals are manly, naked and plain whereas fiction is feminine, dressed, and 'delightful deceit'; yet, there is a desire to construct the narrative in terms of fictional precursors, indeed to construct it as fiction. The possibility of fiction functions in the journals as a barely concealed counter-discourse, a threatening alternative to the plain manliness of the style in evidence. What prevents an outbreak of fiction is, of course, the genre of the exploration journal, but this 'genre' is not simply a set of rules in isolation from material reality; rather it is a norm conditioned and continued by the institutions which gain their legitimacy through its use. Ironically, there are occasions when the genre of the exploration journal actually encourages the production of a description in which realism does not possess the highest priority. In particular, triumphalist narratives of discovery often involve reporting dialogue which has 'official' rather than mimetic value. An example of this occurs in Stokes's journal with this description of the discovery of a river.

> 'This is indeed a noble river!' burst from several lips at the same moment; 'and worthy,' continued I, 'of being honoured with the same name of her most gracious majesty the Queen'. (2: 40)

It is ironic that this 'official' discourse of discovery employs devices which are essentially fictional and, indeed, novelistic (and it is a pretty poor novel at that).

Submitting to the rules

The offering of rewards and career advancement to explorers and the establishment of rules concerning how the journal is to be written, constitute powerful forces controlling the journals' production. There was also a post-exploration review of the field journals that the explorers returned with; indeed, the submission of these journals for government inspection was usually obligatory (see, for example, Giles 2: 71). This highlights how the Colonial Office and the colonial administration appointed themselves centres of information processing, and how this relegated explorers to the role of information-gatherers. More importantly, it meant that journals which contained information or expressed opinions contrary to the interest of the governmental hierarchies could be suppressed. In fact, post-exploration censorship was not necessary because the writing took place under the full knowledge that it was to be inspected. That such a surveillant hierarchy was in place did not mean that the journals expressed uniform opinions; there is a variety of views on all subjects. Yet, attitudes in the journals do fall within a certain range: Aborigines are essentially inferior, the land is rightly appropriated for productive uses, the world consists of objects to be described, measured and owned.

Failure to transmit the information first to the appropriate agency, even if that was the RGS rather than a government department, resulted in censure. The African explorer Richard Burton received an angry rebuke from Roderick Murchison for publishing the narrative of his exploration before it had appeared in the *Journal of the Royal Geographical Society*.[36] The appropriate release of information was also a matter of propriety – privileged information about fertile land, for instance, could obviously advantage speculators. On the return of an expedition led by Augustus Gregory, his brother rode ahead and by accident met the editor of the *Western Australian Inquirer*. Excitedly, he showed him a copy of the field journal before it had been seen by the government. Gregory, as leader of the expedition, was reprimanded by Governor Clarke.[37]

If the explorer as author was restrained by the production process, then other members of the party could always create their own versions of events. However, instructions also took this into account. The instructions given to Sturt for both his 1829–31 Macquarie Marsh and 1844–46 desert explorations included a clause that insisted on the submission of all documents – that is, journals or diaries – kept by any member of the party.

> On your return from your journey, you are to cause all the journals or other written documents belonging to, and curiosities collected by the several individuals comprising the expedition, to be carefully sealed up with your own seal and kept in that state until you shall have made your report in writing of the result of the expedition. (*2Ex* 1: 188)

Again, this is a matter of etiquette designed to prevent the premature release of information about new and possibly valuable lands. But it also operates to produce the explorer as the ultimate authority of the expedition. It is the mechanism for the repression of disagreement of facts observed: the exploration leader's interpretation becomes authoritative because (at least at the time of first release, when most attention is fixed on the expedition) it is unchallenged. As well, the very mechanism of compelling the members of the party to submit their diaries to the leader would have the understandable effect of making them reluctant to record criticisms of, or disagreements with him.

Other voices
Daniel Brock, a member of the expedition to Central Australia, avoided submitting his diary to Sturt by sewing it into the lining of his coat.[38] Brock was the literate malcontent of the party, and his diary contains little that is flattering to the other members. The lone Methodist of the expedition, Brock was outraged at the failure to provide religious services on Sundays (37–38) and scandalised by Sturt's apparent visual impairment (11, 46, 81); but, most significantly, he was sceptical of Sturt's evaluation of the land. Early in his diary he criticises Sturt's

appraisal in *Two Expeditions into … Southern Australia* of the Murray's capacity to support farming.

> The river is evidently rising, what a pity such a wretched country should be watered by so noble a stream – nothing but scrub, sometimes sand, and sometimes stone, but never soil that would raise even a radish – except in the flats, which at seasons are overflowed. When Capt. Sturt published his account of his memorable expedition he stated that this country was adapted (highly so) for pastoral and agricultural purposes. 'Travellers see strange things'. (Brock 14)

The univocal official journal never has to contend with other voices presenting other opinions; its authority, in part, results from its being unchallenged within the journal. Brock's diary is an extra-journal attempt to break this monolithic authority of Sturt the author; it was not published until 1975. Another challenge to the monolithic authority of the official journal is found in Granville Stapylton's journal. Stapylton was second-in-command to Mitchell during the Australia Felix exploration of 1836 and his journal is full of sharp criticisms of Mitchell's personality and professional judgement. Like Brock's diary, Stapylton's journal has only recently been published in its entirety. Alan Andrews, the editor of the journal, suggests it is possible that Mitchell knew of the journal's contents and attempted to restrict its circulation after Stapylton's death in 1840.[39]

As noted, there are few incidents in the journals where other voices are found. In Sturt's journals, particularly, others exist only as functions of the journey. Brock, for example, is mentioned only four times, and these are all in incidental contexts. There is a well-known passage in *Expedition into Central Australia*, however, when one of the party seems to gain a voice separate from that of Sturt. The surgeon, John Harris Browne, is involved in a lengthy discussion with Sturt about the wisdom of continuing the journey. Sturt's report of the collision between Browne and himself is rather absurdly constructed as a series of speeches. This tactic damages Sturt's credibility, as the speeches are reported verbatim, yet only the most naive reader would believe that Sturt could have remembered each word. It is not possible to say why this strategy is used; perhaps it is chosen to increase the drama at this narrative juncture, where Sturt wishes to continue into the desert, while sending back a reluctant Browne with the majority of the party. Sturt, as the protagonist in this drama, begins with a formal and rather abstract statement of his position.

> I am afraid, Browne, from what I have observed, that you have mistaken the object for which I have returned to the Depot, and that you have been

buoying yourself up with the hope that it is done preparatory to our return to
Adelaide; for myself I cannot encourage any such hope for the present, at
least. (*ECA* 2: 15)

Browne's reported reply emphasises the heroism of Sturt's decision to
push on. His 'young friend' points out that Sturt has accomplished all
that he was sent to do, and asks why he wants to penetrate again into that
'horrible desert' (*ECA* 2: 16). That Browne is young allows his objection
to be portrayed as heartfelt, yet ultimately the product of affectionate
immaturity rather than logic. A seeming polyphony is produced briefly,
but only so Sturt can be presented as the most strenuous of explorers,
unwilling to turn his back on the challenge of one last calculated dash
towards the centre of the Stony Desert. The dialogue dramatically
confirms Sturt's bravery, and prepares a defence for his ultimate decision
to discontinue his northward movement.

Browne also wrote a diary of the expedition with Sturt.[40] His version of
the argument with Sturt does not use reported speech, and contradicts
Sturt's version on several points. For example, Sturt's account has him
saying to Browne that your 'health is seriously impaired, – you are in
constant pain, – and your affairs are going to ruin' (*ECA* 2:17). Browne's
version, on the other hand, says that he was the only one of the advance
party who was not obviously suffering from malnutrition (53). Nowhere
does he complain of pain, nor does he evince concerns about his
'affairs'. In Sturt's journal, of course, these contradictions are never
allowed to arise, for the journal's authority and its production of truth
rely on the authority of the one.

The single voice of the explorer

Sturt's version of the opening speech of the dialogue with Browne
constructs Sturt as the 'poised, self-possessed leader calmly doing what is
best for all, after careful consideration in private'.[41] Not all strategies for
enhancing Sturt's superiority are so subtle. His journals are full of
superlatives of praise for himself. He suffers 'as great a heat as man
ever endured' (*ECA* 1: 288), is an unparalleled observer of the Aborigine
(2: 275) and above all is the centre of attention: he tells Browne that the
'eyes of the geographical world are on me' (2: 17). These may simply be
seen as delusions of a man too long in the desert, or as bandages on the
wounds of his disappointment, yet they have a far more important
function within the journal. The central generating force of the
exploration journal genre is the author. In an exploratory journal,
'Sturt', for example, operates both as author and actor. The strategy of all
the journals is to locate a strong, authoritative central observer (Sturt the

explorer), while eschewing the difference between Sturt the explorer and Sturt who narrates the journey. It is crucial for the journal's veracity that there is one voice only in the text, for the objective facts which exist 'out there' can be unified only by being channelled through this sole observer. Two observers or voices would raise the possibility of disagreement and a chaotic uncertainty.

At every turn, the text attempts to reduce the importance of the author's role. It is usually others that ostensibly provide the motivation for writing. Sturt simply wishes to lay the results of his explorations passively before the 'geographical world', which has a right to know the exploration's results, and the appended analysis of New South Wales is a product of Sturt having been 'strenuously urged to give a short description of the colony' (*2Ex* 1: x). He authors *Expedition into Central Australia* because it 'may benefit those who shall hereafter follow my example', and the 'public have a right to demand information' from extenders of geographical information; but it is mostly because, having published a journal of his previous successful exploration, his 'failing to do so in the present instance might be taken as evidence that I lacked the moral firmness which enables men to meet both success and defeat with equal self-possession' (*ECA* 1: iii). The decision to write is taken out of his own hands by his duty to the public and his own reputation. The prefatorial dismissal of literary quality is a staple of the journals. The prefaces vigorously reduce the importance of the writerliness of the journal, part of the way in which the journal constructs itself as innocently mimetic. If the journals are seen as transparent transmitters of the 'real', then they reach this state by the controlling, 'manly' discourse of the explorer. The authority of the journal is assisted by the natural assumption of a unified figure – explorer, author and narrator – who creates the text. Yet, paradoxically, the genre of the exploration journal produces a division between these three functions, which reduces the authority of this unified figure and undermines the explorer as created by imperial mechanisms.

The shifting 'I' of the explorer

Narrator and actor

Any time you write about what you have done you create two identities. One is the 'you' who figures as the actor in the narrative and the other is the 'you' who tells the story. This multiplying of identities is inevitable in all forms of autobiography and adds to the richness and complexity of that form. But doubling of the explorer into actor and narrator works against the generic requirement of univocality in the journals. The journal genre, like autobiography, naturalises the fusion of actor (explorer) and narrator; so, mostly we do not think about the different ways these identities work in the text. This is a fusion we shall now attempt to denaturalise, in this way undermining the author/ity of the journals which are dependent on the unity of this figure.

'I' the explorer

The best way to approach this is through an examination of the first person pronoun, which is instrumental in the journals in constructing a unified explorer/author/narrator on whose unity of perception and judgement the author/ity of the journal depends. Emile Benveniste's pioneering work in *Problems in General Linguistics* enables a critique of the 'I' in the journals. Benveniste argues that the inscription of the 'I' creates two quite different selves – the subject who writes and the subject who is written about.[42] Thus, the 'I' in the sentence 'I sat looking at the Aborigines' utilises 'I' in two separate ways: to identify the subjectivity of the speaker and the subject of the sentence. The splitting of the 'I' at the first moment of its inscription is, as Andrew Hassam has noted, most prominent in autobiography, where the split is usually represented as the present self discussing the past self.[43]

Published journals of exploration are generically more complex than autobiographies or diaries although they share features of each. Yet, there are complicating factors such as prefaces, which treat the author in the third person; there is the frequent difficulty of temporally locating the narrator; there are also retrospective interpolations that may or may not be signalled by a change of tense, or by reference to temporal position.

The journals of Australian exploration can be divided into two types: those which consist mainly of transcriptions from the field-books, and those that are more 'polished', and contain retrospective rewriting. The first category includes the journals of Gregory, Warburton and Stuart; the second, the journals of Mitchell, Sturt and Giles. Those in the first category are primarily structured by day-to-day reports displaying the explorer's mistaken plans, incorrect decisions and lack of foresight; the second type of journal allows the covering up of the faults. In *Narrative Discourse*, Gerard Genette differentiates between four types of narratives: the two which are of direct concern here he calls 'subsequent' and 'interpolated' narrative.[44] The first is the 'classical position of the past-tense narrative' – a position occupied by those journals which are fully narrated from an advanced temporal point. The second narrative type Genette identifies is the 'interpolated' form, where the narrative is constructed 'between the moments of the action'; this is fundamentally the point from which day-to-day journals are narrated (217). The second form certainly has the most 'authority' in terms of producing the text's veracity. The preface to Warburton's journal promises that the 'efforts and struggles of the gallant party . . . are here given exactly as jotted down by the leader, whilst the agony was fresh in his mind. . . . the evident fidelity and absence of exaggeration of Colonel Warburton's style will be an additional charm' (Warburton vii). The authority of the journal which is gained through its 'transparent' style is also attained through the temporal proximity of the writing to the events. The journals tend not to adhere strictly to these rules that they themselves lay down, but are full of retrospective interpolations even when ostensibly transcriptions of the day-to-day field-books. The preface to Warburton's journal actually admits to this practice, saying that Warburton verbally supplied material included in the introduction and interpolated parenthetically into the journal. But 'some few amplifications of Colonel Warburton's own statements or descriptions, supplied in the same way have been incorporated, at the discretion of the Editor, in the text of the Journal itself' (Warburton vii).

The admission of this kind of retrospective interpolation works against the construction of the journal as the spontaneous, simple, written responses to the experiences of the journey; yet, this is a case where one kind of authority is supplementing another. It is in some ways useful for the journal to construct a temporally split narrator, because it provides both the authority of the 'fresh' recording and that of the considered, retrospective judgement, but I will argue that this fragmentation of univocality also costs the journals much of their author/ity.

Ultimately, then, there are some difficulties with strictly categorising the journals as either transcribed field-books or post-exploration testimonies; it is always possible to rewrite retrospectively daily entries to give the impression of infallibility or unusual foresight. A literary archaeologist might approach the problem of categorisation by making a detailed comparison between the field-book and the published journal. On differences being found, the assumption would then be made that Sturt or Mitchell, the real historical personage had, for reasons of vanity or pride, corrected daily entries to fit the facts known at the time of editing. This kind of comparative search usually ends in speculations about the historical person, and is appropriate for biographical investigations, but is lacking as literary analysis.[45] Close examination reveals that not only those journals which are largely transcribed field-books (even those which have later interpolations) but also those which contain proportionally more retrospective matter are created with a different, but necessarily complex relationship between the author and the narrator – a relationship that destroys any simple claims to the unity of author/explorer and narrator, on which the journal's authority is largely dependent.

To read the various Sturts of the journal as a single entity seems an unaffected interpretation, the result of mere commonsense. However, this approach fails to offer an invasive reading, whereby the authority of the figure 'Sturt', for example, can be put into question. At the end of Charles Sturt's *Narrative of an Expedition into Central Australia,* for example, the author apologises for his own incompetence: 'The ideas I would desire to convey are clear enough in my own mind, but I must confess that I feel a great difficulty in placing them so forcibly and so clearly before my readers as I could desire' (*ECA* 1: 416). This logocentric appeal to a pre-linguistic world of ideas might be seen as a traditional defence of a text – a convention of many works of 'fact'. It is more useful, however, to see it as a fragmentation of the monolithic author into author and narrator: the apology creates a split between, on the one hand, the figure of the straining and ultimately unsuccessful author and, on the other, the narrator who explains and apologises for the author's faults.

Certainly, the journals work hard to establish the contiguity of the explorer and author, especially in apologies for inaccuracy. The narrator of *Two Expeditions into . . . Southern Australia* states that exploration has caused bodily harm and begs the reader to remember that as 'I have been unassisted in this work in any one particular, I hope some excuse will be found for its imperfections' (*2Ex* 2: 5). The text seems to draw the 'I' together to produce a uniform persona: the voice of the narrator whose knowledge and control are complete – he knows that the text contains errors. But an insightful reading can once again find the fragmentation of 'Sturt': the knowledge he produces is at the cost of creating an incapacitated and, therefore, error-prone 'Sturt' the author. At the same time an error is admitted the narratorial voice attempts to regain authority, but the text's accuracy nevertheless remains in question. The figure of Sturt is fractured here, and the univocality of the journal collapses; like the autobiographer, the journal-writer 'loses clarity and authority even as he multiplies himself'.[46]

Retrospective re-writing

The retrospectivity of some of the journal entries destroys the facade of the journal as moment-by-moment (or at least end-of-the-day) report, and creates the possibility of memory error. Sturt describes a meeting with a party of Aborigines 'of whom, if I recollect, there were seven' (*ECA* 1: 414). Whether there were seven or eight is perhaps of relatively little importance, but the phrase 'if I recollect', opens the division between narrator and explorer and generates the possibility of more significant errors being present in the text. The retrospectivity of the journals allows interpolations of analysis, passages where the narrator takes on a theoretical voice and does not attempt to reproduce the thoughts of the explorer. An example of this is found in Philip King's journal, where there is a rather sudden temporal shift in the narratorial position. The journal describes the sowing of seeds and an inscription of a tree, but then it says that 'when we visited Oyster Harbour three years and a half afterwards, no signs remained of the garden, and the inscription was scarcely perceptible, from the stump of the tree having been nearly destroyed by fire' (King 1: 18). Here the narratorial voice is quite different to that of the explorer: it is temporally removed and can use retrospective knowledge to inject a particular meaning into events narrated.

Ordinarily in the journals the gap between the author and narrator is quite small; it is really only evident when the process of writing is referred to – when the 'author' emerges as an actor within the narrative and the narrator takes on a separate function. When retrospectivity is utilised, the narrator is superseded by a supra-narratorial voice which is temporally advanced. Often these narrative positions are compacted because retrospectivity allows rewriting, and thus the separation in time between the two narrational voices is expunged. In Forrest's journal it is possible to see these stages presented in different ways. First, there is an example of the simple author/narrator construct, where Forrest has just decided to shoot Aborigines if they attack.

> I thus decide and write in all humility, considering it as a necessity, as the only way of saving our lives. I write this at 4 p.m., just after the occurrence, so that, should anything happen to us, my brother will know how and when it occurred. – 5 p.m. The natives have appeared to move off. (Forrest 189)

The 'I' here is split between the 'I' who is the explorer/author actively engaged in a strategic inscription (the subject of the sentence), and the 'I' who is the narrator telling the story of the author (the subject who writes). The unusual feature of narration in this passage is that it is simultaneous – there is no temporal gap between the story and its narration. Genette points out that within simultaneous narration the text may veer in two quite different directions.

> A present-tense narrative which is 'behaviourist' in type and strictly of the moment can seem like the height of objectivity, since the last trace of enunciating that still subsisted in the Hemingway-style narrative (the mark of temporal interval between story and narrating, which the use of the preterite unavoidably comprises) now disappears in a total transparency of the narrative ...[47]

Ideally, the 'transparency' of the explorer's text is improved by the temporal closeness of the writing to the event, and this proximity is, of course, at its greatest degree in simultaneous narration. The authority of this method of narration inheres in its ability to make itself immediate; but, on close examination, Forrest's narration does nothing of the sort. Rather, writing is itself the subject of the narration, and as a result the 'simultaneous operates in favour of the discourse' at the expense of the action, which 'seems reduced to the condition of a simple pretext'.[48] Simultaneity, then, can operate in both ways: it can create the text as transparent and, thus, in explorers' journals valorise its authority; or it can emphasise the text's density and proclivity to self-reference, reducing its referentiality and, thus, authority to speak objectively of the material world. In the case of Forrest's inscription it is the text's self-reflexivity which is established, rather than its transparency.

Another example of the fragility of the subject and innate complexity of the narration in the journals is found again in Forrest, where there are multiple layers of retrospectivity.

> ... we were now in the very country that had drawn Mr. Gosse back. I have since found it did the same for Mr. Giles ... (Even now, months after this time, sitting down writing this journal, I cannot but recall my feelings of anxiety at the camp.) (Forrest 219)

Here, it seems that there are at least three temporally separate narrative voices. There is the narrator who is 'closest' to the events it describes. There is also a narrative voice with a quite separate viewpoint, one which has knowledge of Giles's retreat. Then, there is a third voice, which indicates its presence by parentheses and locates itself in time the way the second voice does not.

Stuart's journal consists of daily entries. Waiting at Beresford Springs for the return of the men, Stuart indicates frustration at the absence of part of the group: 'No signs of the two men; they must have stopped at some water during the night. It is very tiresome to be delayed in this way: what can they be about? At 12 noon they arrived ...' (92). The journal is constructed so that it seems to be a constant record of the explorer's thoughts, a kind of stream of consciousness. Despite this, the suspicion remains that the puzzlement is retrospectively produced, if not after the exploration then at least at the end of the day. In other places Stuart's journal does bear characteristics of an unfinished record. At one point he rather comically remarks, 'I forgot to mention that the nut we found on the south side of the range is not fit to eat; it caused both men to vomit violently. I ate one, but it had no bad effect on me' (159–60). It is in these dislocations between the generic expectations and the text that the author, narrator and explorer seem closest. The observations on the nut could have been seamlessly woven into the record at the appropriate point, but as it stands it connects the action of observation and the writing of the journal in a way polished narratives do not. In the contravening of the forward motion of the narrative the text successfully creates an effect of a figure who is both explorer and narrator. As it does so, however, it simultaneously reduces the authority of the author/ explorer. He forgets, he makes mistakes.

The author in the third person

Mitchell as author makes no such mistakes, and it is not a coincidence that it is in the preface to *Three Expeditions into ... Eastern Australia* that the most dramatic split between narrator and author occurs. The narrative voice speaks of the author in the third person, a prefatorial convention which vigorously constructs the author as a character of the narrative. The author becomes an identity separate from the narrative voice – it is he who returns at the 'close of many a laborious day, when the energies both of mind and body were almost exhausted' (*3Ex* 1: iii), and this is why some defects may be found. Error, then, is not the narrator's fault, but is the responsibility of the author. As a strategy, this could be successful: whatever faults exist are those of the main character, but the narrator's hegemonic and unquestioned voice continues, and it is this narrator who expresses the events and findings of the exploration.

The narrative voice, however, cannot fully separate the text from the author; indeed, after describing the errors of the author, this narrative voice paradoxically also makes him responsible for the journal's truth. First, he is thoroughly delineated as a character: 'In his expeditions into the interior of Australia, the author was led cheerfully on, by an eager curiosity to examine a country which is yet in the same state as when it was formed by its Maker' (*3Ex* 1: iii). The author becomes the producer of truth, but it is an author whose own volition is curiously controlled.

> With respect to the narrative of those expeditions, the sole merit of which he claims is that of having faithfully described what he attentively observed; neither his pencil nor his pen has been allowed to pass the bounds of truth. (*3Ex* 1: iii–iv)

Who stops his pen passing the bounds of truth? The author here seems to be imbedded in a subordinate position to the narrator, in some hierarchy of power. The author seems to have embodied those tenets of 'accuracy' that the organisations which aid imperial expansion hold as vital; the author has been 'faithful', but it is not clear whether the description is faithful to the objects or to the dictates of the Royal

Geographical Society and the Colonial Office. The author's powers of representation are completely open to the narrator's surveillance, and truth seems to be produced as much through coercion (neither his pencil nor his pen has been allowed), as through the author's complicity with imperial desire.

An analysis of *whose* gaze is presented in the journals, reveals that, at the point of enunciation, both the voice and the gaze are fractured. The gaze is always in danger of being a multiplicity of different gazes: the ethnographic, the landscape, the cartographic gaze, and so on, but these are held together by the construction of the strong, central individual. This construction takes place both 'inside' and 'outside' the journal: 'inside', in its mobilisation of the mythology of the heroic explorer; 'outside', in the institutional practices which determine the shape of exploration. Both these pressures bring into being the journal as the prime method by which exploration is recorded. Ironically, however, the journal is exactly that genre in which the fracturing of the identity of the subject is most evident.

3

Picturesque Visions: Controlling the Seen

Codes of production

Can an explorer describe a new land in a new way?

As we have seen, one of the powerful myths of exploration is that knowledge-gathering takes place through the explorer's seeing 'new' land for the first time. In this myth the explorer accurately describes new land that he sees. But far from being a fresh and innocent transcription of the natural world, the discursive construction in the journals of what is seen by the explorers is generated by already existing cultural formations. It is the task of this chapter to show how vision is constructed in terms of the *picturesque* and the *panoramic* – two European conventions of seeing, which possess ideological agendas of their own.

These conventions are not to be understood as harmless strategies for familiarising the unfamiliar, or – worse – as natural responses. Rather, the picturesque and panoramic deconstruct the journals' claims to the authority of originality and immediacy, for no longer is the vision fresh and unaffected, but it is culturally mediated. Moreover, they are techniques which reveal the nexus between power and surveillance within the journal and, once the existence of this nexus is realised, it is possible to see that 'innocent' aesthetic responses are actually expressions of imperial greed. This nexus can be revealed by examining collisions in the journals, particularly between scientific and aesthetic discourses.

Accuracy and defensiveness

Since the exploration journals had not entirely extricated themselves from the genre of travel writing and its reputation for minimal accuracy, claims for the author's veracity are found in the journals. In the second volume of *Two Expeditions into ... Southern Australia* one can find Sturt's stoutest defence of the truthfulness of the journal. It is interesting that, while accuracy may be the first expectation of a journal, it is the use-value of the information which is presented as of primary importance.

> I trust that this book (whatever be its defects) will be found to contain much valuable information of a practical character, and I may venture to affirm, that it will give a true description of the country, and of the various other subjects of which it treats. (*2Ex* 2: 5)

Accuracy and use-value sit side by side in this analysis of the exploration journal and there is no attempt to connect the two. Rather, the anxiety arises that to be of use at all the journals must be read. Sturt's introduction offers the reader the consolation that 'although he must expect a considerable portion of dry reading in the following pages, I have endeavoured to make the narrative of events, some of which are remarkably striking, as interesting as possible' (*2Ex* 2: 4). In arguing that while an official record of an expedition is necessarily dull it may be embroidered by a lively recitation of the more 'striking' incidents, Sturt opens a generic conflict. On the one hand, the journals are an alliance of scientific investigation and instrumentalist pragmatism; they are documents of fact, information gathered by objective, impersonal (even disembodied) means, quantified, conforming to accuracy and detail in description, and providing useful information. On the other hand, the journals are at least as much the narrative of the expedition as the reporting of observation – the observers are continually kept in view. But Sturt is inconsistent in his theorisation of how journals may be interesting. In *Narrative of an Expedition into Central Australia* he states that distinctness of fact can 'alone secure interest to my narrative' (i–ii), directly contradicting his previous expression that interest may be appended through the lively recollection of striking incidents.

This conflict between the genre's demand for the accurate recitation of fact and the inclusion of 'interesting' and picturesque detail was not the sole property of exploration journals but had arisen in the more serious travel literature of the late eighteenth century. Just as exploration literature had to, it needed to distance itself from the less reputable forms of travel writing; so, a defence of accuracy often prefaces the work. Arthur Young's *A Six Months Tour Through the North of England*, for example, notes that the author's experiments in agriculture have given him the 'plodding merit' of being accurate. And, as in exploration literature, there was a need to excuse the inclusion of objects of interest: their display has a utility of its own, in that 'they are a proof, and a very important one, of the riches and the happiness of this kingdom'.[1]

Young's *Travels in France and Italy* mobilises the Coleridgean tactic of a letter from a 'person, of whose judgment I think highly', which insists that Young include the 'passages that would best please the mass of common readers' – sections which Young characterises as being of a 'trifling nature'.[2]

The theoretician of the picturesque, William Gilpin, found that explorers failed to detail scenes of beauty which would be of interest to the journals' readers. He criticised the naval explorer King for missing opportunities to add 'high colouring' to his descriptions, which would have evinced his taste as well as interested the readers. To King's fairly flat description of travelling along a cliff-bound river, Gilpin responds with indignation.

> It is hardly possible, in so few words, to present more picturesque ideas of the horrid and savage kind. We have a river running up a country broken on both sides with wild and romantic rocks, which we know nature never constructs in a uniform manner. We naturally conclude, therefore, that they ran out in some parts into vast diagonal strata, on the ledges of which a bear or two appeared, sitting on their hams or howling at the boat. In other parts, the rocks would form lofty promontories, hanging over the river and inhabited by numerous wildfowl screaming round them. This is copied from Captain King's sketch, and yet he has no idea that a scene so savage could present any other ideas than such as were disgusting.[3]

In building a description through the conflation of geomorphological speculation and imaginary detail with King's journal, Gilpin renders accuracy secondary to the 'interest' of a scene. Gilpin favours a description which includes the observer and his or her emotions as active participants in the description; indeed, the objects themselves come to be seen as valuable only in their ability to provoke pleased responses – in other words, for their picturesque quality. The generic ambivalence between 'accuracy' and 'interest' which plagued the serious travel narrative is shared by the exploration journal. Despite the assertion by the magistrate and poet Barron Field that Australian nature was un-picturesque,[4] exploration journals do often remark upon the pictur-esque qualities of the scenes they are describing; in fact, the descriptions are constructed through a picturesque vocabulary. These aesthetic responses supply the 'interest' of the journals, resulting in their construc-tion of a reader split between a concern for scientific accuracy and a desire to be fed the adventure and aesthetic excitement of a popular travel narrative.

As Bernard Smith has argued in *European Vision and the South Pacific*, fissures develop between scientific/instrumentalist and aesthetic descrip-tions in journals of exploration. It seems to me that it is the objects of description which determine the mode utilised. For objects such as rocks, shells, fauna and flora, and so on, there is a developed scientific code of illustration, designed to expedite – and, in a published form, justify – their placement within Linnaean and geological classifications. Other objects, on the other hand, such as landscape prospects, have no legitimate or ready-made scientific paradigms into which they can be inserted. The ascendancy of Lyellian geology and the explanation of geological features in terms of huge time-spans supply scientific authority but not a descriptive vocabulary sufficient to textually produce large areas of land. The paradigm which did supply a sufficient vocabulary was the aesthetic of landscape – in particular, the concept of the picturesque. Gilpin himself recognised that there was a difference between the aesthetic and scientific production of land: 'The province of the picturesque is to *survey* nature; *not anatomize matter*. It throws its glances around in the broad-craft style. It comprehends an extreme tract at each sweep. It examines *parts*, but never descends to particles'.[5] Mitchell also understood that the aesthetic and scientific production of land were necessarily opposed. When his vision from an elevation is interfered with, he laments that 'the scene, although sublime enough for the theme of a poet, was not at all suited to the more common-place objects of a surveyor' (*3Ex* 2: 177). Yet, he frames the scene by describing how the lower objects are 'blended in one grey shade, like the dead colouring of a picture' (*3Ex* 2: 176).

Topographical and picturesque representation are confused within the journals, so that ostensibly mimetic pictures can be seen to employ standard picturesque construction and arrangement. As well, I will argue that hidden within picturesque aesthetics is an instrumentalist agenda, which establishes nature solely as an object to be valued according to its ability to please and serve human beings. This mode of landscape production opposed scientific evaluation, but paradoxically already carried with it the same utilitarian ideologies of land function possessed by instrumentalist science, which meant that if the land was picturesque it was ripe for transformation into wealth. Furthermore, when picturesque discourse is not available to the explorers, for example in panoramic or the more 'scientific' cartographic descriptions, the construction of the land is nevertheless a self-centring production of an imperial subjectivity.

Representation and appropriation

Both scientific and picturesque productions of the natural world have an impulse towards appropriation of their objects of study. In the journals this appropriation by scientific representation is the more obvious of the two modes: to be represented at all, the fauna in most cases has to be killed and preserved so that, upon return, it may be displayed, decontextualised; or, if preservation is impossible, it may then be illustrated, again removed from its habitat, or accompanied by a token tree branch, perhaps. It is one of the ironies of the journals that attempts to preserve finds have a particularly high rate of failure. The scientific urge towards acquisition and mensuration is deconstructed in the journals by the irremediably fragile nature of the object that they are attempting to include within their system of knowledge.[6]

Just as the animal is hunted, so is the picturesque scene. In *Three Essays* Gilpin constructs this analogy which draws upon the hunt, an occupation of the landed gentry, to describe another entertainment of the same class.

> The pleasures of the chase are universal. A hare started before dogs is enough to set a whole country in an uproar ... and shall we suppose it a greater pleasure to the sportsman to pursue a trivial animal, than it is to the man of taste to pursue the beauties of nature? (48)

The association of picturesque pleasure with the violent extraction of the scene from nature continues in a quotation from a poem on picturesque aesthetics, which Gilpin uses. The aristocratising of the 'man of taste', who is now one of the 'favoured few', accompanies the intimations of violent appropriation in the poem. The arbiters of picturesque taste are those 'favoured few, whom heaven has lent / The power to *seize*, select, and reunite / Her lovliest features' (53 my italics). Mitchell also uses a particularly interesting phrase to describe the taking of a picture: 'the eye of the eagle and the rich crest of the cockatoo of the desert, could not be preserved in dead specimens, and were too fine to be omitted among the sketches, I endeavoured to snatch from nature' (*3Ex* 2: 264). The 'snatching' of a picture is not confined to scientific illustration but is also present in aesthetic productions of the land. The word 'snatched' appears in James Thomson's poem *The Seasons*, 'Spring', lines 950–52, where the eye is 'snatched o'er hill and dale' (1.952) by the landscape itself. Barrell notes that this implies a surrendering of the gaze to the seductive powers of nature, but a few lines later the eye 'roams' at will over the landscape, exerting final control.[7] Playing with the idea that nature could seduce or control one's vision was not infrequent among aesthetes, but rare in explorers. Giles comes closest when he reverses a cliché of panoramic description: 'At length I reached the summit of a high round mountain in the middle tier, and a most varied and splendid panorama was spread before me, or I was spread before it. (Giles 1: 31) Inverting the usual subject–object relationship between observer and nature might be seen as playing with the assumed dominance of the explorer/observer. Carole Fabricant has noted, however, that these moments are not to be taken seriously but are examples of a 'titillating flirtation with surrender on the part of men who were ... very much in control.[8]

The picturesque is a mode of appreciation that is inherently appropriative. William Gilpin exhorts the followers of picturesque taste not to lose an opportunity to annex nature: 'forms, and colours, in brightest array, fleet before us; and if the transient glance of a good composition happen to unite with them, we should give any price to fix, and appropriate the scene'.[9] Although Gilpin may simply be suggesting that our perceptions have a certain value and should be preserved, the picturesque valorises land only in its ability to produce these sensations. There is a description in Mitchell's *Journal of an Expedition into ... Tropical Australia* which attempts to combine artistic sensibility with the exactitude of scientific nomenclature, and which posits the productions of the country as significant only in their ability to supply artists with raw material.

> At this time, the outlines were wild, the tints sublimely beautiful. Mighty trees of Casuarinae ... contrasted finely with erect Mimosae, with prostrate masses of driftwood, and with perpendicular rocks. The hues of the Anthistria grass, of a red-brown, contrasted most harmoniously with the light green bushes, grey driftwood, blue water, and verdure by its margin; all these again – grass, verdure, driftwood and water – were so opposed to the dark hues of the casuarinae, Mimosae and refted rocks, that a Ruysdael, or a Gainsborough, might there have found an inexhaustible stock of subjects for their pencil ... May the object of our journey be successful, I thought then; and may we also hope that these beauties of nature may no longer 'waste their sweetness in the desert air'; and that more of her graces may thus be brought back within the reach of art. (*EITA* 135–36)

This view that nature is simply a repository of aesthetic productions echoes remarkably accurately a similar description by Oxley.

> Several new birds were seen today of beautiful plumage; none however were procured, so as to enable me to describe them ... some fine and singular plants also enriched our collection: it would seem as if nature here delighted in wasting her most beautiful productions upon the 'desert air', rather than placing them in situations where they would become more easily accessible to the researches of science and taste.(Oxley 230)

Here, nature is a source of materials for scientific as well as aesthetic appropriation. The language of commercial gain is alloyed with that of scientific gain – specimens are 'procured' or 'acquired' (Oxley 294) to 'enrich' the collection. And in an aesthetic consumption – echoing the traveller Young's description of the prospect as 'delicious' – Stokes's journal, recounting Helpman's report, says that he was 'feasting my eyes on a most luxuriant well-watered country' (Stokes 1: 206). Every recording is an appropriation and a fixation, and this chapter will show how picturesque aesthetics is thoroughly imbricated with specific material practices as well as being an appropriative aesthetic in itself.

The explorers' picturesque

The land as picture

The 'picturesque' works to delimit the continuity of the universe, to produce a frame which makes a text of the landscape so that it may be read and compared to the ideal. Framing landscape, and labelling it picturesque, combats its threatening vastness and unfamiliarity and demonstrates the triumphant portability of visual taste; it also defers the opening of the aesthetic process to native adaptations. Indeed the picturesque itself is a mechanism for deferral: while an Australian scene may be judged as like or unlike a particular picturesque British landscape, these British scenes are in turn approved according to how they resemble the landscape of Italy – or, rather, the Italian landscape as represented by Italian artists who, in turn, have their models. The examples of landscapes constructed as paintings are legion; a small sample is sufficient.

> The distant range of the Darling mountains supplies a splendid back ground to the picture ... (Stokes 1: 54)
>
> ... a beautiful looking country, splendidly grassed and ornamented with the fantastic mounds [anthills], and the creek timber as back and fore grounds for the picture. (Giles 1: 150)
>
> ... the treeless hills ... formed the background, and the enamelled and emerald earth ... formed the groundwork of the scene. (Giles 2: 285)

The nineteenth century psychology of sight suggested to the explorers that this notion of a landscape as a picture was more than a conceit. Here, again, there is a difference in emphasis between the accuracy demanded of sight and the aesthetic pleasure the sight can produce. Giles says of one scene that 'the verdure of the glen, the bright foliage of the trees that lined the banks of the stream ... formed a picture in the retina of his eye, which is ever pleasing to the traveller to remember, and a pleasure also to describe' (Giles 2: 295). This analysis of retinal impressions, then, disguises the cultural practice of picturesque aesthetics as an ocular necessity. Another appearance of the notion of seeing as a purely retinal activity can be found in Leichhardt's attempts to analyse the unerring geographical sense of the Aborigines. After he has been led back to camp by 'Brown', Leichhardt theorises that the 'impressions on the retina [for the Aborigines] seem to be naturally more intense than on that of the European; and their recollections are remarkably exact, even to the most minute details ... things ... seem to form a kind of Daguerrotype impression on their minds' (118). It is ironic that it is the Aborigines who are granted this visual accuracy rather than the European scientist/explorer.

More often, however, the construction of a scene as picturesque did not involve an attempted naturalisation by way of the physiology of sight, but was acknowledged to be artificial and at the mercy of individual taste. Mitchell's journal is particularly concerned with defining its author as a man of taste, and takes every opportunity to display his knowledge of landscape art. This results in cartographical traces of landscape artists because the view reminded Mitchell of their work. He writes of the 'beautiful headland which appeared quite isolated, and just such as painters place in middle distance, I named Mount Salvator' (Mitchell 222).

The likening of scenes to those produced by such artists is, as I have mentioned, a way of controlling their otherwise threatening otherness. The imperial strategy of simultaneously creating a semiotic blank from a country and then projecting upon it comfortable and preconceived forms can be seen in these ostensibly innocent descriptions. The landscape itself is deferred; it exists only insofar as it reminds one of a European exemplum. The imperial eye thus forms knowledge of the colony (both for itself and others) on its own terms. The picturesque's view of the earth as raw material for aesthetic appreciation means that no views should go unbeholden by the European man of taste – until they are seen in this way, indeed such views are considered to be, as Oxley said, wasted to the 'desert air'. This precludes the possibility of another (especially Aboriginal) aesthetic appreciation; more than that, however, it may even preclude the existence of a population which could appreciate the scene in another way. Mitchell again names a landscape feature after Salvator Rosa, this time erasing the Aboriginal inhabitation of the area.

> Those beautiful recesses of unpeopled earth, could no longer remain unknown. The better to mark them out on my map, I gave to the valley the name of Salvator Rosa. The rocks stood out sharply, and sublimely, from the thick woods, just as John Martin's fertile imagination would dash them out in his beautiful sepia landscapes. (*EITA* 224)

The erasure of the Aboriginal population in descriptions such as these is a result of the impulse of the picturesque to supply *novel* as well as striking views. The aesthetic connoisseur revelling in a previously unseen vista is a trope which is easily aligned in the journals with that of the explorer first viewing a 'new' land. The novelty, however, is severely compromised by the fact that the scene resembles *already known* pictures; the 'new' landscapes are never seen as new but as versions of previously known ones.

Codes of the picturesque

The picturesque is an avowedly artificial and socially constructed mode. The debates surrounding what could and could not be considered picturesque, and what relations existed between the picturesque, the sublime and the beautiful are adequately summarised elsewhere.[10] The important point is that vigorous debates did take place in the public arenas of published letters, didactic poetry and satires of this poetry. It was not simply the taste for the 'picturesque' that was the subject of controversy but the term itself. In *Three Essays: On Picturesque Beauty; On Picturesque Travel; and On the Art of Sketching Landscapes*, William Gilpin struggled to differentiate 'picturesque' from other aesthetic categories – to find what natural elements could be accorded the term 'picturesque', and what were suited to artificial representation. After advancing several tentative arguments and finding them faulty (26–30), Gilpin admits such searches for first principles 'rarely end in satisfaction' (30). He can find no inherent differences in nature between the picturesque and the beautiful but must fall back upon his original definition, which is object-based: that is, the picturesque denotes 'such objects, as are proper subjects for painting' (36).

Gilpin's definition sidesteps the obvious question of how certain natural qualities came to be considered fit for pictorial representation in the first place. On the one hand, Gilpin locates picturesqueness within the features of the object itself, which may be passively recognised by those who have a knowledge of art. On the other hand, however, obtaining a picturesque view is a matter of selection and framing, of choosing an appropriate viewpoint; if the original landscape is lacking in such qualities, then it is also a matter of changing it. Thus, the 'picturesque' as a concept hovers between that which is identified in an object, and that which is obtained from a particular viewpoint or through a strategic framing. As Gilpin's fellow aesthetician Uvedale Price noted, there are few words whose 'meaning has been less accurately determined than that of the word picturesque'.[11]

What qualities, then, were expected to be present in a painting of a picturesque landscape? Although he was not the sole authority, it is useful to follow Gilpin again here, as he gives a clear delineation of the rules for picturesque composition. As part of the reaction against highly ordered gardens, 'roughness' of presentation was greatly valued. Gilpin's directions in this regard are as explicit for the landscape gardener as they are for the painter: 'turn the lawn into a piece of broken ground: plant rugged oaks instead of flowering shrubs: break the edges of a walk ... instead of making the whole *smooth*, make it rough; and you make it also *picturesque*' (8). 'Smoothness' is inimical to the picturesque, as roughness supplies the necessities of 'variety' and 'contrast' (20) and the effect of light and shade.

The rough objects must be encompassed within the picture by the three-plane composition that Gilpin preferred. The foreground was particularly important in a practical sense as it was the first element in the sketch and the one which spatially positioned all others (69–70); but it also played a vital role compositionally, resembling 'those deep tones in music, which give a value to all the lighter parts; and harmonize the whole'. The centre of interest in the picture, according to Gilpin, should be in the middle ground; the foreground occupied a subsidiary function and 'without any striking object to attract the eye, must plainly show, that it is intended only to introduce the leading subject with more advantage'.[12] The 'leading subject' was the concentration of interest of the picture. Gilpin excoriated landscapes that seemed to have no identifying or unifying feature: 'we often see a landscape, which comes under no denomination, Is it the scenery about a run? Is it a lake scene? Is it a river scene? No: but it is a jumble of all together.'[13] As well as having a subsidiary foreground, a middle ground which contained the central subject and a background, art derived from Gilpin's picturesque principles usually utilised a *coulisse*, a framing device consisting of trees or rocks which were darker than the middle ground and helped to focus attention to the picture's centre.

These rules form a complex network of codifications which must be present in any visual representation before it can be awarded the term 'picturesque'. In their complexity these rules severely limit the kinds of scenes that may be depicted tastefully. Their requirements include: one focus of interest rather than many; a clear planar division to establish the illusion of depth; a certain variety and contrast rather than smoothness; and, above all, a point of view which allows the framing of a limited scene rather than an endless expanse.

Gilpin offers an interesting analysis of the differences between writing and art that is relevant to the explorer's journals. In a footnote he writes:

language, like light, is a medium; and the true philosophic style, like light from a north-window, exhibits objects clearly, and distinctly, without soliciting attention to itself. In painting subjects of amusement indeed, language may guild somewhat more, and colour with the dies of fancy: but where information is of more importance, than entertainment, tho you cannot throw too *strong* a light, you should carefully avoid a *coloured* one. The style of

> some writers resembles a bright light placed between the eye, and the thing to
> be looked at. The light shews itself; and hides the object. (*Three Essays* 18 n.1)

For Gilpin, writing is an illumination of an object, and writing which calls
attention to itself is a light that is no longer projected from the author
onto the object, but has shifted to being between the object and reader
of the text. In his attempt to dematerialise writing, Gilpin runs into a
problem with its relation to art. In the note he says that some painting is
just as intrusive as poor writing, but in the text he makes a fundamental
differentiation of the two. Truths are independent of language: 'a truth
is a truth, whether observed in the language of a philosopher, or a
peasant; and the *intellect* receives it as such' (18). But in painting, the
truth resides not in the veracity of representation but the '*very* truth itself
[is] concerned in [the] *mode* of representing' (18). In Gilpin's model,
informational language is a transparent medium, but painting is
'opaque'. He thought pictures encoded with information that was ostensibly accurate, topographical art, to be a 'plagiarism below the dignity of
painting'.[14] In the explorer's journals, however, the rules Gilpin and
others outline as constitutive of picturesque art also operate in illustrations and descriptions that had generic roles determining them as
mimetic and topographical.

It is not difficult to find illustrations in the journals which obey all
these rules. In the second volume of Mitchell's *Three Expeditions into . . .
Eastern Australia* there is a depiction of the 'Fall of Cobaw', near Mt
Macedon in Victoria, which may serve as point of entry into the relationship between the picturesque and journal illustrations which purport to
obey rules of accuracy.

This illustration of the waterfall complies with picturesque codes: it has
a clear centre of interest, which is brightly lit in contrast to the dark stone
which surrounds it (see plate 1). The rocks supply the requisite 'roughness', their facets reflecting light in different directions and intensities to
provide variety. The picture contains three planes: the foreground
features a rock shelf, a fire, and two Aborigines fishing in a pool; the
middle ground contains the main waterfall pent between two large
outcrops of rock, some subsidiary flows of water and trees standing
against the sky; the background is the smallest component, featuring a
sky with a diffuse light source. Mitchell's description of the waterfall
shows that the picturesque qualities in the picture are not accidental.

> I had visited several waterfalls in Scotland, but this was certainly the most
> picturesque I had witnessed; although the effect was not so much in the body
> of water falling, or the loud noise, as in the bold character of the rocks over
> and amongst which it fell. Their colour and shape were harmonized into a
> more complete scene than nature usually presents, resembling the 'finished
> subject' of an artist, foreground and all. (*3Ex* 2: 286)

Plate 1   *The Fall of Cobaw*, near Mt Macedon, Victoria; an engraving by
G. Barnard after Mitchell's drawing. From Thomas Mitchell, *Three Expeditions
into ... Eastern Australia* (vol. 2, pl.37). Mitchell Library, State Library of New
South Wales.

Mitchell further describes the various colours of the rock, the contrast
between the dark moss and the whiteness of the falling water, and hopes
that 'other picturesque scenery, perhaps finer than this', may yet be
found. However, conscious of the codes of the picturesque, Mitchell does
nothing to step outside them. The full description of the waterfall
actually echoes a picturesque structure, leading the eye from the foreground to the centre, from the moss-darkened rocks to the waterfall and
higher, lighter rocks. Mitchell establishes himself as a qualified judge of
the 'picturesqueness' of waterfalls, creating an aesthetic hierarchy and
placing the Fall of Cobaw on this scale in comparison to European
examples. Thus, a scene is valorised by its difference from European
waterfalls, but is firmly fixed within a European aesthetic framework.
This hierarchy is judged by the qualified individual, the man of taste,
according to the 'effect' it produces upon him. The scene is significant
and valuable then, not simply because of the aesthetic pleasure it gives to
people in general, but because it gives pleasure to, and follows the rules
established by, a privileged and select class who classify themselves as
judges of taste.

The lithograph of the *Fall of Cobaw* may be usefully compared with
Turner's *Fall of Tees, Yorkshire*, or, for a monochromatic comparison, with
Edward Goodall's lithograph of Turner's painting.[15] This depiction of a

waterfall is taken from a slightly higher vantage point than Mitchell's and features a more substantial background of receding mountains and clouds, although many picturesque codes are still present. Turner's painting features a coulisse composed of rock walls, which in the lithograph are rather darker, emphasising the contrast between the gloomy rock and the bright waterfall. The rocks display many enfoldings, creating a complex play of light and shade, and there is a human figure dwarfed by the fall. Ruskin's response to this picture places the picturesque in an interesting relationship to accuracy. In *Modern Painters* the *Fall of Tees* is praised because:

> the whole truth has been given, with all the relations of its parts; so that we can pick and choose our points of pleasure or of thought for ourselves, and reason upon the whole with the same certainty which we should after having climbed and hammered over the rocks bit by bit. With this drawing before him, a geologist could give a lecture upon the whole system of aqueous erosion, and speculate as safely upon the past and future states of this very spot, as if he were standing and getting wet with the spray.[16]

Ruskin accepts that the *Fall of Tees* is a picturesque painting; so, one view of the picturesque commends the accuracy of its depiction. Bernard Smith has praised Mitchell's *Western Extremity of Mount Arapiles* and Sturt's *Desert Glen*, concluding that the use of external notes in Mitchell's picture, and the concentration on geological information in Sturt's, are evidence of the authors' intention to supply information for the scientifically minded reader.[17] If Ruskin's critique can be applied generally to the picturesque, then the codes of scientific, mimetic accuracy and those of the picturesque need not conflict, although the picturesque codes would still determine selection and composition of scenes.

Picturesque and scientific worlds collide

On closer examination, it is obvious that scientific and picturesque codes are in continuous collision. Gilpin does not pretend to accuracy of depiction, instead obeying the conventions of the picturesque.

> I hold myself at perfect liberty, in the first place, to dispose the foreground as I please ... I take up a tree here, and plant there. I pare a knoll, or make an addition to it. I remove a piece of paling – a cottage – a wall – or any removeable object, which I dislike. (68)

It would be expected that the journals, in keeping with their pledge of accuracy would adhere to Ruskinesque respect for accuracy, eschewing liberties with the truth. The *Fall of Cobaw* illustration confounds this expectation in its depiction of two Aborigines in the foreground who are nowhere mentioned in the text. To claim that the picture is false because of the addition of the two apparently imaginary figures would be to privilege the truth of the text over that of the picture. Rather than prioritising the truth of the versions by assuming one to be true, it is more useful to ask what purpose the figures serve in the picture. Whereas their absence serves little function in the text, their presence in the illustration strongly adds to its picturesque qualities: they give scale to the waterfall, provide an interesting and varied foreground, and fulfil the picturesque function of human figures in helping the viewers to imagine themselves in the scene, although this particular function is replaced in this case by the exotic appeal of the figures.

Archival investigation shows that Mitchell experimented with foreground figures in his preliminary sketches. One such attempt at the *Fall of Cobaw*, a watercolour and pencil sketch, positions a lightly pencilled explorer with gun reclining in front of the falls, and another standing on top of the falls on a small outcrop. Yet another sketch shows two Aborigines, one fishing with a spear (rather than using a net as in the final version), and one who has been pasted into the picture, sitting in the foreground (see plate 2).[18] These changes illustrate Mitchell's search for composition, for picturesque foreground figures, as well as a concern for ethnographic value in displaying 'typical' native activities.

Plate 2   Mitchell's preliminary sketch for the *Fall of Cobaw* (watercolour and pencil). Dixson Gallery, State Library of New South Wales.

There exist several examples in the journals of Aborigines being used as artistic props for the formation of a picturesque scene. Stuart's journal includes a description from 'Hermit Hill', which mentions the presence of neither indigenes nor hermits (facing p.53). The corresponding picture, however, has a full complement of foreground figures sitting beside a fire in front of a romantically twisted tree. There is a similar example in William Westall's treatment of King George's Sound. The sketch, a view of the harbour from Peak Head, shows few elements of picturesque construction. The oil painting which resulted, however, is adorned in the foreground with two somewhat Rousseauesque natives, one clad in robes, the other with a head-dress of feathers; the scene has grown a grass tree near the centre, and the sense of depth has been increased by use of alternating bands of light and dark.[19] The change from 'accurate sketch' to picturesque oil painting cannot simply be expressed by an alteration of purpose or intended viewer for the painting, however. Many preliminary sketches utilise the same picturesque constructions as more finished depictions: Westall's sketch of Port Lincoln, for example, makes use of a coulisse of trees.[20]

Not all the illustrations in the exploration journals are structured according to the dictates of the picturesque. The depictions of the landscape in Leichhardt's journal almost totally avoid picturesque characteristics. The frontispiece illustration, *Lagoon near the L. Alligator*, makes some concessions to the picturesque: the foreground includes figures, the middle ground has interesting water scenery, and there is a varied background. But these features take up only a third of the vertical area of the picture, the other two-thirds being the sky. The vestiges of a picturesque structure are done away with in the journal's other illustrations, such as the foldout picture *Ranges of the Camp at the Burdekin*, where there is no foreground, coulisse, or 'object of interest'. Instead, four-fifths of the picture consists of clouds. This does not mean that Leichhardt has shrugged off the straitjacket of pictorial precursors to generate a new and accurate mode of representation; rather, the journal has employed another convention, that of the Dutch landscape, where the sky dominates the land, to structure the illustrations. Likewise, other illustrations utilise non-picturesque conventions, but this does not mean that they approach any closer to 'accuracy'.

In Mitchell's *Journal of an Expedition into . . . Tropical Australia* there is a picture of a member of Mitchell's party reclining in the manner of a shepherd in an Arcadian painting (see plate 3). It is difficult to interpret this without speculating about Mitchell's intentions (it seems a deliberate reference to the pastoral paintings with which he was familiar) but, reproducing this rustic figure presents the land as a nascent world of pastoral bliss, and the exploration party as the first of many settlers.

Plate 3 *Martin's Range*, engraved by T. Picken after Mitchell's drawing. From Thomas Mitchell, *Expedition into . . . Tropical Australia* (pl.5). Mitchell Library, State Library of New South Wales.

Another example of text and picture diverging in Mitchell is found in *Three Expeditions into . . . Eastern Australia*, where his party is attempting to follow the course of the Murray river. His description contains some important elements, which will be seen to be repeated in descriptions of the picturesque, in particular the association of 'rich' with the picturesque. He relates that:

> we came upon a most romantic looking scene, where a flood branch had left a serpentine piece of water, enclosing two wooded islands of rather picturesque character; the whole being overhung by the steep and bushy slope of the hill. The scenery of some lakes thus formed, was very fine, especially when their rich verdure and lofty trees were contrasted with the scrub, which covered the sandhills nearest the river, where a variety of shrubs, such as we had not previously seen, formed a curious foreground. (*3Ex* 2: 132–33)

The novelty of the shrubs does not disqualify the scene from being considered picturesque, showing the transportability and flexibility of the concept. The description of the Murray backwater is accompanied by a lithographic illustration which obeys the rules of picturesque composition, especially in its use of foliage (in this case *Eucarya Murryana*, as Mitchell helpfully notes) as a framing device directing attention to the picture's centre. Just as in the *Fall of Cobaw* the foreground includes Aborigines engaged in hunting, who have no presence in the text. A parenthetical note would seem initially to aid resolution of the disjunction between picture and text, indicating that the lithograph 'represents the general character of the scenery on the Murray' (133). This seems to step away from the particularity that characterises empirical research towards a picturesque generalising approach which admits the taking of licence. But, unless Mitchell is presenting the backwater as typical of the river, which is a rather curious strategy, then the note is strictly nonsensical. The illustration is clearly of the scene Mitchell has described in words, except in its addition of foreground figures. The notion of typicality that the idealism of the picturesque engenders can actually be the cause of a picture being taken. Mitchell's justification for making one particular sketch is that it is 'so characteristic a specimen' (*3Ex* 2: 36). Information-gathering based on this principle can obviously never be more than reflexive of the stereotypes brought to the act by the explorer.

The picturesque vocabulary

The precise meaning allocated by Gilpin to the word 'picturesque' was quickly confused by its synonymous interchange with 'beautiful' and 'sublime'. The journals of exploration use the word surprisingly often in a strictly correct way (as Gilpin would have it) – its most appreciated characteristics being harmony, a variation of light and shade, roughness and a tasteful contrast of colours. Mitchell, especially, has a keen appreciation of the need for 'roughness', and variation of light.[21] His description of the Lachlan celebrates the 'highly picturesque' scenery, noting the 'huge gnarled trunks, [and] wild romantic formed branches' of the 'yarra' tree, and the 'striking and pleasing contrast' between the 'yarra' and the acacia (*3Ex* 2: 54–55). On another occasion he notes the fine contrast between the shadows surrounding the trees of the Peel river and the brightly lit rock on which he stands (*3Ex* 1: 40).

Stuart also used the picturesque in a way of which Gilpin would have approved, describing a gorge which had 'a very picturesque appearance; immense masses of rock – some thousands of tons in weight – which had fallen from the top of a cliff into the bed of a creek' (Stuart 383–84). From a hill which was 'sufficiently elevated to afford me [a] most varied prospect', Oxley praises the way the 'intermingled light and shade formed by the different description of trees and shrubs, the hills but above all, the noble lake before me, gave a character to the scenery highly picturesque and pleasing' (Oxley 126). Stokes describes an 'extremely picturesque' sheet of water, the 'gentle repose' of which 'harmonized exquisitely with the slender motionless boughs of the drooping gums, palms and acacias' – this harmony apparently being undisturbed by the sound of guns which were 'dealing destruction among the quails that here abounded' (2: 312). Grey writes of 'romantic and picturesque estuaries', in which spring, native paths, foliage and swans 'imparted ... a quiet and a charm which was deeply felt' (Grey 2: 3). Even the relatively dry journal of Leichhardt savours a picturesque swamp adorned with 'drooping tea-trees' and a 'rich sward of grasses of the most delicate verdure' (493). That explorers were connoisseurs of the picturesque, then, is not in question. However, the picturesque is not simply an aesthetic question divorced from the colonial moment; it is a way of according land an aesthetic value but is also thoroughly imbricated with notions of the land's economic value.

Beauty and use

Sturt speaks of the land as 'rich and picturesque near the river' and in *Expedition into Central Australia* of how 'the transition from the rich to the barren, from the picturesque to the contrary, was instantaneous' (*ECA* 1: 408). He also often associates beauty with 'richness' (*2Ex* 2: 30–31, 34–35). Grey's descriptions combine 'richness' and 'picturesque' a number of times (Grey 2: 3–4, 14, 28) and Oxley praises the 'beautifully picturesque' scenery which is built upon a soil 'which for richness can nowhere be excelled' (Oxley 184). It is not surprising that aesthetic judgement is related to the land's capacity to support life, but it would be ingenuous to read 'richness' as simply indicative of bountiful flora and fauna, and not of a future wealth.

The association of the picturesque with possible wealth-producing areas is a colonial adaptation of the term; Gilpin had denied this connection between the picturesque and the profitable. Describing a 'barren' prospect, Gilpin qualifies his use of the word: 'I mean *barren* only in a picturesque light; forest affords good pasturage; and is covered with herds of cattle; and a beautiful breed of sheep, with silken fleeces, and without horns'.[22] The explorers' use of the picturesque represents a fusion of aesthetics and appraisal of future use-value, but of course there are many appraisals of the land which do not utilise a vocabulary of the picturesque. In the more advanced stages of the colonial enterprise there is a particularly instrumentalist gaze surveying the land, to which aesthetics is irrelevant. Writing in the 1860s, thirty years after Mitchell's *Three Expeditions into ... Eastern Australia* and twenty years after the publication of Sturt's *Expedition into Central Australia*, Stuart privileges the pragmatic over the picturesque judgement:

> ... the country in the ranges is as fine a pastoral hill-country as a man would wish to possess ... (159)
> ... it is a splendid feeding country for cattle. (239)
> ... [the grass is] fit for the scythe to go into, and an abundant crop of hay could be obtained. (272)
> ... a splendid country for producing cotton. (408)

But these are *appraisals* of the land's capacity for producing wealth; they are not *descriptions*. More detailed land evaluations inevitably take on picturesque themes to construct the land as ready for exploitation.

Owning the picturesque

Aesthetics and ownership

Although ostensibly a set of aesthetics which one applied to natural scenes, the picturesque was closely connected with the transformation of the English countryside by the landed aristocracy. As the fashion of the French formal garden declined, the land of the estates was refashioned according to picturesque aesthetics – a reworking involving the shifting of trees, of mountains of earth, of villages and the creation of lakes and streams to produce the 'effect' required. This was a reification of aesthetic principles – a putting into practice of the ideal – that did not alter, but simply extended the attitude to nature which the picturesque engendered. The idea that nature should be judged according to highly conventional terms and altered if found lacking implied that the relationship of society to nature was similar to the relationship of consumer to consumable. This increasingly proprietorial view of land was being enacted on a massive scale by the enclosure laws; these allowed individual appropriation of hitherto common land, which was subsequently guarded by fences of stone or vegetation. The 'natural' landscape of the commons, lost to the increasing regularisation of the countryside, could be reproduced within the boundaries of the estate.

The picturesque landscape of nature, as Ann Bermingham has shown in *Landscape and Ideology*, became the prerogative of the estate, allowing for a conventionally ambiguous signification, so that 'nature was the sign of property and property the sign of nature'.[23] Humphry Repton pointed out that there was no need to differentiate the landscape garden from any other chattel of the landowner, and argued that if the display of 'magnificent or of picturesque scenery be made without ostentation, it can be no more at variance with good taste than the display of superior affluence in the houses, the equipage, the furniture, or the habiliment of wealthy individuals'.[24] The construction of a picturesque 'nature' within an estate nostalgically sought to recapture the pre-enclosure landscape, but by doing so it emphasised the wealth and privilege of the owners: the non-instrumental landscape garden signified the luxury of being able to possess unproductive land. The estate sought to disguise the delimiting feature of fencing which implies enclosed land – the ha-ha (a fence resting within a depression to hide it from the eye), for instance, effectively enclosed the land and demarcated property rights while giving the land the appearance of being commonly owned.[25]

Picturesque estates were signifiers of one's own taste and, of course, wealth, but they operated also as signifiers of a more general cultural superiority. Landscape gardening, Humphry Repton argued, distinguished 'the pleasures of civilized society from the pursuits of savage and barbarous nations'.[26] The disbelief in the indigene's power to transform the landscape plays a large role in the journals' construction of the 'park-like' lands they describe as the products of accident, or as areas divinely intended for colonial settlement.

The Australian picturesque

When the explorers discuss 'picturesque' scenes they are not, of course, speaking of picturesque estates. Yet the proprietorial attitude to nature extends from the actual transformation of the land according to picturesque values to viewing the Australian landscape as prefabricated in the picturesque mode, and therefore fit for the inhabitance of the colonising power. Though there are many complaints concerning the 'gloomy wood' of the continent, juxtaposed with the happy white cottages of civilisation, there is a good deal of praise in the journals for natural scenery. The descriptions initially appear innocent enough, but one point of commonality, the seeming design of the natural scenery, is the departure point for a rhetoric of self-justification. As with all picturesque descriptions, nature exists primarily to please the viewer: 'the scenery ... was much improved by "pine" trees (*Callitris pyramidalis*), whose deep green contrasted beautifully with the red and grey tinges of the granite rocks, while their respective outlines were opposed to each other with equally good effect.' (*3Ex* 1: 166) Mitchell's use of the word 'effect' in this context, and Sturt's use of 'clump'[27] (*ECA* 1: 108) to describe a group of trees is proof of a general familiarity with the vocabulary of the picturesque. Mitchell's description posits nature as a provider of composed scenes designed to give visual pleasure.

Aesthetic descriptions which show pleasure in the way nature has 'arranged itself' move easily into speculations about the suitability of these arrangements for the colonising enterprise. Often, the Australian landscape is seen as ready-made for the occupation of a European power and its agriculture. It is this feature of recognition which is a generally unacknowledged characteristic of the imperial process; for, while analyses of early European responses to the landscape have emphasised how different and strange the land seemed, the construction of it as familiar has received less attention. The recognition of its picturesque qualities is a fundamentally intentionalist stance, which projects English class privilege onto the Australian landscape, and is particularly prevalent in Sturt's journals. In the *Expedition into Central Australia* he again interprets the land in terms of intent.

> We passed flat after flat of the most vivid green, ornamented by clumps of trees, sufficiently apart to give a most picturesque finish to the landscape. Trees of denser foliage and deeper shade drooped over the river, forming long dark avenues, and the banks of the river, grassed to the water, had the appearance of having been made so by art. (*ECA* 1: 108)

This teleological view of the land justified the occupation and ownership by those who could appreciate its picturesque qualities. If the land resembled an estate, then surely the appropriation of land had received a natural confirmation.

The 'well adapted' land

To suggest that land was well adapted for the settlement of a European population avoided the question of *who* had adapted it – and for whose benefit. Explorers used the word 'adapted' with great frequency to describe the many areas they saw as fit for agriculture. Forrest mentions 'fine grassy plains, well adapted for sheep runs' (170); Leichhardt writes similarly of plains and riverbanks which were 'adapted for cattle and horses' (369); Gosse speaks of lands 'well adapted' for pastoral purposes (12). Oxley, looking at an area which had a 'fine park-like appearance', writes that he 'never saw a country better adapted for the grazing of all kinds of stock than that we had passed over this day' (6). Such a view of the land indicates a belief that the land is suitable, or adapted, for the encroaching colonial enterprise. That lands are 'naturally' suited for agricultural or pastoral purposes is taken as a sign that such an enterprise is, probably divinely, blessed.

The key feature of these 'well adapted' areas is their relative openness; this, of course, is a great advantage for both agricultural and pastoral exercises and is also an aesthetic requirement of 'park-like' areas. The production of land as 'park-like' is common to many explorers of the late eighteenth century and early nineteenth century. I. S. MacLaren has noted how Franklin's expedition into what is now British Columbia found landscapes, quite unlike any in Australia, also 'park-like'.[28] In two passages Oxley expresses both the use-value of these open areas and the visual pleasure that they afford.

> ... although the soil and character of the country rendered it fit for all agricultural purposes, yet I think from its general clearness from brush, or underwood of any kind, that such tracts must be peculiarly adapted for sheep-grazing ... our dogs had some excellent runs, and killed two large kangaroos;

the clearness of the country affording us a view of the chase from the beginning to the end. (Oxley 174–75)

We proceeded about nine miles farther through the finest open country, or rather park, imaginable ... I think the most fastidious sportsman would have derived ample amusement during our day's journey. He might without moving have seen the finest coursing, from the commencement of the chase to the death of the game: and when tired of killing kangaroos he might have seen emus hunted with equal success. (Oxley 291–92)

This visual pleasure is implicated with park-like scenery, and the opportunity it creates to see across wide tracts of land in the bush is a power in itself – a power that licenses colonial adaptations of activities belonging in the estates of Britain. Grey notes on one occasion that he had 'never enjoyed a better day's pheasant hunting in any preserve in England' (Grey 1: 102). The park-like features of the landscape were not accidental, however. The land had in fact already been adapted, but by indigenous means for indigenous purposes; its adaptation was not intended as a sign to be self-servingly read as an encouragement to exploitation. Mitchell describes a 'beautiful plain; covered with shining verdure and ornamented with trees, which, although "dropt in nature's careless haste", gave the country the appearance of an extensive park' (*3Ex* 1: 90). Commenting on this passage in Mitchell's journal, the 1838 review of *Three Expeditions into ... Eastern Australia* in *Blackwood's Edinburgh Magazine* states that this will be the 'hunting-ground of some future Australian potentate' (708), thus positioning Australia's future as an antipodal revision of Britain's past.

The alignment between aesthetics and economics in Australia slightly alters the qualities of the picturesque. Whereas in Britain the parklands often were purely for pleasure – an ostentatious display of surplus wealth – in Australia the functions of production and pleasure were seen to be combined. A comparison between a description of a 'natural' and a settled landscape demonstrates a slim separation between a land arranged for exploitation and one already under that process.

I looked to the west and saw a beautiful park-like plain covered with grass, having groups of ornamental trees scattered over it ... I never saw a more beautiful spot. (*ECA* 1: 286–87)

I ... was highly delighted at the really park-like appearance of the scenery. This pretty locality is now occupied as a cattle run, and must be a place of amusement as well as pleasure. (*ECA* 1: 95)

The actual pasturing of cattle fulfils the land's promise without altering its appearance. The welcome combination of profit and visual splendour ('amusement') is the final justification of the appropriation of land for agriculture; in the picturesque the utilitarian pressures of agriculture and aesthetic demands are reconciled. Mitchell echoes this belief in the possibility of an operational yet picturesque farm.

> Certainly a land more favourable for colonization could not be found. Flocks might be turned out upon its hills, or the plough at once set to work in the plains. No primeval forests required to be first rooted out, although there was enough of wood for all purposes of utility, and as much also for embellishment as even a painter could wish. (*3Ex* 2: 271)

There is, of course, employed here a logic of having one's cake and eating it; Mitchell's assumption is that utility and aesthetics can be combined, and that the (limited) fecundity of the wood allows it to be used and yet reserved for picturesque clumps. More importantly, the peculiar utilitarianism and fragmented view of nature that the picturesque itself generates is here in evidence. Rather than being an integral element of the environment, connected in complex ways to the land, vegetation is an 'embellishment' and 'ornamental', necessary only because of its importance to the economy of the aesthetic, as wood is to the economy of agriculture.

Castles in the air

Ruined towers of the imagination

As Gilpin opined in his *Three Essays* (46), the 'picturesque eye is perhaps most inquisitive after the elegant relics of ancient architecture; the ruined tower, the Gothic arch, the remains of castles, and abbeys. They are the richest legacies of art ... Thus universal are the objects of picturesque travel.' Australia, of course, did not provide these 'universal' objects of picturesque appreciation; despite this, castles make surprisingly frequent appearances in the journals. William Hodges begins this trend in South Pacific exploration literature by including a burning castle in his painting of the New Zealand coastline, *A View of Cape Stephens (New Zealand) with Waterspout* (1776, National Maritime Museum, London). Although picturesque codes dictated the selection and composition of many of the explorer's illustrations and descriptions, to include a romantic flaming castle in picture or text in a factual description would have been a career-terminating choice.

Nevertheless, castles do serve a function within the journals as items to which natural formations are often compared and their picturesque acknowledgment tends to legitimise this presence. Mitchell likens one formation to the drawings of John Martin (*EITA* 237) and praises another one as picturesque (224); Eyre, describing the cliffs of the Great

Australian Bight as having the 'romantic appearance of massy battle-
ments of masonry', echoes the familiar complaint that the view offered
the painter an excellent opportunity, and it was unfortunate that he
himself was not one (Eyre 1: 327).[29] Stuart observes to the north and
north-east of Chamber's Pillar 'numerous remarkable hills, which have a
very striking effect in the landscape; they resemble nothing so much as a
number of old castles in ruins' (151–52). Comparisons such as this one
by Stuart utilise easily accepted codes of picturesque comparison which
retain their valency for the modern reader, thus hiding their Euro-
centrism. When Stuart compares a formation of rocks to a locomotive
(150), however, what is most apparent is the arbitrary nature of the
comparison, with its localised cultural and temporal connotations.

The inclusion of castles as a picturesque detail for comparative
purposes is another way in which the land is accorded significance only
in relation to a European history. A land, it seems, possesses picturesque
value because it has remnants of a particular history and a particular
kind of history. In the Australian context castle comparisons make the
unfamiliar familiar, provide a shorthand and 'interesting' description of
geological formations otherwise difficult to describe, but they also
reinforce the idea of the land as without a history. Castles occur in the
journals but their existence is always anomalous, a trick of vision.

> As we were standing across from one shore to the other, our attention was
> drawn to a most singular object. It started suddenly up, as above the waters to
> the south, and strikingly resembled an isolated castle. Behind it, a dense
> column of smoke rose into the sky, and the effect was most remarkable. (*2Ex*
> 2: 163–164)

There is a fairly obvious reading available which undermines the
Eurocentric construction of Australia as without a history that the
phantom nature of these castles reinforces. The fact that the castle's
appearance is a mirage allows the land's existence as a mysterious
presence which confounds sight, permitting only a solipsistic vision of
the explorer's own familiar world.

The appearance of castles is also taken as an opportunity to remind the
reader of the uncivilised state of the country's inhabitants. Mitchell's
descriptions of castle-like features are full of praise for their picturesque
qualities, and simultaneously erase Aboriginal knowledge and skills.
Once again the landscape is once again seen through prior experience
with a particular artist – the mountains' rating as a picturesque scene is
high (see plate 4), as they have Mitchell:

> recalling to my memory the most imaginative efforts of Mr. Martin's sepia
> drawing, and showing how far the painter's fancy may anticipate nature. But
> at the gorge of this valley, there stood a sort of watch-tower, as if to guard the

Plate 4   *Tower Almond,* engraved by T. Picken after Mitchell's
drawing. From Thomas Mitchell, *Expedition into . . . Tropical Australia*
(pl.16). Mitchell Library, State Library of New South Wales.

entrance, so like a work of art, that even here, where men and kangaroos are equally wild and artless, I was obliged to look very attentively, to be quite convinced that the tower was the work of nature only ... I named this valley 'Glen Turret,' and this feature 'Tower Almond,' after an ancient castle, the scene of many early associations, and now quite as uninhabited as this. (*EITA* 237)

Meditations on ephemerality were intended to be provoked by the textual presence of castles; in tourist narratives their appearance would often be accompanied by a homily from the author on the transience of life. Mitchell has juxtaposed castles with Aborigines, reminding the reader that they are incapable of building such a permanent structure, but in the same description discounting Aborigines as a populace at all – the imaginary castle is uninhabited. The combination of ephemerality and Aboriginal absence subtly constructs a history in which the Aborigines are destined to be placed within the nostalgic domain of history with other obsolete races. Both real and imaginary castles are deserted – the ruins (real and imaginary alike) being evidence of the failure of the people – and this absence demands replenishment. Mitchell's other detailed description of a geological formation as a castle again erases Aboriginal presence and constructs a future in which these 'deserted' areas, now discovered, may be re-peopled.

The hills overhanging it surpassed any I had ever seen in picturesque outline. Some resembled gothic cathedrals in ruins; others forts ... it was the discovery worthy of the toils of a pilgrimage. Those beautiful recesses of unpeopled earth, could no longer remain unknown. (*EITA* 224)

These areas were, of course, neither 'unknown' nor 'unpeopled': on the page immediately following this description Mitchell notes clear signs of Aboriginal inhabitance (*EITA* 225).

The city or the bush

As clothes are the chief markers of civilisation and nakedness signifies savagery, so too is the uncivilised land, the wilderness, 'naked' (*3Ex* 1: 23). When responding to the settled landscape of cities, the explorers can no longer satisfactorily utilise the picturesque, for towns do not include objects that signify within the realm of the picturesque. There are occasions when an explorer will use the word 'picturesque' in a way of which Gilpin, at least, would not have approved. For example, Sturt describes towns which 'embossomed in trees, and picturesque in scenery, bear a strong resemblance to the quiet and secluded villages of England' (*ECA* 2: 200). The traditional picturesque aesthetic, of course, when employed by estate owners made exactly the opposite demands of towns – that instead of being constructed they be removed entirely.[30] The attempt to produce towns as picturesque is a colonial variant but occurs less commonly than productions in which the city is contrasted to an unpicturesque land. Picturesque landscapes are described in such a way as to invite colonisation; once a colony is implanted, however, the land is then constructed according to the 'gloomy, melancholy and monotonous' paradigms of description. The 'whitewashed buildings [which] bore outward testimony to the cleanliness and regularity of the inhabitants' (*2Ex* 1: 6) stand in opposition to the gloomy forest. Sturt, examining the progress of Sydney, utilises the stereotypes of the opposition between city and bush.

> A single glance was sufficient to tell me that the hills upon the southern shore of the port, the outlines of which were broken by houses and spires, must once have been covered with the same dense and gloomy wood which abounded everywhere else. The contrast was indeed very great – the improvement singularly striking … success has been complete: it is the very triumph of human skill and industry over Nature herself. The cornfield and the orchard have supplanted the wild grass and the brush; a flourishing town stands over the ruins of the forest; the lowing of herds has succeeded the wild whoop of the savage; and the stillness of that once desert shore is now broken by the sound of the bugle and the busy hum of commerce. (*2Ex* 1: xv)

The central structure of this description is that of succession: the buildings replace the forest; food crops 'supplant' the natural vegetation; bovine exclamations displace human voices; the sounds of civilisation 'succeed' silence. The legitimacy of succession – that natural progression whereby the 'old' is replaced by the 'new' of the historical narrative – is striven for, but undercut in a number of ways. The land echoed to the 'wild whoop' of the savage and yet it was empty and silent – a stillness that now is filled with the call of the military bugle. Such contradictions result from the anxiety about the legitimacy of succession, occurring at the point of overlap between competing discourses which supply a superfluity of narrative logic: the disordered wild whoop is replaced by herds, the emptiness of the desert shore is replaced by the joint military/commercial endeavour. The original inhabitants are not supplanted by the military, but rather by innocent and productive cows. Most significantly, the presentation of a commercial and military order as a creative force is deconstructed by the description of the forest as being in 'ruins' – the violence of the forced succession is not fully suppressed.

Civilisation and the regularised landscape that results are anathema to the code of 'roughness' that Gilpin argued was necessary for picturesque effect. Stokes laments that the 'picturesque wilderness had given place to the unromantic realities of industry; and the region of business had superseded that of poetry and romance' (Stokes 2: 482). But the explorers often created aesthetic sanctions for buildings and, in particular, fences; in this way, therefore, European encroachment was sanctioned by recourse to the picturesque. Stokes approves of the beautifying skill of the axe, which caused the landscape to wear 'a most English aspect' (Stokes 1: 238) – the anglicisation of the land is also, of course, a transformation towards the picturesque. Enclosure is constructed as an addition to the aesthetic of the natural – Oxley, for instance, praising the 'industrious hand of man [which] had been busy in improving the works of nature' in fencing in government grounds (Oxley 2). Mitchell notes of one establishment that 'the symmetrical appearance of their stock-yard fence, when it first caught my eye, so long accustomed to the wavy lines of simple nature, looked quite charming as a work of art' (*3Ex* 1: 330).

'A work of art' obviously refers to the fence's human-made status, but also partakes of the aestheticisation of nature in terms of a pictorial object. As prestige items, paintings were indicators of wealth and property: when an enclosed piece of land becomes a picture it is its own display of wealth. Arthur Young, travelling through Italy, sees the enclosed lands on a mountain as an exhibition: 'in several places the view is picturesque and pleasing: enclosures seem hung against the mountain sides as a picture is suspended to the wall of a room'.[31] The uncultivated nature is the 'wall' or meaningless background – the only significance is generated by human presence. Topographical paintings of colonised areas are often constructed in such a way that the surrounding nature is significant solely in terms of the emplaced buildings. The surveyor and explorer G. W. Evans produced *A View of Sydney, New South Wales, on Entering the Heads*, which, although ostensibly purely topographical, shares many of the structures of the picturesque, including the dark foreground, a three-plane schema, foreground figures and a limited coulisse. Here, it is clear that the bush is an undifferentiated mass, important only because it frames the object of concern, Sydney, which, with clean white buildings stands contrasted to the dark surrounds. Thus, the actual process of colonisation comes to be considered as a detail in a picturesque composition, carrying with it connotations of approval. The coulisse itself has the strong ideological function of constructing nature as, simply, curtains partially withdrawn to display the real scene. In the final analysis, therfore, nature is simply irrelevant to the visual embodiment of imperial progress. The finest example of this is the illustration of Stuart's arrival on the northern coast, where the exploration party is framed by a riotous mass of vegetation which occupies fully half the breadth of the picture (410). The gap in the vegetation looks suspiciously like a pathway an exploration party would need to cut to get through to the beach so that the picture could be taken, which would be a case of the party's activities creating the possibility of vision. The flag-raising in Stuart's picture and the city in Evans's view of Sydney were constructed using picturesque codes but this process went beyond the two dimensions of painting.

The Royal Botanic Gardens

The gubernatorial reserve in Sydney aped the landscape conventions of British estates. The Upper Garden of what is now the Royal Botanic Gardens was purely functional and consisted of rectangular plots which initially provided vegetables; later it was used as a propagating ground for seeds collected by explorers and accompanying botanists, such as Allan Cunningham.[32] The Lower Garden, however, was laid out in its final form according to picturesque principles and with advice from Mitchell in 1833.[33] Tanner has noted how this arrangement met with the approval of Colonel Mundy, who described the Lower Garden as designed in 'English pleasure-ground style, embracing a wide circle of the picturesque Farm Cove'.[34] Fabricant has observed that the terms by which nature gives pleasure and the means by which it is redesigned to do so, 'underscore the economic aspect of control and identify power with the gratification of appetite'.[35]

In the colonial context this satisfaction of the eye required the visual and subsequently physical appropriation of land, which denied the original inhabitants that particular pleasure – and, indeed, their subsistence. That the park-like scenery in Australia, so frequently commented upon, was a result of Aboriginal firing practice and was not 'natural' (in the sense of being uninfluenced by humans) is an irony, underlined by an incident which took place in 1828 in the Domain, Sydney, then part of the governor's reserve along with the Botanic Gardens. A party of Aborigines camped in the Domain started a fire which threatened the Botanic Gardens but, to the general relief of the citizenry, was quickly quenched: how ironic it is that the very tool which created the park-like, picturesque scenery threatened the Botanic Gardens' carefully designed simulacrum. The *Sydney Gazette* benignly argued that no action should be taken against the blacks, pointing out that 'after all, the poor blacks are the legitimate lords of the soil' (4 August 1828, 3 March 1829).

Exploration as agent of change

The gardens avoided transformation by the Aborigines, and instead came under Mitchell's cultivated and cultivating hand. In helping to arrange the Botanic Gardens, Mitchell was not by any means the only explorer to alter the land because of a pictorial or visual necessity. The very act of exploring required the large-scale destruction of the country

through which the exploring party moved. Grey records an occasion
when his exploring party was caught in thick bushland; his solution was
to 'set fire to the bush, and being thus enabled to see our way a little, we
commenced moving rocks and stones' (Grey 1: 87).

The construction of a pathway is necessary not simply for travel but for
sight – the creation of the possibility of a view is frequently mentioned in
the journals. Surveying required triangulation of points from summits,
which were often, unhelpfully, densely vegetated. Mitchell regretfully
records that on one occasion he had to be 'content to cut off the top
branches only of a tree on the summit I had endeavoured to cut down,
and to erect a sort of platform on the remainder, whence I took my
angles' (*EITA* 176). He also writes of two occasions on which the large-
scale clearing of trees on a hill was necessary to obtain a panoramic view
(*3Ex* 1: 9 *&* 2: 222). The first description, in particular, emphasises the
destructive effort needed to establish a view: 'it was desirable to clear the
summit, at least partly, of trees, a work which was accomplished after
considerable labour – the trees having been very large' (*3Ex* 1: 9). Many
of the views described and illustrated are thus manufactured; the coulisse
of trees in some of the illustrations is present because of the creation of
the possibility of the view itself. The scenes obtained are not natural,
therefore: the observation itself alters what is observed. Sturt's journal
gives an insight into how the exploration party inevitably transformed
the landscape as they travelled: 'our animals had laid the ground bare for
miles around the camp, and never came towards it but to drink. The axe
had made a broad gap in the line of gum-trees which ornamented the
creek, and had destroyed its appearance'. (*ECA* 1: 321)

If the power relationship seems entirely with the explorers in the
cutting down of forests in order to obtain knowledge of the countryside,
this advantage often seems missing from the resultant descriptions. Here,
the land seems to emerge as a threat to language, revealing linguistic
limitations by its novelty and strangeness. However, it is possible to see
some of the ostensible failures of vision and words as carefully crafted,
working to establish a limit to the knowledge gained at that particular
moment, but in no way acting as a critique of the production of
knowledge through sight.

Struck speechless

Language and the 'new' land

It is an axiom that the discovery of a 'new' land creates immense
pressures on the language of the newcomers, especially explorers, and as
professional describers Australian explorers are struck speechless an

embarrassing number of times. It is possible to read these moments as failures, admissions that the scientific cataloguing of land is based on methods and language inappropriate to their surroundings. But to assume these confessions of failure are productions of the landscape as a true other – something outside the limit of the explorer's language to which only oblique reference may be made – is to underestimate the powerful stabilising function of language. An allowance that the land is indescribable is found repeatedly in Sturt's journal, though he is not the only explorer who used this trope.

> It is impossible for me to describe the kind of country we were now traversing, or the dreariness of the view it presented. (*2Ex* 2: 59)

> It is impossible for me to convey to the reader's mind an idea of the nature of the country through which we passed. (*2Ex* 2: 79–80)

> It is impossible for me to describe the effect of so instantaneous a change of circumstances upon us. (*2Ex* 2: 86)

> Broad and striking as were the features of the landscape over which the eye wandered from the summit of this hill, I have much difficulty in describing them. (*ECA* 1: 379)

These stunned confessions of linguistic ineptitude hardly seem to be part of the imperial construction of the land, yet they serve an important purpose in policing the stability of the construct. They accomplish this task by compartmentalising the threatening within that sub-field of aesthetic perception called 'the sublime'.

Edmund Burke's *A Philosophical Enquiry into the Origins of Our Idea of the Sublime and Beautiful* remained the prime guide towards emotional responses to nature during the nineteenth century. It attempted to formulate those objects which would give rise to feelings of awe associated with the sublime, but also analysed in detail the feelings themselves.

> The passion caused by the great and sublime in *nature*, when those causes operate most powerfully, is Astonishment; and Astonishment is that state of the soul, in which all its motions are suspended, with some degree of horror.[36]

Responses to vertical inclines were especially likely to include a Burkean horror; indeed, Forrest's response to the cliffs of the Great Australian Bight provides a textbook example of the formulation of a viewer's response to a sublime scene. The cliffs 'which fell perpendicularly into the sea, and, although grand in the extreme, were terrible to gaze from. After looking very cautiously over the precipice, we all ran back quite terror-stricken by the dreadful view.' (Forrest 99). The sublime provokes a wordlessness in the viewer, giving rise to 'feelings that I cannot attempt to describe' (Leichhardt 123). But the view itself, as in the examples from Sturt's journals above, may also be indescribable. Burke held that a flat plain, like the desert through which Sturt travelled, could not be considered sublime (72). Yet, on examining Burke's requirements for sublimity, one finds ample space for a colonial adaptation of his rules. He remarks that to:

> things of great dimensions, if we annex an adventitious idea of terror, they become without comparison greater. A level plain of a great extension on land, is certainly no mean idea; the prospect of such a plain may be as extensive as a prospect of an ocean; but can it ever fill the mind with any thing so great as the ocean itself? This is owing to several causes, but it is owing to none more than this, that the ocean is an object of no small terror. (Burke 57–58)

The sublime is a way of capturing and annulling this terror by including it within a system of European aesthetics. The plains of the desert, it may be argued, were indeed a source of terror and the response was to construct the desert in terms of the Burkean sublime. The sublime is a recognisable other: it is by definition ineffable, yet occupies a niche in a familiar and stable Eurocentric code. To say that it is 'impossible to describe' the land is to invoke a *topos* familiar to readers of travel literature and, by doing so, to absolve oneself of any individual deficiency in descriptive powers.

Malcolm Andrews has drawn attention to just how tired the picturesque vocabulary became and how this accounts for some of the problems of description in this mode. In particular, he notes the rather comical attempts of Bishop Percy to describe mountainous scenes found on his Scottish tour in 1773. In his manuscript 'Observanda', Percy writes:

> the immense Group of stupendous Mountains beyond it to the North, rising up in gigantic scenery beyond one another, form a succession of Picturesque wonderfully great, astonishing & ~~picturesque~~ fine ~~Picturesque~~ beyond all description, & to which no Language can do justice.[37]

Designating something as 'beyond all description' does not avoid the problem of a clichéd vocabulary, as this phrase becomes a cliché in itself. Thus, explorers not only capture the disturbing within a pre-existent category called 'the ineffable', but signal its safe entrapment with a conventional phrase.

The journals often employ the rhetorical strategy of declaring the impossibility of describing a scene before going on to do just that.

Speech, following a declaration of speechlessness may contravene the rules of ineffability, but a more important point is how this oxymoronic process works in favour of the journal's authority. Indicating the difficulty of describing a scene and then going on to describe it constructs the explorer as a surmounter of linguistic, as well as geographical, obstacles. In most cases when a declaration of ineffability is followed by a description, the landscape is constructed in terms of a lack. It is not the describer at fault, but the land's failure to provide recognisable difference on which language may operate. The land is described as 'blank and desolate' (*2Ex* 1: 144); there is literally nothing to say, and yet description proceeds. After declaring it 'impossible to describe' the land, Sturt gives quite an extensive description.

> The plains were still open to the horizon, but here and there a stunted gum-tree, or a gloomy cypress, seemed placed by nature as mourners over the surrounding desolation. Neither beast nor bird inhabited these lonely and inhospitable regions, over which the silence of the grave seemed to reign. (*2Ex* 2: 59)

Later in the same volume of the journal Sturt again confesses the impossibility of describing the scene, which is also followed by a description structured by absence.

> ... reeds lined the banks of the river on both sides, without any break, and waved like gloomy streamers over its turbid waters; while the trees stood leafless and sapless in the midst of them. Wherever we landed, the same view presented itself – a waving expanse of reeds, and a country as flat as it is possible to imagine one. The eye could seldom penetrate beyond three quarters of a mile, and the labour of walking through the reeds was immense... (*2Ex* 2: 80)

The impenetrability of the land, its rejection of imperial scrutiny, constitutes, as I have said, a site of resistance; but here it is within the two-stage strategy of, firstly, declaring the land's ineffability (thus placing it comfortably within the category of the sublime) and, secondly, assuaging any doubts concerning the adequacy of language or the explorer by triumphantly producing a description.

Resistance to sight

Despite the triumph of the sublime there are moments when the land produces resistance to sight. The mirage destroys the party's attempts to form geographical order out of visual impression. The disturbance of sight may be described, but it remains a deconstruction of the authoritative statements concerning length, height and spatial relationship, and also challenges exploration methodology's heavy reliance on sight. Sturt describes a mirage which 'floated in a light tremulous vapour on the ground, and not only deceived us with regard to the extent of the plains, and the appearance of objects, but hid the trees, in fact, from our view altogether' (*2Ex* 2: 56). Occasionally the land resists the spectators directly when it emerges as a threat, its apparent lack of difference ceasing to be merely monotony and becoming life-endangering. Sturt grows suspicious of the power of the landscape: 'it appeared as if the river was decoying us into a desert, there to leave us in difficulty and distress. The very mirage had the effect of boundlessness in it, by blending objects in one general hue.' (*2Ex* 2: 58).

Blindness is another way in which the resistance of the land is present in the journals. Sturt's mention of his blindness (*2Ex* 2: 5) and, in particular, his excusing himself from giving a sketch because of his inability to see (2: 227) are cases of the land's power, not just over the explorers, but over their instruments of information-gathering. The explorer's destruction of the forest to obtain views, and the desert's glare causing blindness are both occasions of a collapse of the separation of observer and object observed that realism in particular demands; but in the second case it is the power of the object that is exercised in causing blindness.

Once the picturesque structures inherent in many of the journals' illustrations and descriptions are revealed, the pretence of objectivity and mimeticism begins to break down. The explorer's 'taste' is already imbricated with the scene depicted and the ostensible goal of the illustrations – truth – seems rather secondary. Other illustrations, however, such as scientifically directed depictions of fossils, flora and fauna, and topographical views of the land seem less easily criticised, and require more analysis of the relation between observer and observed demanded by realism.

The eyes have it

The explorer's perspective

One of the fundamental assumptions of Western art is that there is a separation of viewer and object viewed – of the 'fully subjectified eye (or 'I')' and the represented scene.[38] The picturesque establishes a value for the object according to the observer's position in space, while paradoxically holding to the idea that the objects/scenes possess an inherent picturesque merit. Non-picturesque depictions of scenes also operate to establish value, but one based on mimetic achievement, by how closely illustrations resemble the 'real' scene. The central code which mimetic art uses to achieve verisimilitude is perspective.

Linear perspective creates the illusion of depth in a flat representation and, unlike what occurs in non-mimetic art, creates a very specific relationship between spectator and picture. The spectator is in a particularly privileged position: although outside the painting s/he determines the position and arrangement of the objects within. Terdiman, in 'Ideological Voyages', has pointed out how perspective does not operate solely by determining the relationships of the objects depicted to each other but 'crucially, to one privileged element *outside* it; that is, to the source of the perceiving consciousness' (28). Objects are arranged and depicted in terms of their difference in space to each other, but above all to their distance from the observer; thus, the space created by linear perspective is a controlled space, dominated by the viewer, who is nevertheless placed outside it. Terdiman has utilised the metaphoric possibilities of 'perspective', and how it positions 'differences as a hierarchical mode of relation' (28), to investigate the power relationship between seer and seen. He uses this metaphor to investigate the relationship of the European knowledge-gatherer to his oriental object, but it is useful to partially return it to the sphere of the visual, to help understand the role of the observer in the pictorial production of the land.

The illusion of reality which perspective creates can be maintained only when the viewer's eye is at a fixed distance from the picture; the Renaissance painter Brunelleschi's first perspective picture used a peep-hole set at a particular height and distance from the painting for the full illusion to be transmitted.[39] In analysing the addressee of Abraham Ortelius's *Theatrum Orbis Terrarum*, Rabasa interprets the mapmaker's presentation of his map as a device which may be used, in Ortelius's own words, to 'peepe upon those places, townes and Forts, which lye most advantagious and commodius to satisfy ... ambition'.[40] Perspective dictates a position for this 'peeping'. Brunelleschi's peep-hole accommodates one eye only; in respect of Ortelius's map the eye is that of the Renaissance man, who may travel and survey his enemy while closeted; in the case of the explorer it is the objectifying and masculine eye of the European which views the feminised land before him. The cartographical necessity of gaining elevation and seeing great distances offers a particular point of view and demands the arrogation of a visual power over the land, opening it for inspection.

It must be emphasised that the explorative practice of finding places from which to view the country was not simply a foible nor frivolous pleasure-seeking on the part of the explorer but was an essential element in the discovery and mensuration of the land. Mitchell writes that 'the visible possibility of overlooking the country from any eminence, is refreshing at all times, but to an explorer it is everything' (*EITA* 157–58). This does not prevent the vision gained from being expressed in terms of pleasure, however. There are innumerable examples of explorers constructing the ascent of hills in terms of the 'reward' of the vision at the summit. Moreover, the description of visual 'reward' reveals that the gaze employed is a peculiarly masculine one; what is being offered is a recumbent feminised land open to the penetrative gaze.

Commanding views

The connotations of control are constantly present in the descriptions of the views obtained and have a decidedly military flavour, the word 'command', in particular, being frequently present. Gilpin, describing Volney's account of mountain-climbing in Lebanon, says that 'there on every side you see an horizon almost without bounds ... you seem to command the whole world'.[41] Cowper also celebrates the command of the visual:

> Now roves the eye;
> And posted on this spectacular height.
> Exults in its command.[42]

The 'commanding' eye is also glorified in the exploration journals; the word 'command' being in widespread use. Grey writes of a 'commanding position' (Grey 1: 371); Stokes congratulates himself on the fact that he 'commanded an extensive view' (Stokes 1: 150); and Mitchell finds 'an elevated point, which seemed to command an extensive view' (*EITA* 237). The military connotations of the word 'command' are particularly evident whenever there is a contest for height, and thus power of surveillance, between the explorers and the Aborigines. After a number of strategic manoeuvres to gain altitude, Eyre congratulates himself on securing 'the best and most commanding station in the neighborhood' (Eyre 1: 226–27). Stokes's journal also employs the territorial connotations of command; he is careful to land in a 'position not directly commanded by the natives' (Stokes 1: 98).

The implication of the word 'command' is that the view is brought under control by the explorative gaze. But the control of the view is also a kind of ownership, and the vantage points that provide these views are presented as particularly desirable; they offer not only spatial but future prospects. Oxley, for example, describing the 'beautiful and extensive prospect' from Mount Molle, notes that it is 'a fine rich hill, favourably situated for a commanding prospect' (Oxley 4–5). Exploration necessitates a temporary taking possession of the land, often in those areas of greatest desirability; Oxley chooses to pitch his tent upon a well-grassed and watered piece of land 'commanding a fine view of the interior of the port and surrounding country' (Oxley 327). Such a view presented the elements of a location for an aristocratic manor – elevation and views of land mixed with water to 'relieve' the eye. But this manorial point of view did not simply have to be foreshadowed by explorers but could be described as it already existed. Writing of the land of the Australian Agricultural Company, which had appropriated huge areas for its wealthy shareholders, Stokes describes the home of one of them: 'Mr. Ebsworth the treasurer of the Company resides there in a charming cottage, almost covered with roses and honeysuckle, and commanding two picturesque reaches of the Karuah' (Stokes 1: 315). In this case the commanding view is one with the picturesque: a controlling discourse of the visual, it is embodied as a material practice in the alienation of land and the reproduction of a British estate system in Australia.

Generally, I will differentiate the panoramic from the picturesque gaze, but their essential similarities are occasionally revealed. While panoramic descriptions by the explorers are not coded according to picturesque requirements but have rules of their own, picturesque views often in practice did take place from elevations. William Mason complained about the manipulation of picturesque rules by estate owners in order to monumentalise their property: 'the *Picturesque Point* is always thus low in all prospects: A truth, which though the Landscape Painter knows, he cannot always observe; since the Patron who employs him to take a view of his place usually carries him to some elevation for that purpose'.[43] But the picturesque inevitably lent itself to this kind of purpose since it was, as I have argued, an innately appropriative mode. Appended to Gilpin's *Three Essays* (ll 216–33), there is a poem on landscape painting which criticises this tendency of landowners to force painters to fix views of their property so that their possessions may be displayed without the inconvenience of returning to the summit where the view is obtained. The property-owner, having 'fix'd the point of amplest prospect' instructs an 'obedient son of Art' thus:

>   ... 'Take thy stand
> Just here,' he cry'd, 'and paint me all thou seest,
> Omit no single object.' It was done;
> And soon the live-long landscape clothes his hall,
> And spreads from base to ceiling. All was there;
> As to his guests, while dinner cool'd the knight
> Full oft would prove; and with uplifted cane
> Point to the distant spire, where slept entomb'd
> His ancestry; beyond, where lay the town,
> Skirted with wood, that gave him place and voice
> In Britain's senate ...

... Heedless he, meanwhile,
That what he deems the triumph of his taste,
Is but a painted survey, a mere map;
Which light and shade and perspective misplac'd,
But serve to spoil.

Gilpin acutely portrays the landowner's anxiety to legitimise his ownership by displaying his ancestral tombs and the role that pictorial monumentalisation of his ownership plays in this. Gilpin's concern is with the lack of composition in such a picture and this leads him to oppose art and cartography. Yet, the picturesque is exactly suited to its employment in this way: a mode designed to 'fix' appealing natural scenes can also 'fix' estates, which are, in any case, imitating a picturesque model of nature. The composition of the picturesque and panoramic scenes differ, but they are both implicated with property-owning, vision and power.

Elevation and surveillance

The effacement of the eye's immediate presence is necessary for claims of scientific detachment and objectivity, but this detachment is continually broken down by the alteration of the land needed to obtain views, and also by the cartographic method itself, which needs to include the surveyor's position to produce an accurate map.[44] The separation of observer and observed is also seemingly collapsed by the inclusion of the explorers within pictorial studies of the landscape. In part, this is another facet of the whole epistemological enterprise of exploring, where the knowledge-gatherers and their difficulties form part of the information presented in the journal. It is also a Romantic technique, such as found in the paintings of Caspar David Friedrich, where a figure's back only is seen as he or she looks out to a panoramic view. Furthermore, it is a case of the observer also being observed, and seemingly being reduced to another element of the landscape. *Mitchell's Mitre Rock and Lake, From Mount Arapiles* (plate 5) positions the explorers on the far left, overlooking the land, but humbled by its scale.

In its positioning of the explorers below the point of view the picture represents, such a depiction constructs another, higher point of view, in effect creating a hierarchy of vision. Ultimately, this hierarchy of verticality includes God, who looks down on the explorers, from an even higher eminence: 'The eye of God looking down on the solitary caravan, as with its slow, and snake-like motion, it presents the only living thing around, must have contemplated its appearance on such a scene with pitying admiration ...' (Giles 2: 318). The point of view of the eye of God is not simply a well-worn trope, but continues in the explorers' texts the

Plate 5   *Mitre Rock and Lake, From Mount Arapiles,* engraved by G. Barnard after
Mitchell's drawing. From Thomas Mitchell, *Three Expeditions into . . . Eastern
Australia* (pl.31). Mitchell Library, State Library of New South Wales.

association of height and surveillance. Giles's text, describing the appearance of the exploration caravan from above, is constructing God's view as
simply an extension of the explorer's. The explorers fashion a world
saturated with levels of surveillance, with God the ultimate surveillant,
his benevolent watchfulness serving as evidence of the righteousness of
the explorer's task. Writing of his survival, Sturt states:

> in the wide field of nature, we see the hand of an over-ruling Providence,
> evidence of care and protection from some unseen quarter, which strike the
> mind with overwhelming conviction, that whether in the palace or in the
> cottage, in the garden, or in the desert, there is an eye upon us. (*ECA* 1: 9–10)

This is a particularly democratic surveillance, penetrating both palace
and cottage, but in invading these relatively safe places, it is intimated
that it has a judgemental as well as benevolently watchful function. The
explorers' survival is usually taken as evidence of divine approval of their
activities: Stokes confesses that he believes that '*His Eye* to whom the
darkness and light are both alike, watched over our safety' (2: 88) and
that 'our preservation can only be attributed to Him whose eye is on all
his creatures and who disposes of our lives as it seemeth good in his sight'
(2: 282). Divine surveillance is constructed as a larger version of explora-

tive practices; the vision of the explorer echoes the greater vision of God. Stokes climbs a hill to look over the country, and remembers that it is the same hill that Cook climbed to try to see if there was a passage out of the reefs which had imprisoned his ship. Cook's watchfulness is rewarded by his discovery of Providence Channel – a name, Stokes alerts the reader, 'which must ever remind us of Him, who in moments when our lives hang by a thread, is ever watchful, and spares us in the exercise of his inscrutable will' (Stokes 1: 347). The explorative gaze is a microform of the divine gaze; the flow of the gaze cannot be reversed, however, and must always be directed from the 'higher' point to the 'lower'. The 'higher' surveillant is invisible to those below, or at least shrouded in an impenetrable mystery – God's will is 'inscrutable'.

The compass seems to offer an absolute frame of reference which avoids the subjectivity of the individual percipient in favour of the universal and undebatable referents of direction. This, however, ignores how direction is culturally produced, mediated by technology and representational convention and how it cheerfully embodies the disjunction between magnetic and 'true' north. The fixity of the compass as a source of direction is undermined by the problems that the explorers have with it. Stokes describes a panoramic view from 'Compass Hill', so named not because of the compass's use in aiding description but because the compass was lost there (Stokes 1: 159). He also notes that boundary disputes originated in the fact that in the interregnum between the surveying and settling of land, magnetic north, with which the boundaries were laid down, had varied: thus, the compass is deconstructed as a source of a priori fixity (Stokes 2: 245–47).

While the compass directions are usually represented as absolute and independent, in the text they inevitably revolve around the central figure of the explorer. This is particularly so in panoramic descriptions, which are structured as circles centred on the eye of the beholder. Panoramas are the classic moments of the journals: the explorer gains elevation for the quotidian duty of triangulation of points, but this is always at the same time a celebration of the visual.

Panoramas

The panoramic description is unlike the picturesque construction of nature, in that natural objects are not ordered according to a pre-existent aesthetic which was self-consciously artificial. Panoramas are concerned with the establishment of topographical accuracy through a wide field of vision. This 'accuracy' does not consist of fidelity to a pre-textual reality but is a product of the ways in which the panorama is used and understood. Again, nature is seen through a cultural construct, although this construct is – unlike the picturesque – obsessively concerned with detail. The art form comes to dominate description of the real. Stokes, for instance, describes a scene as if it is, in fact, a panorama: 'Under any circumstances the discovery would have been delightful, but the time of the previous darkness, the moon rising and spreading the whole before us like a panorama, made the scene ... unusually exciting' (Stokes 2: 40). The panorama as popular art form demanded the complete success of the illusion that the viewer was part of the scene. This required a number of effects, but most importantly the vivid delineation of the scene and a convincing reproduction of daylight.[45] Discussing scenery in Timor, Stokes enthusiastically describes how 'the whole scene appears before you clear and bright, with every line sharply drawn, every patch of colour properly discriminated, a splendid panorama of towering hills and wavering forests' (Stokes 2: 195). He continues, 'whilst I was gazing at this picture ...', revealing that the scene is being described as a work of art, and 'panorama' is not simply referring to breadth of vision.

The panorama (as a technical device) positions the viewer centrally to the picture. At the same time she or he must always be kept at a certain distance from the painting to maintain the illusion of reality.[46] Eyre, describing a scene where Aborigines are gathered, bemoans their tendency to self-decoration; he notes that this is for effect and remarks that, however, 'like the scenery of a panorama, they are then seen to most advantage at a distance' (Eyre 2: 209–10).

The picture which accompanies this (see plate 6) features just such a distanced viewpoint, displaying a field of dancing, costumed natives lit by the combined effects of moon and fire. This picture successfully reduces the intricacies and particularities of an Aboriginal activity to a stereotypical scene of native ritual, a scene which exists only to please the (European) viewer.

The notion of a panorama implies a fixed spectacle with a large range of vision, usually 360 degrees. But there were moving panoramas, 'canvases of often enormous length wound round a concealed spool which were unwound horizontally across prosceniums onto a second concealed spool'.[47] Some of these lateral panoramas depicted river or sea voyages – indeed, they were perfectly suited to such a display. Grey characterises one journey as just such a panorama: 'Amidst such scenes and thoughts we were swept along, whilst this unknown coast, which so many had anxiously yet vainly wished to see, passed before our eyes like a panorama ... '(Grey 1: 400–01). The idea that the observer is stationary while the scenery is moving is not uncommon, but it nevertheless positions the explorer as the immobile centre of viewing, and reduces what is seen to the moving scenery of a visual amusement, although the panorama had pretensions to being considered an educational tool.

Plate 6   *Kangaroo Dance of King George's Sound*; drawing by J. Neil. From Edward John Eyre, *Expeditions of Discovery into Central Australia* (vol. 2, facing p.229).

The panorama provided a spectacle by which colonial progress could be demonstrated at 'home'. Robert Burford's panorama of Sydney, exhibited at Leicester Square, allowed the viewer a 360 degree view of the young town, the harbour and the surrounding country, which was minutely detailed with extraordinary care, constructing for itself the impression of extreme accuracy. It is is possible, however, to examine the original drawing for this panorama by Augustus Earle, which is contained in the small booklet, *Description of A View of the Town of Sydney, New South Wales*. From that, it can be seen that this ostensibly accurate panorama is in fact a compendium of discrete scenes. The view is not just a catalogue of civic amenities, such as churches, roads and distilleries; it also features small dramas which reveal the everyday 'life' of the town. There are scenes of 'typical' Aboriginal activities such as fighting with spears, and climbing gum trees, as well as Governor Darling and Colonel Dumaresq out for a ride being greeted by 'King' Boongaree. The improbability of these things happening simultaneously – or being seen to be happening simultaneously – betrays the claims to accuracy that panoramas implicitly make. Instead, it reveals that the panorama is an inherently duplicitous genre; not only is its basic premise that of the illusionistic reproduction of presence, but the picture itself includes temporally distinct events while ostensibly being a synchronic depiction.

Of the many panoramic descriptions in the journals which are constructed using the points of the compass, one example is sufficient. After describing the scene as impossible to describe, Sturt produces the land in terms of compass direction.

> The dark and broken line of the Barrier Range lay behind us to the south; eastward the horizon was bounded by the hills I had lately visited, and the only break in the otherwise monotonous colour of the landscape was caused by the plains we had crossed before entering the pine forest. From the south-west round to the east northwards, the whole face of the country was covered with a gloomy scrub that extended like a sea to the very horizon. To the north-west, at a great distance, we saw a long line of dust . . . knowing it to be raised by the party. . . (*ECA* 1: 222)

Such a principle of ordering seems as natural to the modern reader as it undoubtedly would have to Sturt; nor does it seem particularly surprising that cartographic codes should be utilised in the textual production of a scene. However, compass direction is not a natural feature of the land, but is rather part of its cultural production. And the panorama is not a unified 'scene' – nobody can see 360 degrees simultaneously – but a conglomeration of particular perceptions produced as a continuum, the joinings between the pieces erased. Moreover, on close inspection, the production of the panorama is far more complex than simply a matter of listing objects in relation to their directional referents. Direction is adopted as a natural way of relating objects (always to the observer), but the method varies between giving one particular direction and an arc of degrees.

In Sturt's description the arcs of horizon south and east are only cursorily described by referring to one particular direction, the arc of land from the south to east being unmentioned, and it is difficult thereby to picture the full circumference of the vision. In contrast, the arc of land from the south-west clockwise to the north-east is described, but it happens to be a virtually undetailed homogeneity to which the usual simile, 'like a sea', may be attached, the only differentiating feature being the trail of dust the explorers themselves raise. The detail of the mountains, which Sturt's description carefully avoids, may have been dealt with by pictorial means. But the only form which adequately relates the objects to each other is purely cartographic – the uncertainty engendered by Sturt's description of the country to the south-east is relieved by reference to his map. The cartographic influence on Sturt's panorama does not at all remove the I/eye centredness of the description: rather, Sturt stands in the centre of the compass and is the point from which direction emanates. He stands, as he says, 'in the centre of barrenness'. A panorama is often structured in terms of its being a view 'round the compass' (Oxley 136); but the word 'compass' has a second meaning, that of 'embracing what is seen'. Thus, Oxley's description of a panoramic view from a hill considers the panorama in terms of visual possession as well as rotation: the 'whole landscape', he writes, 'within the compass of our view was clear and open, resembling diversified pleasure grounds' (Oxley 174).

The construction of Mitchell in his journals provides an excellent example of several of the tropes of what might tautologically be called the surveyor's surveillance. In *Three Expeditions into ... Eastern Australia* he is presented as the surveyor who accomplishes what his predecessors say is impossible: describing how he 'clambered over rocks and measured from cliff to cliff with the pocket sextant' Mitchell says that he 'had encompassed those wild recesses' (*3Ex* 2: 323). This encompassing of the wilderness is the embrace of knowledge; the 'wild recesses' are 'opened' by being captured within triangulation lines. This is possible, not because of the labour of Mitchell alone, but through his attaining a position for authoritative gazing. 'I made the most of each station when it had once been cleared', he writes, 'by taking an exact panoramic view with the theodolite, of the nameless features it commanded' (*3Ex* 2: 323 n.). Here, then, is the intersection of three central tropes of the explorative gaze in its self-formulation. The gaze 'encompasses' the land, it 'commands' what is seen, and it borrows the prestige of accuracy belonging to the panorama to assert its own authority.

Perspectives in cartography

The map seems to offer a way that relieves this explorer-centredness and the possessiveness which seems to be involved with 'commanding' and panoramic views, as it is a form which ostensibly depicts objects' relationship to each other without the controlling aspect of a single observer.

Unlike a verbal description, which may always be suspected of subjectivity, a map offers a seemingly indisputable representation of the world. Details may be argued, but the essential method of representation rarely comes into question. In producing the land as it does, a topographical map aggressively positions the observer in space: the earth is below, open to investigation. Yet, the normal perspective is absent; the land is not proportioned in any particular direction, seemingly constructing a generalised viewer rather than a single eye in space. The map is two-dimensional, composed of symbols that vaguely resemble objects seen from space, and offers a simulacrum of three-dimensionality by use of the same codes of shading which Mitchell, for example, uses to represent sea shells.

Interpreters of the history of cartography have drawn attention to the connections between art and cartography, and especially to the problem of point of view. Of particular interest is the development from panoramic vistas to elevated and bird's-eye views, then to cartography. The traveller William Bingley recorded how he was able to obtain a bird's-eye view of a town, the area seeming to be 'spread out like a map beneath the eye'.[48] Svetlana Alpers has pointed to a kind of middle-ground between landscape and cartography in the painting of a *View of Amsterdam* by the Dutch artist Jan Micker.[49] Here, the city is presented from the nearly vertical, the unseen clouds casting shadows across the streets and neighbouring fields. This was, of course, an impossible point of view at the time, although possible (and popular) in the nineteenth century,[50] but the viewpoint could be imagined. Another impossible point of view, and one which was specifically cartographical, was offered by James Wyld's Great Globe in Leicester Square. Just as Robert Burford's panorama was, it was ostensibly aimed at education, but provided entertainment during the year of the Great Exhibition and an outlet for Wyld's products – he was a globe-maker and map-salesman by trade.[51] His Great Globe displayed a relief map of the world on the inside of the sphere rather than, which was more normal, the outside. The concavity of this representation of the world positions the observer directly at the centre: as with the panorama, the world is revealed to the central eye.

Two-dimensional maps also depend on an imaginary position, but one that is complicated by the mathematical transposition of projection. Ptolemy's 'third method' for the representation of the curved sphere of the earth in two dimensions depends upon imagining an observer external to the earth. The length of the axis between this observer's eye and the centre of that section of the earth examined determines the visual angle from which it is possible to calculate perspectival distortion.[52] The projection which results from Ptolemy's method was later modified by Mercator and remains one of the standard projections. The construction of a topographical map, then, attributes a privileged position – in much the same way as does perspective – to the imagined observer as well as to the map's addressee. In promising that the 'Noble-man and Gentle-man by speculation, may travell through every Province of the World', Henry Hexham, Ortelius's English translator, constructs the addressee, European man, as naturally visually privileged, and a man who has no need to travel himself.[53]

Moreover, the map as a construction of space depends upon the (imagined) external observer; this observer's position above the earth determines the arrangement of objects within the representation. Other possible arrangements, including those which are not determined by a privileged observer are eschewed, because of the convenience of the Mercator projection. Its two-dimensional nature means it is transport-

able, and that its instrumentalist value is increased, even though its
'accuracy' is necessarily reduced by a system of projection. Ultimately, the
map is a successful tool of imperial knowledge-compilation because it
convinces people that it represents 'the' world and that, except for
improvements in accuracy and the development of thematic maps, there
are no other worlds that can be depicted. It gains this authority because
it 'effaces the orthogonality, the perspectival projection (intended both
for depictions as pictures and as maps, which are also, of course,
pictures) of who is declaring *that* view ... to be *thus*'.[54]

Exploration literature can never efface the role of the explorer as
point of view as well as a map can, although Grey's description of country
which 'lay like a map at our feet' attempts to arrogate to his view the
certainty that is provided by cartographical representation (Grey 1: 180).
The view, of course, is nothing like a map with its codes, colouring and
two-dimensionality; yet, the highest praise that a view can have is that it is
like a map. This is again the tendency towards treating the seen in terms
of a cultural construct. This is not, as in the picturesque, an affirmation
of the vision's picturesqueness; rather, it is the self-confirmatory
construction of the explorer's point of view as one of unequalled access
to the real. That the real is approached through a comparison with
cartography is a strategy to enhance the explorer's claim to accuracy, and
also adopt the technique of map-reading advised by Ortelius, who defines the map as a military tool.[55] After noting that he can read the land
like a map, Grey catalogues the 'natural riches', 'the finest harbours' of
the land and states that it is 'singularly favoured by nature' (Grey 1: 180).
'Singularly favoured' for what purpose the text does not say, yet it is clear
that the land is being surveyed by this distant eye for possible future
exploitation. This is not particularly surprising in an explorer; but it is
surprising how often the spatialisation of land, through maps and
descriptions of vistas, is intimately connected with its temporalisation.

The word 'prospect' plays a dual role in many of the explorers'
descriptions: it embodies the idea of looking out into space and the idea
of looking forward into time. When explorers speak of the journey itself,
it is often the case that the prospect spatially ahead is the prospect of
travel the explorers have before them in time (for example, Eyre 1: 59 &
1: 356). A prospect is often taken as a moment in which it is appropriate
to comment on the future of the colony. Grey says, after describing a
'beautiful prospect', that he 'painted in fancy the rapid progress that this
country would ere long make in commerce and civilization' (Grey 1:
163). Contemplations on the future are not simply associated with seeing
distances but the very word 'prospect' encourages the temporalisation of
a spatial perspective. Mitchell writes that the 'prospect of an open

country has a double charm in regions for the most part covered with primeval forests, calling up pleasing reminiscences of the past, brighter prospects for the future' (*EITA* 309).

These private reminiscences of the English countryside, provoked by the open country are again part of the self-serving reading of the Australian landscape, a view of it as ready-made for the colonial enterprise, which the 'brighter prospects' suggest. The hierarchy of vision is not forgotten when prospects of the future are discussed. Stokes writes that 'men of the highest eminence have foreseen and foretold the ultimate importance of that vast continent o'er which, within the memory of living man, the roving savage held precarious though unquestioned empire' (Stokes 1: 1). These men of the 'highest eminence' are able to see furthest into the future because of their 'high' position; the future is seen clearly belonging to that imperial narrative which informs history. As Grey cannot see the land except as a map, so too is the future seen through the equally culturally constructed imperial narrative. No other history outside this history can be imagined; thus, through the temporalisation of a spatial construction of the land, the 'orthogonality, the perspectival projection' of this history is forgotten.

4

Maps and their Cultural Constructedness

He had bought a large map representing the sea,
Without the least vestige of land:
And the crew were much pleased when they found it to be
A map they could all understand ...

'Other maps are such shapes, with their islands and capes!
But we've got our brave Captain to thank'
(So the crew would protest) 'that he's bought us the best
– A perfect and absolute blank!'

Lewis Carroll, *The Hunting of the Snark*

Maps and Reality
The philosophy of Western cartography

An interesting example of a textual reference to maps is found in Sturt's journal of his 1844–45 exploration.

Let any man lay the map of Australia before him, and regard the blank upon its surface, and then let me ask him if it would not be an honourable achievement to be the first to place foot in its centre. (*ECA* 2: 1)

It seems to me that interpreting this in such a way that Sturt is left with his foot in the centre of a map can be more than a vexatious misreading. There is a slippage here between map and reality that attests to the peculiar authority that maps possess: there can be few representational objects that are so often confused with the things they are meant to represent. The creation of an outline of Australia as a blank is also a construction of a continent as empty, uninhabited, locationless. When the map has a foot placed in the centre of it, it is not impossible that a mark will be left upon its previously blank surface, thus echoing the many footprints which occur in the journals. This chapter is about these two aspects of mapping in the journals: the sliding between maps and reality, and the construction of Australia as a blank to be drawn on.

Chapter 3 of this work concluded by arguing that the specular position constructed within Western cartography is essentially the same as that for panoramas, picturesque pictures and other visual delights. Separate from the 'seen', the viewer (as textually constructed) is at the same time at its centre; this can be either literally, as when viewing a panorama, or else central in the sense of possessing a controlling and privileged viewpoint. Cartography's philosophy is that of scientific positivism, which rejects the notion that knowledge is socially produced, or that it is a reflection of the power of the mapmakers. Cartographers do not claim that any one map displays reality; rather, traditional cartography assumes the superiority of the positivist agenda, and any suggestion that mapmaking involves 'non-scientific' or 'non-objective techniques' is rejected.[1]

Traditional historians of cartography have often castigated certain categories of maps as being compilations of hypotheses and suppositions rather than veracious representations. This argument imposes a progressivist view of mapping, and establishes a hierarchy which privileges one mode of representation (post-seventeenth century European, mimeticist and realist) over alternative modes. Thus, not only are non-European cartographies – such as those used by Polynesians and Aborigines – ignored, but those elements within the Western cartographic tradition which can be labelled 'inaccurate' are assigned to marginal areas of 'myth' and 'imaginary geography'.[2] To establish this critical stance is to insist on the anteriority of the 'real' while reducing the map to a purely transparent or mimetic re-presentation of this reality. It is important for modern cartography to suppress its precursors by labelling them 'mythical' and therefore dismissable, for it is in these medieval maps that is most clearly revealed that cartography is a social practice – a fact modern cartography is often reluctant to admit. Modern cartography encourages a reading of maps which effaces their own cultural production (that is, both how they are consumed and understood as objects) while reinforcing the authority of the producer. We believe that a map is 'innocent, a servant of the eye that sees things as they really are';[3] it is through this belief in the innocence of maps, their capacity for transparency, that they gain their authority. Constructing maps as innocently mimetic disallows reading them as productions of complex social forces; instead, the authority of the map resides in its claim to show the 'real', and that the map is the best way in which this can be shown.

Maps do not bear any simple relationship to a pre-existent reality, nor is this reality available in any unmediated way. Maps do possess a use-value – that is, when compared with objects of vision, there may be *some* relationship. This does not mean that any aspect of a fundamental 'reality' has been successfully traced on a map, but rather that one cultural construct (maps) is used to negotiate another (the seen). A map's accuracy is, in part, produced by this relationship, but accuracy (or its ability to convince the map user that it is accurate) is also a function of the representational devices a map uses.

The founding assumption of cartography is that it presents the user with a view of the land from above. There are highly refined methods for accomplishing this perspective, including conventions of shading, colouring and iconographical codes for objects as seen from above. Maps present mountains, for example, with shading codes that attempt to signify their three-dimensionality in two dimensions. This does not occur in relief maps alone but in most maps, except topographical maps, where vertical variations are represented by contour lines. Colouring is used to represent the earth's surface: green for vegetation, blue for water, and so on. These are in part iconographical – that is, they are codes which signify the objects – but they seem to be based in the real colours of the objects. This is true also for maps that include symbols which signify objects as seen from above. There are codes for trees, buildings, roads, and these are intended to signify by convention the presence of the objects; but they do so through a quasi-mimetic representation of how these objects are supposed to appear from above. This appeal to the 'real' in the colouring of maps, for example, disintegrates as soon as it is examined closely. Blue only conventionally represents the sea; the sea is many colours – occasionally blue, but at other times grey, silver or green. The conventionality of these signs is exactly what is forgotten in most map reading, and in the forgetting arises the peculiar access to the real granted to maps. This use of cartographic codes helps ensure maps are not simply consumed as purely codified objects, but are understood as representing the real in an immediate way.[4]

The general attack on Cartesian notions of space as embodied in maps has joined a surge of interest in the ways in which maps create and reinforce power relations. J. B. Harley has drawn connections between various approaches such as Foucauldian, semiotic and iconological to conclude that cartographic discourse, dominated by 'elite or powerful groups and individuals' is primarily a 'language of power, not of protest'.[5] He points out that there are advantages to be gained when 'maps cease to be understood primarily as inert records of morphological landscapes or passive reflections of the world of objects, but are regarded as refracted images contributing to dialogue in a socially constructed world'.[6] In the light of the rejection of the reflectionist or mimetic model of cartography, the question of whether certain maps are accurate or not becomes largely irrelevant. Instead of re-inscribing the old dialectic of representation/real in empiricist terms, it is more useful to see mapping as a semiotic practice temporally embedded and transformative of previous maps, rather than as an innocent inscription started afresh on blank paper. This allows the map critic to compare modern maps with medieval *mappae mundi* (world maps), not in terms of which is superior in representing the real, but in terms of what political and social agendas are present in both, and what continuities exist from one to the other.

In practice, then, maps are not recognised as highly codified texts which have an uncertain relationship with geographical 'reality', both producing and being produced by it; rather, they are seen as at least semi-transparent of reality. As they are read this way, the cartographic practice of representing the unknown as a blank does not simply or innocently reflect gaps in European knowledge but actively erases (and legitimises the erasure of) existing social and geo-cultural formations in preparation for the subsequent emplacement of a new order. As this section will argue, the construction of Australia as *tabula rasa* joins with its production as antipode to produce the continent as an empty, inverted space desperately requiring rectification and occupation. This is firstly a semiotic practice, taking place upon the cartographic space I have argued is especially privileged; but it does not remain a purely textual practice, as imperial inscription soon becomes all too material for the indigenes whose presence is erased.

Ideology in maps

Readings, then, that do not simply privilege maps' verisimilitude reveal their ideological and political function. Not only have maps played an important role in offering necessary information, they have also been used for propaganda and religious purposes, and have served as symbols of imperial destiny. The globe is often featured in depictions of rulers – the Holy Roman Emperor, Charles IV, for example, is pictured with a tripartite globe signifying his political dominance.[7] The proprietorial relationship that the emperor has with the globe suggests the picture acts as a projection of imperial power and offers an implicit argument that Charles IV is the rightful ruler of the globe he holds. This interpretation is reinforced by similar uses of the globe in pictures of Christ, where there is no question of a limit of sovereignty.[8] The religious symbolism of medieval *mappae mundi* also prefigured the spread of empire and its missionary justification. Woodward notes that the thirteenth century Ebstorf map of the world, the central structure of which is the body of Christ, has Christ's left hand reaching out to embrace even the twenty-four monstrous races of the antipodes.[9] The body in the map presents a world structurally dependent on Christ, and by extension on his earthly institution, the church. The map also projects the inevitability of the institution's homogenising rule – Christ's left hand is a sinister prefiguration of the missionary enterprise.

Maps do not simply serve as locations for symbolic displays of power but become directly involved in political rivalries. The most obvious example of this is Pope Alexander's division of the New World in two, an operation which was entirely cartographic, ignoring geographical and indigenous differences in favour of a solution which reflected the European balance of power: the same could be said for the nineteenth century division of Africa. The reaching hand of Christ, and the apparent inconsequentiality of indigenous and geographic differences to the division of the New World are evidence of the powerful homogenising effect of maps. The 'universal' applicability of one cartographic practice allows the transportation of power to a worldwide empire, in which maps perform the function of allowing power to be 'gained, administered, given legitimacy, and codified'.[10]

The Austral continent, from before its discovery, is seen as a place of perversity, where the norms and nature of Europe are inverted. Already, then, the southern continent exists only in relation to Europe: it is part of a European search for identity, rather than possessing independent status. Its blankness is a representation of European ignorance, but works semiotically to form the antipodal landmass as empty, unsettled, and inviting European inscription. The form itself creates meaning. Representations of Australia as an upside-down blank are unavoidable given the founding assumptions of European cartography, and are best understood as part of the European process of 'othering', whereby European self-identification can only proceed by the identification of other places and cultures as 'different'. This difference is produced by the creation of a semiotic *tabula rasa* and subsequently projecting upon it fantasies of difference that emerge from the European imaginative archive. Africa, Asia and America have all been subject to this process. The maps created them as semiotic voids, which are immediately filled by exotica. So immediate is this projection that the blanks of these continents are rarely seen; what is forgotten amongst the elephants, trees, skiapods, and imaginary cities, is the fact that the creation of 'Africa' or 'America' was initiated by the construction of an empty space, subsequently filled. Australia in this regard is unique. It is formed as a blank and is filled occasionally by fantasy, but one of these projections is blankness itself. Thus, Australia is semiotically 'filled in' by projections of blankness – both cartographically and in explorers' aesthetic descriptions. It is because maps act as a semiotic field that they need to be subject to a kind of investigation which denies them their commonsense foundational assumptions and instead views them primarily as cultural productions.

Antipodality and conceptions of the world

A history of the upside-down

A network of classical and medieval myths is found in explorers' constructions of Australia, and especially in the metaphoric references to mapping within their texts. The imaginative construction of a *terra australis*, an antipodean continent which served to balance the Eurasian landmass, was not simply the result of an aesthetic or pseudo-scientific desire for symmetry. Nor was it some charming but errant myth, whimsically utilised in the early European responses to Australia, to be soon discarded for more realistic appraisals. Brian Elliot has recognised that the word 'antipodes' still carries 'hints of oddity, of perverse variations from the civilized norm'; but, having decided that the antipodal construction of Australia is a 'foolish prejudice', Elliot himself somewhat perversely says that 'we need not stay to examine it'.[11] The cartographic discourse that gives rise to the notion of the antipodes begins long before the expansion of European empires; it is part of the imaginative preparation for empire and is also useful in the administering of the empire once founded.

Ambrosius Theodosius Macrobius (AD 399–422) revived notions held by Crates of an equatorial ocean dividing the earth's north and south landmasses. In his *Commentary on the Dream of Scipio*, Macrobius presents the southern hemisphere as basically isomorphic of the northern. His argument proceeds by dividing the world into five zones: the southern and northern frigid zones, the inhabitable temperate zones, and the uninhabitable central zone, the main feature of which is an impassable torrid ocean. The difficulty faced by this proposal was, of course, that which faced all theories propounding the sphericity of the earth – why the people on the other side did not fall off. Macrobius neatly combats this by sidestepping the question of gravity and instead repeating his geographic isomorphism in terms of the thoughts of the antipodal inhabitants: 'I can assure you that the uninformed among them think the same thing about us and believe that it is impossible for us to be where we are; they too, feel that anyone who tried to stand in the region beneath them would fall'.[12]

Latitudinal zones of climate were one of the few ancient geographical notions to be supported by voyages of discovery, though the equatorial zone was found to be habitable. But the idea of the existence of an antipodal region was not always accepted. Cicero, referring to the original meaning of 'antipodes', attacked those who alleged that 'directly opposite to us on the farther side of the earth are people who stand with feet against our feet, and these men you call antipodes'.[13] Lucretius condemned those who maintained 'that living things walk head downwards, and cannot fall off the earth into the spaces of heaven beneath any more than our bodies can of their own free will fly up into the quarters of heaven', and he characterised the theory as resulting from 'twisted reason'.[14] The idea of the antipodes as perverse or against reason was argued also by Cosmas Indicopleuestes (Indian traveller), an Egyptian monk writing in the sixth century.

> But should one wish to examine more elaborately the question of the Antipodes, he would easily find them to be old wives' fables. For if two men on

opposite sides placed the soles of their feet each against each, whether they chose to stand on earth, or water, or air, or fire, or any other kind of body, how could both be found standing upright? The one would assuredly be found in the natural upright position, and the other, contrary to nature, head downward. Such notions are opposed to reason, and alien to our nature and condition ... [15]

Although attempts by Cosmas in his *Christian Topography* to reconcile models of the world with the Bible resulted in a flat four-cornered earth with a vaulted roof (Rev. 7:1, Isa. 40:22), the shape of the earth was generally accepted to be spherical and it was the existence of the antipodes, rather than the earth's supposed sphericity, which was the cause of conflict. McCrindle notes, in *Christian Topography*, that the opposition to the notion of the antipodes was shared by most of the Christian Fathers, including Augustine, Chrysostom and Severianus of Gabala.[16] Much of this opposition came from the concern about the origin of the people who, it was assumed, would inhabit these regions. Augustine reasoned that either these races, likely monstrous, did not exist, or if they did they were not human, or if demonstrably human they must be descended from Adam.[17]

The perverse antipodes

The 'upside-downness' of the antipodes encouraged its construction as a place where everything was reversed. This joined with the geographical prejudice of medieval maps, where Europe embodied the norms which dictated what was 'human', and all that was not human belonged to Asia or, more likely, Africa. The 'extreme' regions of the earth were the repository of all that was abnormal or perverse. This was not seen as semiotic play – as are the later utopian fantasies which use other continents as convenient stages onto which may be projected an inverted Europe – but rather as a natural condition that was objectively there in the world.

In his fourteenth century *Polychronicon*, Ranulf Higden urges the reader to note that 'at the farthest reaches of the world often occur new marvels and wonders, as though Nature plays with greater freedom secretly at the edges of the world than she does openly and nearer us in the middle'.[18] The remarkable continuity of this trope can be seen by comparing it to an 1817 description by Sydney Smith, who writes that 'in this remotest part of the earth, Nature (having made horses, oxen, ducks, geese, oaks, elms, and all regular productions for the rest of the world) seems determined to have a bit of play, and to amuse herself as she pleases'.[19] Ranulf Higden's description of extremities circumscribes a paradigm of possible descriptions from which Smith's description is directly drawn, foreshadowing responses to Australian fauna and flora as examples of nature's more frivolous productions. Also, of course, it puts Europe naturally at the centre, and everything else at the periphery. The discourses of Australia as periphery, antipode and *tabula rasa* can all be found most famously in a description of a painting by Louis Buvelot by Marcus Clarke, who later employed it in his preface to Adam Linsday Gordon's volume of poetry *Sea Spray and Smoke Drift*.

> In Australia alone is to be found the Grotesque, the Weird, – the strange scribblings of Nature learning how to write. Some see no beauty in our trees without shade, our flowers without perfume, our birds who cannot fly, and our beasts who have not yet learned to walk on all fours. But the dweller in the wilderness acknowledges the subtle charm of this fantastic land of monstrosities.[20]

The maps become places where aberrations are first (literally) marginalised. The Hereford and Ebstorf *mappae mundi* both push to the extreme south a collection of blemmyae, cynocephalae, skiapods, antipodes, panotti, donestre, four-eyed maritime Ethiopians, and other curiosities. The southernmost areas of the world, then, become a stage on which European fantasies of difference, aberration and monstrousness can be played out.

The common idea about the antipodes was that its inhabitants would have their feet where their heads should naturally be. Tommaso Campanella's socialist utopian story, *The City of the Sun*, includes a list of penalties the imaginary society imposes on aberrant behaviour. Those who are homosexuals are 'made to walk about for two days with a shoe tied to their necks as a sign that they perverted natural order, putting their feet where the head belongs'.[21] Published long after many voyages south of the equator, Campanella's story can still utilise the easy transference from antipodes as opposite to antipodes as perverse. Richard Brome's play, *Antipodes*, written in 1636, constructs the southern hemisphere as isomorphic of the northern:

> They walk upon firm earth, as we do here,
> And have the firmament over their heads,
> As we have here ... [22]

But the antipodes are also 'contrary' – a place where the natural order is reversed and women overrule the men, parents and masters obey the child and servant, and, in a reflection of Campanella's alignment of antipodality with perversity, the 'wives lie uppermost'.[23]

Joseph Hall's *Another World and Yet the Same (Mundis alter et Idem)* of 1605 includes a comprehensive map of the imagined southern continent, divided into different territories and governments. *Terra Australis* is used by Hall to satirise European society, its 'upside-downness' encouraging the projection onto it of cultures the reverse of Europe. As in *The City of the Sun*, antipodality means perversion. Viraginia, a land ruled by women, is at war with Locania, a country where men 'are so lecherous and so much inclined to sex that their lust burns with desire for boys, for whores, and perhaps even for mules and cattle'. Perhaps even worse than the occasional cohabitation with farm animals is the southern continent's island of Hermaphrodita, populated with doubly gifted people who, on finding anyone of only one sex 'display the person as a great monstrosity'.[24] The idea of the other continents as repositories for hermaphroditic populations begins with Pliny, who located them in Africa[25]; it continues to George Sandys's 1626 edition of Ovid's *Metamorphoses*, in which Sandys argued that Florida was especially replete with hermaphrodites.[26] The view that Australia was inhabited by hermaphrodites is expressed in the 1676 French travel fantasy, *La Terre Australe Connue* by Gabriel Foigny.[27] *Another World and Yet the Same* also imagined Amazonia, a province of Viraginia where 'the women wear the breeches and sport long beards, and it is the men who wear petticoats and are beardless' (64). Long before the antipodes was 'discovered' cross-dressing was already popular there.

Hall's rather witty story is a parody of many a collection of wild travellers' tales, yet it shares the problem of parody that it tends to reproduce, even honour, that which it criticises. Even though none of these fantastic projections is meant to be taken seriously, the southern continent is still being used as a stage where dreams of difference are played out. Indeed, these fantasies of antipodal difference do not disappear with discovery, but carry on after contact with the land and its inhabitants. And theories of the antipodes as opposite were understood by explorers to be more than just obsolete and amusing tropes.

Australia as perverse

Initially, it might seem that some details of the fantasies were accurate. In the region of Crapulia that Hall outlines, the population 'walk about nearly naked; nor do they care for clothes' (29). When Aborigines are described, there is often the preconception that their nakedness is somehow perverse, or odd. Of course, Hall's fantasy utilises the already extant notion that savages have few clothes, so *Another World and Yet the Same* is not an originary moment for nakedness as sign of the other, but focuses this trope of otherness with the lens of antipodality. Other depictions of the inhabitants of the southern continent in Hall's work are more obviously reliant upon previous 'authorities'. There is a description of the inhabitants of Codicia, in Lavernia, which is an example of Hall's indebtedness.

> Monstrous men inhabit the province of Codicia, whom Munster and Mandeville depict with a hog's head. They walk like quadrupeds, face always downwards, so that they don't neglect anything worth picking up; nor do they ever look up at the sky. In terms of their speech, they grunt, indeed, rather than talk. (116)

This is remarkably similar to later descriptions of Aborigines by explorers and others. I am not suggesting that any particular explorer read Hall, or even had any of these fantasies in mind when describing Australia; rather, Hall's work extended the general currency of *terra australis* as a repository of perversity, and explorers worked with this as one possible descriptive paradigm. The very notion of oppositeness is conflated with perversity, so that differences – especially in the natural world – are seen as aberrations.

Australia as a repository of perversity is, of course, one of the central tropes of early landscape description. The animals are bizarre, the trees peculiar and even monstrous, the vegetation continually green; indeed, the country in its entirety seems to be the product of whimsy and an affront to good taste. The French explorer, Péron, evinced considerable confusion at the failure of the Blue Mountains to cool the wind which passed over them – that mountains cool air is:

> so natural and so conformable to all the principles of natural philosophy, that it would seem not to admit of any kind of modification; and, nevertheless, it receives, in the case in question, the most decided and absolute exception; as if the atmosphere of New Holland, as well as the animals and vegetables of this singular continent, has its peculiar laws ... [28]

By the 1840s the various peculiarities of the continent had become commonplaces. The 'strange contrasts to the rest of the world' Australia offered, 'its cherries with their stones growing outside – its trees, which shed their bark instead of their leaves – its strange animals – its still stranger population' were 'enumerated and commented upon' by John Lort Stokes and his companions (Stokes 2: 519). There are examples of strikingly similar descriptions: J. Martin observed that the 'trees retained their leaves and shed their bark instead, the swans were black, the eagles white, the bees were stingless, some mammals had pockets, others laid eggs, it was warmest on the hills and coolest in the valleys, [and] even the blackberries were red'.[29]

The perversity of Australia is already known before contact because the 'authorities' had predicted it. Speaking of the scarcity of fresh water,

Stokes constructs a feminised antipodal land, as fey and 'capricious' as any woman. As:

> the voyager knows, from the best authority, that upon the coasts, and within the heart of Australia, nature seems to delight in contradiction, and that she is more than usually capricious with respect to the supply of what is ordinarily her most common ... gifts. (Stokes 1: 96–97)

What is interesting in this description is that it is not experiential contact with the continent that is referred to when speaking of the land's antipodality, but rather 'the best authority'. The paradigm through which the land is discursively formed already exists, and actual contact is described within this matrix.

The very 'perversity' of the land and the animals posed a challenge to the geography and the Linnaean biology of the time. Péron notes that the continent's peculiar laws 'differ from all the principles of our sciences and all the laws of our systems' and that 'experience of every kind is always to be overturned in this singular part of the world'.[30] Likewise, Oxley remarks that 'the whole form, character, and composition of this part of the country is so extremely singular, that a conjecture on the subject is hardly hazarded before it is overturned; everything seems to run counter to the ordinary course of nature in other countries' (81). For biologists, however, Australian fauna and flora's stubborn refusal to fit into existing Linnaean categories meant the necessity for a paradigm shift in their discipline. Richard White and Geoffrey Serle have both noted that the scientists who contributed to the obsolescence of the 'great chain of being' biology – Darwin, T. H. Huxley and J. D. Hooker – all visited Australia.[31]

Perversity and the anomalous Aborigine

The increasing trend towards the consideration of the relationship between animals and their environment was, in part, a result of the novel flora and fauna of the southern continent. But the construction of the land, and particularly its inhabitants, as perverse demonstrates the ease with which biological theories could be transformed for political use. As late as 1927 the anthropologist Baldwin Spencer could argue that the Aboriginal race was as perverse, and outmoded as Australian fauna: 'Australia is the present home and refuge of creatures, often crude and quaint, that have elsewhere passed away and given place to higher forms. This applies equally to the Aboriginal as to the platypus and kangaroo'.[32] In Spencer's formulation, the Aborigines have survived only because they have been sheltered from the progressive outside world, and their 'extinction' is naturalised through an implicit mobilisation of the inevitability of evolution.

Explorers often see the Aborigines as incongruous, and thus unfit to possess the land. There is one particular description of George Grey's in which antipodeanism is the silent partner in the construction of the Aborigine as perverse, excessive, and strictly unnecessary: 'I wondered that so fair a land should only be the abode of savage men; and then I thought ... of their anomalous position in so fertile a country ...' (Grey 1: 207). The Aborigines are, like other strange productions of the country, an anomaly. The other notable occasion when Grey uses the word 'anomalous' is to describe a lungfish, 'the uncouth gambols and leaps' of which 'were very singular' (Grey 1: 90). Like the lungfish, which can survive out of water for a considerable time, Aborigines are in an unnatural position, inhabiting a continent they cannot fully exploit. The discourse of antipodeanism works to establish the indigene as perverse and strange like the rest of the continent and what it contains, but whereas the odd fauna is merely a curiosity, the Aborigine is an insult to the natural ownership of resources by those who judge themselves best able to exploit them.

It is not surprising that the colonisation process should activate the discourse of antipodeanism that works in its favour. It is perhaps surprising that, from the earliest age of imperial expansion onwards, the antipodes had been seen as a legitimate field for ambition. Marlowe's Tamburlaine swears that:

> ... when holy Fates
> Shall stablish me in strong Egyptia,
> We mean to travel to th' Antarctic pole,
> Conquering the people underneath our feet ... [33]

The desire for the antipodal empire that Tamburlaine feels is in no way inhibited by the perversity of southern lands. This perversity, and the anomalous states of the inhabitants, is, in imperial discourses, rectifiable by British enterprise, which can make the continent a normal, productive element of empire.

The blank land of the south

Imagining the fourth part of the world

Terra australis as a concept must negotiate changing paradigms in mapmaking and the power structures which enable and license these methods. The southern continent can be seen to have been repressed in certain medieval cosmographies, but reappears, being a central function in disallowing an easy stability of worldviews based on the Bible. The dominant *mappa mundi* of the middle ages was the T-O (*orbis terrarum*) map (plate 7) – a useful name, as the map is constructed by placing a 'T' within a circle. The horizontal arms of the 'T' are formed by the Nile and the Don (Tanais) rivers, the vertical arm by the Mediterranean. The orientation is usually towards the east and so Europe is in the bottom left-hand corner, Africa in the bottom right, and Asia covers the top hemisphere.

The division of the world into three parts is significant, in that it supports the Biblical story of the post-diluvian world being divided between the three sons of Noah (Gen. 10). The pictorial/cartographic depiction of this shows the overlordship of Shem in Asia, Ham in Africa, and Japheth in Europe, leaving little room for a fourth continent.[34]

There is a hybrid type of *mappa mundi*, which conflates the Macrobian zonal map and the tripartite T-O map; this may be categorised as quadripartite. This type of world map retains the tripartite division of the northern hemisphere and adds a southern hemispheric continent. The so-called Beatus maps, the characteristics of which can be traced back to the *Commentary on the Apocalypse of Saint John* by Beatus of Liébana (eighth century) are often of this type. Here, a fourth continent is placed on the far right (south) of the map. Woodward translates the inscription on the otherwise blank antipodal continent on a Turin copy of the map thus:

> outside the three parts of the world there is a fourth part, the farthest from the world, beyond the ocean, which is unknown to us on account of the heat of the sun. We are told that the Antipodeans, around whom revolve many fables, live within its confines.[35]

In another version of this type of map from the eleventh century, the so-called *Osma Beatus* (Cathedral of Burgo de Osma copy), the austral continent is occupied by a reclining skiapod – a creature who uses his oversize foot to shade him from the fierce sun of the torrid zone.[36] Lambert of Saint-Omer's map (plate 8) has an antipodes roughly equal in area to the landmass of the northern hemisphere. This map is also heavily inscribed, describing the torrid zone which separates the northern hemisphere from the southern, and speculating on the races that may live in the antipodes.

The Giovanni Contarini map of 1506 is well-known for its incorporation of the Columbian ideas of Asia being a short distance from Europe, but it also includes a 'Terra S. Crucis', which is positioned south-west of Africa, largely below the tropic of Capricorn.[37] The unmodified Ptolemaic *Geography* depicted an antarctic continent, but the presence of

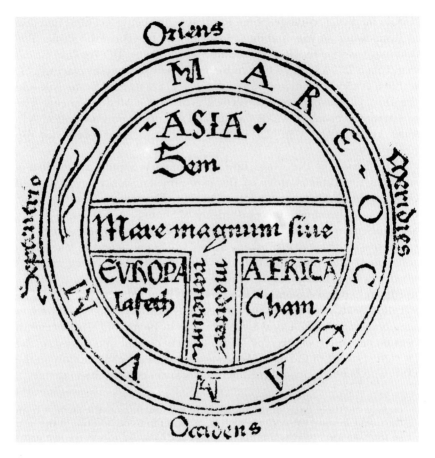

Plate 7 An example of a medieval *orbis terrarum* (or T-O) map, which divided the world into three sectors.

an antipodal world was by no means obligatory. Martin Waldseemuller's 1507 world map, while displaying the newly-discovered Americas, has no suggestion of a *terra incognita* in the southern regions. Patricia Gilmartin has noted, however, that after 1540 'almost all maps and globes showed some kind of antarctic continent'. This was to be expected after the sighting of land below South America on Magellan's 1522 voyage and the exaggerated continent of the imagination that resulted.[38]

The Mercatorial revolution in cartography failed to dislodge the notion of the necessity of an antipodal balancing landmass. Mercator's 'World Chart' of 1569 declares that 'under the Antarctic Pole [lay] a continent so great that, with the southern parts of Asia, and the new India or America, it should be a weight equal to other lands'.[39] The

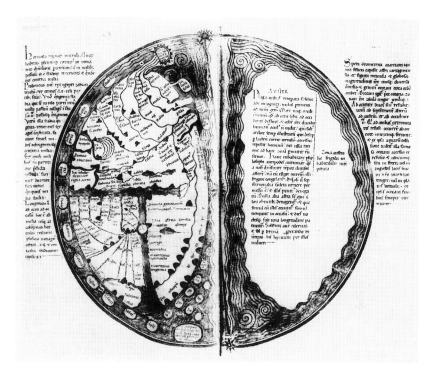

Plate 8   Lambert of Saint-Omer's *mappa mundi*, a medieval map of the
so-called *Beatus* type, which divided the world into four sectors.

tenacity of this idea can be appreciated when Alexander Dalrymple is
found repeating it two centuries later, saying the weight was needed to
'counterpoise the land on the North, and to maintain the equilibrium
necessary for the earth's motion'.[40] Mercator inherited a variety of place
names, for instance Marco Polo's 'Lucach' or 'Beach', and sites for the
antipodal land. Whatever he adds to the southern continent, and despite
the new scientificity of his projection, Mercator repeats the construction
of a southern landmass as a blank to be filled in by European inscription.
The 1569 map of the world has a legend describing 'Beach' as a land of
gold, and the neighbouring 'Maletur' as a land of spices. Maps hold
desperately to the notion that there must be a balancing landmass, and
project dreams of difference or wealth upon it.

Australia as a blank

The fractures in the logic of mapping, where a continent is declared
blank because it is unknown, and then is written over in legend, was

apparent to the cartographer's contemporaries. Joseph Hall's *Another World and Yet the Same* has the character Beroaldus complain bitterly about the delineation of an unknown continent.

> It has always disturbed me to meet constantly with Terra Australis Incognita on geographical maps, and indeed, is there anyone who is not completely senseless who would read this without some silent indignation? For if they know it to be a *continent*, and a *southern* one, how can they call it *unknown*? And if it be unknown, why have all the geographers described it after one form and location to me? (12)

The practice of creating a blank to represent ignorance, and filling that blank with a legend (both in the sense of a myth and a cartographic inscription) continued into the eighteenth century. The mapmaker Emmanuel Bowen produced in 1744 a map of Australia which shows the collision between the evolving claims for accuracy and the use of new discoveries as sites for mythic projections. There are two legends (inscriptions) spread across the otherwise blank outline of what was known of the continent. The first emphasises the accuracy of the cartographic reproduction: 'this map is very exactly copied from the original and therefore the Dutch names have been preserved ... the reader is desired to observe that nothing is marked here but what has has [*sic*] been actually discovered'.[41] The second and rather longer legend creates the southern continent as a place of great and readily accessible riches. It provides a patina of scientific justification by pointing to the equally rich countries sharing the same latitude. Swift had satirised this practice of using the blank areas on maps as an area for fantasy.

> So Geographers in *Afric*-Maps
> With Savage-Pictures fill their Gaps;
> And o'er uninhabitable Downs
> Place elephants for want of towns[42]

Bowen had not used the blank spaces on the Australian map for simple pachydermal fancies, but to project the possibility of profit from, and control of, the new land.

> It is impossible to conceive a Country that promises fairer from its Situation, than this of *Terra Australis*; no longer incognita, as this map demonstrates, but the Southern Continent Discovered ... whoever perfectly discovers & settles it will become infalliably possessed of Territories as Rich, as fruitful, & as capable of Improvement, as any that have been hitherto found out ...[43]

The explicit inscription of desire upon maps is relatively rare. More often the blank areas on maps serve as a place where the cartographer's imagination may have free rein. But it is a mistake to see the projection of fantasy as harmless decoration; rather, it is at this point that cartography offers the clearest display possible of the European erasure of, and subsequent projection upon, other cultures. The map semiotically creates a *tabula rasa* out of the Australian continent simply by rendering it. This initial creation of a blank is not an intentional strategy, designed to erase indigenous presence and culture, but is integral to the cartographic representation of knowledge. The blankness represents ignorance, but when included on a map it does more than this: it constructs the continent as a screen on which European fantasies may be projected.

These fantasies are not the products of an individual's imagination, but are dredged from the European archive of monsters, Orientals, hyperboreans and antipodeans. On maps these spaces come to exist only as a place where these fantasies may find a home. Thus, Justus Danckerts's map of 1690 uses exactly that illustration which Swift criticises. Danckerts's map shows the northern half of Australia as then understood and includes two elephants, a group of natives with spears, and rather European-like trees. This cartographic projection allows the emplacement of a safely familiar 'other' upon the shores of the continent: the map promises that although the inhabitants will not be like us, they will be some mixture of exactly those categories we know as other. These kinds of projections are not the isolated feature of one particular map but gain a momentum and a currency of their own. Coronelli's map of 1696 is obviously heavily influenced by the Danckerts map: it also includes a remarkably similar grouping of natives with spears surrounding an elephant, and has the simple shelters Danckerts's map shows. The vegetation is somewhat different, however; no longer are there the European trees but exotic palms, which signify that this is an/other country. But even this simple projection of difference is disturbed by the two deer which wander out of a grove of palms: this is a difference with peculiarly familiar elements.

Reading the desert oceans

Describing the desert

To realise the possible profits it was necessary, as Emmanuel Bowen notes, to discover physically the continent. The complex arguments surrounding the actual discovery of Australia by Europeans are too well-known to be repeated here.[44] What is of more interest is how the outline of Australia, once formed in maps by a thin line and a halo of names, is filled in by the terrestrial explorers. Pre-discovery 'filling in' took place via various fantastic projections upon the continent. But post-discovery inscription upon the map is not simply achieved by the cartographic transference of hills that are objectively 'out there' onto the map. Surveying is an agonistic practice involving the transformation of the 'seen' (already codified, as I have argued) onto the map (a place of written codes). Pre-discovery establishment of a southern continent meant its construction as a blank stage for the projection of European fantasies. One of these fantasies is 'blankness' itself, and it is possible to see this trope at work in explorers' accounts.

One of the more surprising elements of the explorers' descriptions of the interior is the recurrence of the image of the desert as a sea. One interpretation of this might suggest that the frequency of these descriptions indicates a wish fulfilment on the part of the authors – that is, in lieu of the mythic, expected sea, they are forced to create one linguistically through metaphor and simile. This kind of reading emphasises how the tropes of myth, when the myth cannot be reconciled with empirical observation, are interpolated with the new descriptions. In fact, the examination of the land for signs of the inland sea are mixed in the journals with tropic descriptions of the land as sea. When Sturt is forced to accept that an inland sea does not exist, he places it in the past. Finding regular sandhills which follow each other 'like the waves of the sea in endless succession', he concludes that 'the whole of the low interior I had traversed was formerly a sea-bed, since raised from its sub-marine position by natural though hidden causes' (*ECA* 1: 380–81). Sturt presents himself as belated, rather than incorrect about the existence of the sea; in a sense he was correct, in that if he had visited the area several hundreds of thousand of years previously he would have found a use for the boat his party had painstakingly dragged with them. His argument is also interesting in constructing those things not open to simple empirical observation as 'hidden', as if they have been intentionally positioned to avoid the explorers' gaze. The desert itself is described this way – as 'veiled' (*ECA* 2: 2) or surrounded in 'mist' (2: 3).

Sturt continues to project his oceanic theories upon the landscape he describes. The inland sea that he concludes from experience exists (1: 258), and later decides must have once existed, is reconstructed imaginatively in his descriptions in two different journals. Both construct the desert as ocean, and hills as islands. The *Two Expeditions into ... Southern Australia* (published 1833) describes D'Urbans group of hills projecting from the sea-like desert:

> It rises like an island from the midst of the ocean, and as I looked upon it from the plains below, I could without any great stretch of the imagination, picture to myself that it really was such. Bold and precipitous, it only wanted the sea to lave its base; and I cannot but think that such must at no very remote

period have been the case, and that the immense flat we had been traversing, is of comparatively recent formation. (*2Ex* 1: 80)

It is worth comparing this with a similar description in the *Expedition into Central Australia* (published 1849).

I must confess that they looked to me as if they had been so many small islands, off the point of the larger one. They rose in detached groups from the midst of the plains, as such islands from the midst of the sea, and their aspect altogether bore such a striking resemblance to many of the flat-topped islands round the Australian continent described by other travellers, that I could not but think they had once been similarly situated. (*ECA* 1: 248)

Both descriptions use the image of hills rising above the desert as islands do above the sea. But it would be a mistake to suggest that this is all the descriptions do; they are more than similes aiding the reader's understanding by recourse to the familiar. The passages construct the explorer as somewhat helpless before the monumental theories which make themselves evident. Sturt 'could not help but think' and 'cannot but think' that a sea once existed at these points; he 'must confess' that the hills look to him to have been islands. These suggestions of the explorer's helplessness in the face of overwhelming evidence for certain geographical theories efface his role in constructing the land in a particular way. Sturt's use of recognition of similitude as a kind of proof is, at best, scientifically dubious, but an attack aimed at this would ignore the politically strategic effect of images of the desert as a sea.

Sturt's description of the land as ocean has the effect of homogenising the landscape surveyed. Constructing the desert as sea produces it in terms of its essential undifferentiatedness, as if all the desert, and indeed all deserts, are the same. In these descriptions, by no means solely the production of Sturt, that traditional complaint of the monotony of landscape recurs; though in this case the complaints concern land covered by vegetation rather than desert.

From this our view is most extensive, over a complete sea of white grassy plains. (Stuart 315)

A dark gloomy sea of scrub without a break in its monotonous surface met our gaze. (*ECA* 1: 252)

The view from the summit was just as I had described it before – an ocean of scrubs, with isolated hills or ranges appearing like islands in most directions. (Giles 1: 58)

Descriptions of the land as a sea homogenise the land in two ways. First, the differences within the individual landscapes are erased. Second, the differences between quite divergent landscapes are repressed by describing them as oceans. The scrub which forms a 'gloomy sea' for Sturt is obviously different to the stony plain whose horizon is 'like that of the ocean' (*ECA* 1: 373) into which ridges of land abut like 'so many head lands projecting into the sea' (1: 372). The repetition of the image of the sea may simply be the struggle to express the vastness and levelness of the scenery, but it has the effect of reducing the land into an undifferentiated mass.

Perhaps it could be argued that the simile of the desert as being like a sea is an inevitable construct of one aesthetic perceptive system attempting to deal with an unfamiliar landscape. This may be so; but, when explorers describe the landscape, aesthetic and cartographic practices are not separate – they are intertwined. The cartographic and aesthetic gazes both attempt to construct landscape as a text which may be read. If the landscape fails to provide variegated signs which may be interpreted, then the land is considered a 'blank' – this, in essence, is what a description of the land as a sea accomplishes. In the absence of either cartographic or aesthetic signs, such a description may give the impression that there has still been a cartographic and aesthetic response to the landscape, but its result will only be the construction of the land as a text which is a 'perfect and absolute blank'.

The inability of the explorers to perceive difference within a flat land is certainly the result of a European landscape aesthetic which privileges variation of vegetation and elevation, but these elements also have a practical importance for explorers. Particular kinds of vegetation are signs of water: Sturt finds one scene is pervaded by a 'dark brown sombre hue', but perceives some 'gumtrees in the plains below us, to the N.E., indicating the course of the creek over them' (*ECA* 1: 177). Elevation is important for availability of water; but it is also necessary for the surveying requirements of the exploration parties. Without elevation to provide either a view or at least points for triangulation, the land resists not only mensuration but also the exploration which both produces and depends on this measurement. Sturt's journal expresses frustration:

> From the spot on which we stopped no object of any kind broke the line of the horizon; we were as lonely as a ship at sea, and as a navigator seeking for land, only that we had the disadvantage of an unsteady compass, without any fixed point on which to steer. (*ECA* 1: 375)

It is ironic that in the middle of the desert Sturt is returned to the condition of the European discoverers of Australia. But the difficulties he expresses are the differences between charting a coastline, where there is a clear delineation of the extremes of the land and limits of the sea, and the mapping of the desert, where no such difference is immediately recognisable to European eyes.

The gaining of height to read the land does not always mean that the eye will be 'rewarded' by the view. Oxley describes a position from which there was 'nothing relieving the eye but a few scattered bushes, and occasionally some dwarf box-trees: the view was as boundless as the ocean' (Oxley 93). In the absence of signs Leichhardt also mobilises the notion of desert as sea. 'There was no smoke', he writes, 'no sign of water, no sign of the neighborhood of the sea coast; – but all was one immense sea of forest and scrub' (153). Explorers also deploy the trope when attempting to describe the particular type of mirage that does not simply distort vision, but renders it inoperable. Stuart, completely blinded by a mirage, says that he 'never saw it so bright nor continuous as it is now; one would think that the whole country was under water' (Stuart 20). And, of course, there is the classic desert mirage, where the plain appears transformed into an ocean (for example, Leichhardt 501). A reading of these descriptions should not involve the acceptance of these aesthetic responses as if, in some objective way, the lands described do resemble a sea; rather, what needs to be examined is how homogenising constructions like this are involved with the textualisation of the land. A land without legible signs to a European, may be full of signs to an Aborigine; moreover, the indigene may not even see the land in terms of written 'signs' at all.

Land as a system of signs

As the discipline of surveying leads the explorers to valorise verticality over horizontality of landscape, so too does it encourage this construction of the land as a system of signs, or as a language. This might initially seem an innocent activity, and certainly one of immediate practical benefit. If signs such as a line of gum trees, a bird flying in a particular direction, or the presence of a certain formation of land can be interpreted correctly, then it is possible to determine the existence, probability or location of water. Giles finds tracks of wild animals leading to water and writes that 'such characters in the book of Nature the explorer cannot fail to read' (Giles 2: 200). Even though I have argued that the 'land as sea' trope is used to homogenise the land and aid its construction as a blank, the sea and sea weather are themselves often read as texts. Grey writes of the decipherment of signs of weather at sea.

> These omens have a meaning. – Down to the southward, somewhere off Cape Horn, there blows a furious gale. The wind will draw round shortly to the northward. – That is the interpretation and the reading. (Grey 1: 31)

The explorers' production of the land as a system of signs provides a method for determining the nature and geological history of the land as well as what their next advance should be. 'Many a sign and token', Grey writes, 'might lead the practical explorer to hope, that he was about to enter upon a tract of extent and fertility' (Grey 2: 5). Exploration is promoted as a 'shedding of light', a 'lifting of the veil' and an 'opening up' of the land. The commentary to Warburton's journal suggests that what is 'opened up' is the land as a text. Warburton 'with enduring camels, was enabled to traverse ground that had hitherto remained a sealed book to Europeans' (198). Once open, the book may be read in ways that are immediately useful to exploration, but the very notion that the land *can* be read is an arrogation of power, and an exhibition of the belief that a European methodology has universal applicability.

In many ways the land defies this kind of textualisation process and makes reading difficult or aberrant. Mirages interfere with perception, as do haze and smoke, instruments (particularly the barometer) are broken and compasses are unreliable. A set of signs which may have been readable and reliable becomes inconsistent. For example, various signs of Aboriginal inhabitance such as hatchet marks on trees may be read as indicating the presence of water (Oxley 168). But often signs of Aboriginal inhabitance are found in exactly those areas where no water is to be found. Moreover, some Aboriginal signs, which are felt to be deliberate significatory artifacts (apart from incidental marks such as tree scars or shell middens), are seen but resist reading. Grey finds that Aborigines have placed rocks in trees. These are genuinely disturbing as they are understood to be signs, but Grey cannot even guess at what they may mean. But often it is the land itself which refuses to follow the textual logic placed on it. The sand hills that Sturt believes 'precisely resembled a low and barren sea coast' (*ECA* 1: 252) are read as signalling an inland sea. When the reading of the land fails in such a spectacular way, neither the particular mode of interpretation nor the overall creation of the land as text comes under question. Rather, the discourse of Australia as a perversity is reinvoked – in its peculiarity it avoids normal interpretation – and thus the central methodology of exploration is left largely unscathed.

The idea of nature as a system of signs is part of the scientific method that exploration uses, but the more specific notion of nature as a book is also utilised in the journals. Nature as a text, an idea with a long history, gained special vigour as interest in the natural world increased. Akenside's *Pleasures of the Imagination* describes 'the world's harmonious volume, there to read / The transcript of Himself. On every part / They trace the bright impressions of his hand'.[45] The philosopher Bishop Berkeley considered that the 'phenomena of nature [form] a most coherent, entertaining, and instructive discourse'. Berkeley considered that there was a 'natural connexion of signs with the thing signified', and that the 'proper objects of vision constitute a universal language of the Author of nature'.[46] The divine intentionality with which the language of nature is imbued underwrites its connectivity and denies arbitrariness in the sign. When the signs that the explorers read sometimes seem arbitrary – that is, where the signifier and referent fail to connect – then the notion of land as a decipherable text is put under some stress. However, the antipodeanism of the continent is invoked to explain this failure of interpretation; so, what is needed is not an abandoning of the idea of land as text, but merely an adaptation of the reading strategy to the colonial situation. However different the language used in the antipodal continent, Sturt maintains that God is the author of nature in Australia (*ECA* 2: 21). This kind of hermeneutics of the land partakes of the Paleyan mixture of scientific methodology and religious belief that leads to 'justificatory' investigations of the natural world, but it possesses more immediate dangers. To posit the land as a text is to claim an ability to read it in a certain way and thence to arrogate power over it.

Writing on the blankness

Gayatri Spivak observes that the assumption of an uninscribed earth establishes the conditions of the possibility of 'worlding a world'.[47] The textualisation of the landscape by the explorers reifies space as a *blank text*, ready to be inscribed on by the impending colonial process. I have argued that maps have played a significant role in the visual production of the continent as a *tabula rasa*, and that the cartographic emptiness is not simply a display of geographical ignorance but has important political implications. Indeed, the blank on the map is often taken as a direct insult to British enterprise, and presents a perfect opportunity for an introduction to the journal. The introduction to Warburton's journal notes that 'a glance at the map shows us what an immense tract of land is entirely unknown ... this is ... the greatest absolute blank on the face of the globe' (Warburton 5). In these discussions it is unclear whether the 'blank' is purely cartographical ignorance or is read as expressing some aspect of 'reality'. Slippages of this kind, a peculiar characteristic of writing about cartography is evident in texts other than exploration journals. Eliza Berry's *Australian Explorers* dwells upon the blank of the continent, and leaves the question of whether the blank is purely cartographic or not unanswered.

> Cook proclaimed 'midst ringing cheers,
> The new abode for man.
> The edge in light, within, a blank,
> A broad and mysterious wild.[48]

Is the edge in light simply because it is known, or is it because it is inhabited by Europeans? Even when detailed cartographic results are brought back destroying the complete blankness of the interior, the suspicion remains that it was possible to think of the actual country as blank: 'Ernest Giles has shown that the interior is not the blank wilderness that we have hitherto supposed, and who knows what future explorations may not bring forth?' (Warburton 9).

Occasionally, the creation of Australia as a blank text, while ostensibly representing the unfulfilled (yet soon to be sated) hunger of apparently disinterested science, will, by juxtaposition, reveal the direct economic imperatives motivating exploration. Sturt praises the explorations of Ludwig Leichhardt, hoping that the present journey will 'complete the discovery of the internal features of the Australian continent, and when we look at the great blank in the map of that vast territory, we cannot but admit the service that intrepid traveller is doing to the cause of Geography and Natural History' (*ECA* 2: 307). Immediately following this, Sturt notes that it is doubtful whether Leichhardt's 'investigations and labours will greatly extend the pastoral interests of the Australian colonies' (307). That the explorers and their financial supporters were interested in the extension of pastoral holdings through explored districts is well known. Less commented upon is the way in which the representations of land, while still produced in the 'cause' of geography and natural history, operate for the direct pecuniary interests of the expanding pastoralists and are, of course, prejudicial to the indigenous inhabitants, who are entirely omitted from the maps. As a result of this omission, the maps efface the Aboriginal cultures contacted by explorers, and about which some knowledge is possessed, at the same time as they carefully include locations of white settlement.

In this sense the maps produced by the explorers can be criticised as failing to reflect the land, and failing to reflect, as well, the empirical knowledge produced by exploration. This is in part the fault of the map genre itself, as there was no readily available iconography which could indicate nomadic inhabitance.[49] One could argue that, even if specific populations could not be represented, tribal areas at least might be outlined. But exploration as a discipline does not lend itself to this kind of knowledge-gathering: exploration's first concern is getting from point to point alive and gathering the maximum amount of information about the physical geography. Exploration ethnography is rarely patient enough, or sufficiently linguistically skilled, to inquire about tribal boundaries – if, indeed, the explorers realise there is such a thing. Instead of describing native geo-cultural formations, the map acts as an incitement to the alteration of ownership. Sturt once again links the appropriation of knowledge with the appropriation of land:

An ample field is open to enterprise and to ambition, and it is to be hoped that some more decisive measures will be carried into effect, both for the sake of the colony and of geography, to fill up the blank upon the face of the chart of Australia, and remove from us the reproach of indifference and inaction. (*2Ex* 1: 160)

Ostensibly, the filling up of the blank will be a matter of exploration and discovery; there is the expectation, however, that the 'enterprise and ambition' will take the course of an energetic emplacement of civilisation and that the blank will be filled up this way. In their roles as surveyors, of course, the explorers did not just record the expansion; they enabled it. For Mitchell the land's existence as *tabula rasa* is both cartographic and real – in fact, there is little difference: 'this territory, still for the most part in a state of nature, presents a fair blank sheet, for any geographical arrangement, whether of country divisions – lines of communication – or sites of towns' (*3Ex* 2: 333).

For surveying purposes the construction of the land as a blank sheet is necessary. In the erasure of the land, not only is prior Aboriginal occupation and ownership ignored, but the land itself is inserted into a particular narrativisation of history. A blank sheet, of course, intimates that there has been no previous history, but also constructs the future as a place/time for writing.

The particular narrative of history the explorers construct positions them as at the beginning of a long and glorious history. This is noticeable in the possession ceremonies, where Stuart hopes that the raising of the flag 'may be the first sign of the dawn of approaching civilization' (410). In following the course of the Peel River, Mitchell describes how he:

advanced with feelings of intense interest into the country before us, and impressed with the responsibility of commencing the first chapter of its history. All was still new and nameless, but by this beginning, we were to open a way for the many other beginnings of civilized man, and thus extend his dominion over some of the last holds of barbarism. (*3Ex* 1: 36)

The privileging of written over oral history is here so strong that the existence of a history previous to white incursion is utterly effaced. Mitchell's emphasis on the 'nameless' nature of the *tabula rasa* he constructs is that of the mapmaker. It should be mentioned that the idea of Australia as a *tabula rasa*, and the historicising of this notion, is by no means the province of explorers alone. The idea can also be found in fiction – in Catherine Martin's *An Australian Girl* (1890), for example. There, the narrator combines some of the commonplace descriptions of the country as a melancholy, monotonous waste with constructions of it as a *tabula rasa* awaiting future inscription:

> These great unpeopled spaces ... call up thoughts of the early dawn of creation. Under some aspects, they are sombre in their monotony, melancholy in their primeval solitude; their strange silence weighs on the heart at times with a sense of indefinite anguish. It is as though one had come upon a waste world sealed against the traditions and presence of the human race. There is no trace of the immemorial past – no buried record of the ages that have gone. But the unstoried blank stirs the imagination curiously with dim guesses at the chronicles which may be written of this land in days to come.[50]

The Aborigines and the signs of their existence are excluded from the construction of the land as text; thus, when this text is read, they are absent. The French-Australian writer Paul Wenz also activated the trope of a storyless Australia. History for Wenz is necessarily productive of myths and permanent structures. Australia is deficient in this regard, as its:

> forests are generally not dense enough to shelter elves or ghosts; no Red Ridinghood could gather strawberries in them, or meet a wolf or doe in them, for the shade of the tall eucalyptuses is too scanty for strawberries; wolves and does have never existed in Australia ... There is no history; the childish primitive legends that peopled the great deserts died with the tribes ... In Australia there is a total lack of ruins that are the tangible past, of the old castles and the old temples that form part of the history of a people.[51]

The land has not been written about, but it has also not been written *on* by its inhabitants. Wenz can imagine only that there is one type of history – the history that he is familiar with – and constructs Australia through the antipodal paradigm in conferring upon it a particular strangeness in this 'lack' he identifies. Wenz's description begs for deconstruction (how the Aboriginal legends are more 'childish' than Red Ridinghood he sadly fails to examine); but the denigration of Aboriginal legends and the assumption of their disappearance with the presumed (and unexplained) extinction of their creators is simply another way of creating a *tabula rasa* from the land. The discourse of Australia as a blank slate is also found in D. H. Lawrence's *Kangaroo*.

> The soft, blue, humanless sky of Australia, the pale, white unwritten atmosphere of Australia. *Tabula rasa.* The world a new leaf. And on the new leaf, nothing. The white clarity of the Australian, fragile atmosphere. Without a mark, without a record.[52]

That Australia possesses the 'white clarity' of the empty page repeats exactly the explorers' descriptions. It might be possible to excuse Lawrence's erasure of the marks of Aboriginal inhabitance as the result of ignorance; no such excuse is possible for the explorers. The 'Milmeridien' burial ground is described by Mitchell as a 'fairy-like spot'

(*3Ex* 1: 321), which is rather ironic in the light of Wenz's construction of Australia as deficient in fairy tales. Mitchell may structure his description in such Eurocentric ways, but the journals display in the text and accompanying picture a full awareness of how the land was constructed by the Aborigines for a particular purpose. Grey's descriptions of the cave paintings he finds are an example of an explorer encountering Aboriginal pictorial inscription upon the land (1: 201–07). There are of course countless example of the explorers finding and describing Aboriginal constructions – monoliths, wells and encampments – yet, their significance is violently erased by the preference for certain types of structures. It is possible to subvert this logic by inversion.

In 'Ordering the Landscape' Rhys Jones describes the reactions of a northern Australian Aborigine on seeing a large city (Canberra) for the first time.

> The idea of buying and selling land like any other commodity and of attach-ment to the land only as a matter of transient convenience was totally alien to Gurrmanamana, and he regarded it with a mixture of suspended belief and with some mild revulsion, as if there were something deeply wrong with this state of affairs. Here was a land empty of religious affiliation; there were no wells, no names of the totemic ancestors, no immutable links between land, people and the rest of the natural and supernatural worlds. Here was just a vast *tabula rasa*, cauterized of meaning.[53]

One wonders if this is the kind of sentimentalist or nostalgic inversion of imperial crimes through which imaginary rectification of historic wrongs and, therefore, forgiveness are sought. In seeking some recuperation via inversion, Rhys Jones's Eurocentric construction of Gurrmanamana's response perhaps displays the depth of guilt associated with cartographic erasure that still exists in Australia.

5

Seeing the Aborigines put in their Place

Focusing on the Aborigines

The theatre of contact

The two founding assumptions of ethnography are that the 'natives' will be seen and described without preconception and that the ethnographer should not interfere with their behaviour. What we find in the proto-ethnography texts is that the explorer is neither able to disentangle himself from pre-existing stereotypes of the 'native', nor is he able to avoid interfering with the very objects he wishes to observe.

It is appropriate to begin the discussion on the nexus between surveillance, power and ethnographic description in the journals of exploration with two illustrations of the pleasure/pain economy of investigation by sight. The coastal surveyor, Philip Parker King, carried with him a sextant for fixing his position at sea, a theodolite to measure the earth when on inland surveys, and a magnifying glass, the most significant use of which seems to have been to ignite Aborigines. King writes that an Aborigine:

> was a good deal surprised at my collecting the rays of the sun on my own hand, supposing that I was callous to the pain, from which he had himself before shrunk; but as I held the glass within the focus distance, no painful sensation was produced; after which he presented me his own arm, and allowed me to burn it as long as I chose to hold the glass, without flinching in the least, which, with greater reason, equally astounded us in our turn. (King 2: 142–43)

Sight, as this book has discussed, is a principal method by which the earth is delineated, and the instrument of vision which enables knowledge generation about microcosmic levels – the magnifying glass – is here (mis)used to establish an economy of pain and visual pleasure. King is the master of the experiment, administering the burn as long as he chooses to hold the glass, while the Aborigine exists only as a passive object of investigation. The Aborigine's subjectivity is never presented and he is neither described as exhibiting, nor is assumed to feel, pain. Moreover, the Aborigine as observing subject is not presented in this episode. Even when King is illuminated with out-of-focus light, the Aborigine is not constructed as an intelligent independent observer, though his surprise is noted. The sovereign subjectivity of King the experimenter is never threatened by a return gaze which might express a subjectivity of its own. Rather, the Aborigine is an object of examination as he burns, and his stoicism results in the 'astonishment' of the party. The visual novelty and pleasure of astonishment is similar to that when the explorers ascend an eminence and are, by the splendid view, 'repaid' for their efforts. This economy of pleasure is present when King burns the Aborigine: the pleasure is still the explorer's, but the burden of payment is on the Aborigine.

The second example of the confluence of sight and power is somewhat more complex, and needs to be prefaced by two short descriptions which utilise the same topos. Coming upon a tribe of indigenes, Mitchell notes that they had 'exactly the appearance of savages as I have seen them represented in theatres' (*3Ex* 2: 108). The confirmation of the accuracy of the theatre ignores the preparatory role that theatrical representation has had on Mitchell's perception: since the Aborigines have already been prefigured in theatre, their appearance (as well as a host of other aspects such as motivation, behaviour and beliefs) is already *known* by European observers, including Mitchell. The theatre utilises the codes of savagery, semi-nakedness, blackness, and so on, for the purposes of display. Mitchell's comparison of their real and theatrical appearance produces the indigenes in exactly the same way – as objects to be seen, enjoyed, and understood as confirming those generalised codes constitutive of savagery. The pleasure of viewing Aborigines and their activities as theatre is also expressed by Sturt, whose description of an Aboriginal camp as picturesque emphasises that it had the 'effect of a fine scene in a play' (*ECA* 2: 79). The importance placed on the observer's enjoyment also raises the question of the observer's metaphorical point of view.

In the first volume of *Narrative of an Expedition into Central Australia*, Sturt includes a long and somewhat tourist-like description of a corroboree. He begins by defending its inclusion, aware that a corroboree description is already a clichéd element in travel narratives.

> The several descriptions which have been given by others of these scenes, might render it unnecessary for me to give my account here; but as my ideas

of these ceremonies may differ from that of other travellers, I shall trespass on the patience of my readers for a few moments to describe them. However rude and savage as a corrobori may appear to those whom they are new, they are, in truth, plays or rather dramas ... (*ECA* 1: 83–84)

The text seems weighed down by the influence of previous descriptions. One might extend the geographical metaphor of 'trespassing', used here to excuse infringement on the reader's patience, to say that this descriptive passage must create a space for itself, ensuring its significance by holding that it is the product of a new point of view. In fact, the passage creates a particularly privileged point of view for Sturt: he is not simply an observer beyond the proscenium arch; but, as he attends a 'family corrobori, or private theatricals', he is 'let into the secrets of what takes place behind the scenes' (*ECA* 1: 84). Sturt's intimacy with the Aborigines, then, allows him 'stage access', where the mechanics of production are revealed to him. Having moved from a regular audience member to a behind-the-scenes observer, Sturt finally emerges as stage manager of the entire display.

> We had some difficulty in persuading our friends to exhibit, and we owed success rather to Mr. Eyre's influence than any anxiety on the part of the natives themselves. However, at last we persuaded the men to go and paint themselves, whilst the women prepared the ground ... on their commencing their chanting, the men came forward, emerging from the darkness into the obscure light shed by the yet uncherished fires, like spectres. After some performance, at a given signal, a handful of dry leaves was thrown on each fire, which instantly blazing up lighted the whole scene, and shewed the dusky figures of the performers painted and agitated with admirable effect ... (*ECA* 1: 84–85)

The description evinces a relishing of the visual consumption of the dance. The performance, safely contained and framed by the pros-cenium arches of the dominant metaphor, exists in the description for the pleasure of the explorer, who may with trained eye admire the effect of the scene in which the painted figures, frozen by the fire's sudden blazing, resemble elements in a picturesque composition.

Sturt's construction of the corroboree as play is not simply a method of understanding; it is a strategy of control, as it reduces the ritual's suggest-iveness, obscurity and threat to the observer's universal knowledge. Produced as a tame piece of exotica, the corroboree is returned to the sphere of Western knowledge as, first, another native 'ceremony' and, secondly, just like a 'Covent Garden' drama. This two-step process – constructing the corroboree as 'strange' though known, and then as something well-understood – is paralleled by a pleasure economy of sight. The corroboree is valorised according to its aesthetic effect on the explorer's cultured eye and achieves the ultimate accolade of the tourist attraction – it is 'well worth seeing'. Like the nobleman's park it is arranged for visual pleasure, and the Aborigines are coerced so that they may become exhibits.

Satisfying visually, the corroboree as ceremony disappoints Sturt. He notes a certain lack of enthusiasm, which he tentatively ascribes to the Aborigines' only having recently learned the particular dance. However, he finds his own explanation unsatisfactory and the poor performance remains a puzzle: 'but, as I have observed, for some reason or other the thing was not carried on with spirit, and we soon retired from it; nevertheless, it is a ceremony well worth seeing, and which in truth requires some little nerve to witness for the first time' (*ECA* 1: 85). The most obvious reason for the corroboree's poor success can be discovered by misconstruing the first sentence above – it is because 'I have observed' that there is an understandable lack of commitment on the Aborigines' part. King's and Sturt's observations are both manipulations of the objects of study. The interference with the Aborigine for purposes of study undermines the separation of the observer and the observed that empiricism – and the facile claims to accuracy of the journals – depends on. Each observation can be produced only with an interference with the Aborigine and Aboriginal lives; thus, the ethnography produced can only be a record of the Aborigines' action as they react to the explorer's presence and attempts at manipulation.

That the observation usually involves an active intervention on the part of the explorer, it may be argued, detracts from claims of objectivity. But another problem emerging in the explorer's account is the thoroughly textualised status of the indigenes. Rather than being part of the 'unknown' land, they are strangely familiar – Sturt has seen them before in the theatre. Noting Flaubert's despair that everything he finds in Egypt is a rediscovery rather than a discovery, Richard Terdiman has analysed the cause for this 'banality of the exotic'.[1] Rather than adopting or attempting to assimilate indigenous epistemes, colonial discourse uses a double structure Terdiman calls penetration (the forcible imposition of the dominator and of his discursive system within the dominated space), and appropriation (the consumption enforced by the dominator of what belongs to the dominated).[2] Flaubert is able to ironise the Western penetration of the 'Orient', embodied by inscriptions made by European travellers upon Egyptian monuments, allowing him a false separation from the process; but in explorers' texts there is little irony.

Sturt's organisation of the corroboree is a manipulative intervention of the explorer into Aboriginal culture, a 'forcible imposition', as are virtually all ethnographic descriptions in the journals – they are impositions and celebrations of dominance. Sturt's description of the corroboree is an insertion of a foreign discourse which can only ever construct observations in its own terms. This penetration becomes an appropriation of the Aborigine, an absorption of her and her culture into a sub-set of scientific knowledge via the objectifying gaze or via a return of implements or skeletons to the central scientific institutions. A scientific description of the corroboree would involve particular codes, including reference perhaps to other 'savage rituals', but Sturt elects to construct the corroboree according to the different, but also pre-fabricated knowledge of theatre. The consumption of Aboriginal culture is, in fact, dominated by its textual production: the corroboree cannot speak for itself, but must be spoken for.

The domination of an event by the pre-formulated discourse of theatre, and the consumption of the event within these terms is the reason why, as Edward Said writes, 'a new median category emerges, a category that allows one to see new things, things seen for the first time, as versions of previously known things'.[3] This is a way of forming new knowledge. King, for example, notes that a 'curious mound, constructed entirely of shells, rudely heaped together, and fourteen feet in height ... was supposed to be a burying-place of the Indians' (87). The terminology 'Indians' does not need alteration and the mounds – which are, in fact, shell middens – are mistaken for grave sites. But Said notes that representing things as a version of the already known is not merely a way of producing new knowledge, but of controlling the threat it represents to the established view of the world.[4] The corroboree is quickly brought under the aegis of 'native ritual' by Sturt, reducing its threatening mystery, and reassuring the reader that all elements of Aboriginal life are open to European inspection.

Seeing without being seen
The journals sporadically express the difficulties of observing without interfering. The solution is usually to efface the explorer by having him come 'suddenly' upon Aborigines who are supposedly unaware of his presence. He observes without being observed, or may be welcomed into camps, where (he assumes) life carries on as normal. Sturt laments the 'degraded position in the scale of human species' into which the Aborigines have been placed, arguing that he has 'come suddenly upon them in a state of uncontrolled freedom – have passed tribe after tribe under the protection of envoys – have visited them in their huts ... and I am, in candour, obliged to confess that the most unfavourable light in which I have seen them, has been when mixed up with Europeans' (*ECA* 2: 212). The Aborigine who mixed with King and his magnifying glass might suggest that King certainly produced an 'unfavourable light'.

Sturt's description is remarkable for its self-effacement – others are Europeans, but he is the invisible observer, moving over the land seeing everything, understanding everything. However invisible Sturt may have initially been to his objects of study, the writing of these episodes of 'suddenly coming upon' indigenes places them within an already well-constructed field. Mary Louise Pratt has described the similarities in the 'arrival scene' in Louis de Bougainville's eighteenth century journal and Raymond Firth's twentieth century ethnographic writing.[5] These episodes are important in the textual demonstration that the native informants are not corrupted by 'civilization' nor by the explorer himself. In the generalised 'manners and customs' descriptions, where the (usually male) Aborigine is depicted going about his quotidian duties without regard to the explorer, there is no sense of an interactive observer whose presence might alter 'traditional' Aboriginal patterns of behaviour; rather, there is an extreme self-effacement that Johannes Fabian has called the 'denial of coevalness'.[6]

The construction of the explorer as invisible observer is a superb example of the project of Panopticism explicated by Michel Foucault. He describes in *Discipline and Punish* the Benthamite architectural design that allows constant surveillance of the prisoner/patient/madman by a central authority: a peripheral building surrounds a central observation tower, organised in such a way that the caged are perfectly visible, but the observing authority cannot be seen by the inmates (201–02).

> By the effect of backlighting, one can observe from the tower, standing out precisely against the light, the small captive shadows in the cells of the periphery. They are like so many cages, so many small theatres, in which each actor is alone, perfectly individualized and constantly visible.[7]

Such a building represents a dissociation of the see/being seen dyad. The Panopticon's central tower can be seen by the prisoner, and so the consciousness of surveillance is an important part of the process: the surveillance is internalised as an element in the disciplinary machinery. This model is unlike colonial surveillance, where the indigene ostensibly has no awareness of the explorer's presence, and presumably the explorer's main task is knowledge accumulation rather than discipline. But Foucault specifies that the intention of the observer is irrelevant and that he might well be a 'philosopher who wishes to visit this museum of human nature' (202). The Panopticon represents the visual desire of the explorer to reduce the threatening complexity of interactive observation by distancing the observer from the observed, and to construct observing moments as a 'small theatre' and the indigene as an 'object of information, never a subject in communication' (200). The distanced observer that the explorer wishes to be collapses under the contingencies of exploration and the returning gaze of the indigene.

Allegories of understanding

The conventional story of the unseen arrival bestows a special visual power upon the explorer, who might seem to embody the objective, fresh observer of realist philosophy. But the very conventionality of the arrival story undermines any claims for the novelty and objectivity of the viewer's observations. The journal's story of the unseen observer complements and displaces previous narratives of unseen watchers, and Sturt's story is intricated with these previous stories in constructing his own observational practices. As a story which may be read back to other stories, Sturt's description is fundamentally allegorical in nature. The inevitable intrication of any story with others breaks down the naive claims that any piece of writing can be transparent or can innocently reproduce what is observed. Instead, meaning is created by reference to these other narratives, to the significances and valorisations they contain.

Jose Rabasa has observed that maps operate as narratives in this sense, repeating and displacing previous figurations.[8] Such a view opens the way to an allegorical rather than realist reading. Mercator's *Atlas* can be seen as 'constituting a world where all possible "surprises" have been pre-codified'[9] – the incomplete Mercatorial projection systematises all space awaiting further inscriptions without itself being altered. Likewise, the ethnography of the explorers takes place in a similarly systematised 'space', where constructions of the indigene can be drawn from the medieval catalogue of anthropophagi and similar weird creatures.

Space has to be regulated and rendered blank before it can be inscribed; the indigene also is constructed as a blank. Stephen Slemon has pointed out that allegory works by 'constituting a semiotic lack in the space of figurative otherness', which is immediately filled.[10] The 'filling in' of the indigene disguises the original erasure, where the semiotic field is formed as a receptacle for the projection of European images. Native Americans were also likened to blank slates. Richard Eden's *The Decades of the Newe Worlde* (1555) posits Indians as being like a 'smooth and bare table unpainted, or a white paper unwritten, upon the which you may at the first paint or write what you list; as you cannot upon tables already painted, unless you raze or blot out the first forms'.[11] The concept of the indigene as open to what might be called 'managerial inscription' is also present in constructions of the Aborigine. James Grant, for instance, writes that 'the mind of the Aborigine seems to be the "resa tabula" of the philosophers; it has not been wrought upon by education; it is wax, of the purest and softest kind, fit to receive and preserve any impression' (170) – a description which seems to suggest that the Aborigines may be ameliorated or rather, entirely reconstructed, by the Europeans. Mostly, however, the erasure of the indigene is hidden. The subsequent projection upon the Aborigine of images, behaviours and motivations drawn from the European archive of the monstrous and alien disguises this erasure and the allegorical nature of the semiotic positioning of the indigene.

The rhetoric of presence which underwrites all ethnographic description is deconstructed by this view of language as intractably allegorical. As James Clifford has written, 'allegory prompts us to say of any cultural description not "this represents, or symbolizes, that" but rather, "this is a (morally charged) story about that"'.[12] The next section of this chapter will show how 'innocent' observations are inherently allegorical in nature. The black skin of the indigene, for example, already in existence in the European archive, is endowed with several meanings – treachery, laziness and mental inferiority. Sturt's construction of himself as an unseen observer is the keystone for these allegorical presentations of the indigene, for he can pose as the distanced and objective observer, reducing all that he sees into neutral scientific data, while these observations act as 'morally charged' stories, retelling and complementing the already known narrative of the indigenes. The credibility of any statement about the Aborigine relies on the way it connects with these multiple discourses of the indigene, rather than on any correspondence to reality. The ethnography of the explorer, therefore, says more about the European and his knowledge-gathering systems than it does about the original inhabitants of the Australian continent.

Othering the indigene

How stereotypes work

As I have argued, the descriptions of Aborigines in the journals are the products of semiotic fields within which much of the labour necessary to construct 'the native' had already been completed. Robert Dixon and Bernard Smith have discussed the Hellenised portrayal of Aborigines.[13] The first volume of Mitchell's *Three Expeditions into ... Eastern Australia* has a picture, *First Meeting With the Chief of the Bogan*, which demonstrates how, pictorially, Aborigines are produced through pre-existent images (see plate 9). Throughout the journals a green bough of leaves is understood to be a universal sign of benign intentions, and Mitchell sees the boy-chief's costume of leaves as a sign of peace: 'I received him in this appropriate costume, as a personification of the green bough, or

Plate 9   *First Meeting with the Chief of the Bogan*, engraved by G. Barnard after Mitchell's drawing. From Thomas Mitchell, *Three Expeditions into . . . Eastern Australia* (vol. 1, pl.12). Mitchell Library, State Library of New South Wales.

emblem of peace'. And in a note Mitchell explains, 'the Greeks used to supplicate with green boughs in their hands, and crowns upon their heads, chiefly of olive or laurel . . .' (*3Ex* 1:194).

As well as being hellenised, or understood through comparisons with classical culture, Aborigines are orientalised. Said's *Orientalism* is at pains to demonstrate that Orientalist studies are a self-contained system of generation of knowledge about the Orient, often proceeding without reference to the East's view of its own reality. The same Orientalist scholasticism leaks into investigations into the Aborigines. Some corroborees, writes Stokes, 'express feats of hunting and war, while others are very indecent and remind us of similar exhibitions in the East' (1: 394). Giles argues that the practice of spousal disfigurement is an 'ancient and Oriental custom' (2: 103), and there are innumerable parallels of biblical and Aboriginal cultural elements (for example, Eyre 1: 104). Again the strange familiarity occurs, the tired exotica of the corroboree being already 'known'. But here Aborigines are differentiated from the observer through their cultural alignment with the group perhaps most thoroughly othered, the 'Orientals'. This is another way of reducing the threatening obscurity of the corroboree, and constituting the Aborigine within the generalised field of knowledge of the 'others'.

Simultaneous with the creation of utter, irreducible difference, is colonial discourse's need to create the Aborigine as entirely known and familiar. I have suggested that this is inevitable, as the Aborigine is textually engineered by use of semiotic paradigms existing in the European archive. But this creation of the Aborigine as *knowledge* also enables their *judgement* by the explorer. Giles repeatedly characterises Aborigines as lower on the scale of humanity, but they can be placed on that scale only because they are essentially similar to Europeans – just poorer performers. Giles seems almost surprised that in 'an existence totally distinct from ours of civilisation, men and women live and love, and eat and drink, and sleep and die', but concludes that 'the passions are the same in all phases of the life of the human family, the two great master motives, of love and hunger, being the mainspring of all the actions of mankind' (2: 147). The Aborigines are in the family but less mature than the European. Stephen Greenblatt has argued that colonial discourse has a 'fundamental inability to sustain the simultaneous perception of likeness and difference',[14] either producing utter difference or a collapse of the indigenes' particular identity. Utter difference, however, is only illusory, for the tropes that constitute difference are well-known. The explorers' discourse becomes trapped within these stereotypes, recirculating everything already known about indigenes and indigenous culture. Sturt's *Two Expeditions into ... Southern Australia* alone, for example, manages to mention the laziness of Aborigines and their sullen nature and cannibalistic tendencies (*2Ex* 1: 10, 19, 114; 2: 228) – all stereotypes used in regard to indigenous peoples in many parts of the world.

The colonisation and subjectification of an indigenous people uses set structuring devices, which are identifiable across a number of particular historical instances and locations. The first and most important of these structures is what Abdul Jan Mohamad has called the Manichean allegory.[15] This Manichean struggle divides coloniser and indigene into a number of binary oppositions: White/Black, civilised/savage, Christian/heathen, rational/instinctive, progressive/regressive and self/other. The first of these oppositions is derived directly from observation and can therefore claim to be empirically sound, objective and neutral. But the epidermal metonymy cannot remain as simply an association of colour with race or as something which is noted and then taken for granted. In the explorers' journals the blackness of the Aborigine is emphasised, urged and repeated countless times. Australian explorers, of course, did not invent the association of black skin with evil, treachery and barbarity, but utilise a pre-existing discourse often without questioning its logical or historical basis. In one way this makes the frequency of the repetitions of epidermal descriptions all the more remarkable: in

spite of the notion that black skin represents racial backwardness being
something that 'goes without saying', it is said over and over again. In
part, this stems from treating skin as a racial signifier and, thus, identifier
of racial homogeneity – Sturt's summary of the Aborigines of the interior
notes that the colour of their skin was fairly uniform (*ECA* 2: 136). The
endless use of the adjectives, 'black', 'sable' and 'dark', however, creates
an excess of what needs to be empirically proven or what is of scientific
interest.

This fetishisation of epidermal colouring, in conjunction with reliance
on the European archive of associations, leads to a metonymic relationship between colour and race, which is used to continue the allegorical
construction by which colour stands for all elements in the secondary
oppositions. To be black then, means to be irremediably savage, heathen,
regressive and other. Homi Bhabha has taken up this issue of fetishisation, using the Freudian fable of the fetish to probe the dynamics of
othering. The stereotype results from the initial disavowal of difference
in the subject's search for a unified self, and the subsequent recognition
of difference in the indigene. As the search for a uniform identity
collapses with this recognition of difference, the stereotype gives access
to an ' "identity" which is predicated as much on mastery and pleasure as
it is on anxiety and defence'[16] – it offers an antitype against which identity
of the coloniser may be formed. This means that the indigene is trapped
within this discourse of colonial self-identification, rendered as a safe
alterity, and the stereotype remains a fixed category.

The remarkable stability of the stereotypical images of the indigene –
the cannibal, the savage, the 'wild' man – can be explained by their use
in the formation of the colonisers' subjectivity as an aid to their positioning of themselves as everything opposite to the indigene. Stereotypical
discourse also rationalises the erection of institutional and disciplinary
control of the indigenes so that they may be parted from their land,
allowing the full identification of the colonisers as productive agricul-
turalists and settlers. Ultimately, the success of the construction of the
Aborigine is a reflection of its self-fulfilling effect: the destruction of a
native culture itself validates many of the stereotypical categorisations.

Judging by appearances

The recognition of epidermal difference is initially presented as a purely
scientific judgement, in that it aids efficient categorisation of the
indigene. John Lort Stokes evinces concern that language is too
inaccurate to convey the fine shades of meaning (and colour) that he
desires. He observes that the Aborigines are 'almost black, – in fact, for
ordinary description, that word, unqualified by the adverb, serves the

purpose best' (Stokes 1: 98). Attempts to scientifically describe the skin of Aborigines, limited as the explorers generally are to monochrome illustrations, results in a certain frustration which is generally soothed as the epidermal discourse slides into a number of ancillary observations. One of these, aesthetic judgement, firmly places the Aborigine in the category of the inferior. Blackness itself is an aesthetic drawback: Mitchell finds that the most attractive female he sees is also the least black (*3Ex* 2: 93). Sturt finds the Aborigines 'the most miserable human beings I ever saw' and the men, at least in part because of their skin colour, 'anything but good looking' (*ECA* 1: 209). His harshest criticism, however, is reserved for Aboriginal women; they are 'hideous and loathsome' (*2Ex* 2: 46), 'very ugly' (50), and would 'disgust my readers' (135) if pictorially represented.

There are many admiring descriptions, but these are often of Aborigines who are not 'typical'. Eyre's generalised description of Aboriginal women is notable for its emphasis on female charms, as judged by a European, but also because the reason these charms are said to exist is that the Aboriginal features are not fully formed. He writes that 'the jet-black eyes, shaded by their long, dark lashes, and the delicate and scarcely-formed features of incipient womanhood give a soft and pleasing countenance that might often be called good-looking – occasionally even pretty' (Eyre 2: 208). There is, of course, no indication that aesthetic criteria of cultures other than European might apply or even exist, but rather the aesthetic judgment is extended into a hierarchisation of the races.

It is possible to see the subtle movement back and forth between aesthetic and scientific descriptive discourse; attempts to describe skin scientifically become aesthetic judgements, which in turn lead to the 'scientific' field of phrenology. According to Sturt the best-looking males have 'pleasingly intelligent countenances' (*2Ex* 1: 21); this observation opens the way to a purely phrenological interpretation, which, as a 'science', will carry with it a certain authority that perceptive readers might find lacking in the aesthetic judgements. But phrenological discourse is not separate from aesthetic judgements. Pretending to be the results of 'objective' or disinterested observation, phrenology uses existing aesthetic understandings which position 'other' cranial features as signifying ugliness or, in the Aborigines' case, a lower stage of development. Describing the Aborigine 'Pulcanti', who, while being transported by the police to Adelaide made a daring escape attempt, Sturt says:

> he was the most repulsive native in aspect that I ever saw, and had a most ferocious countenance. The thick lip and white teeth, the lowering brow, and deep set but sharp eye, with the rapidly retiring forehead all betrayed the

savage with the least intellect, but his demeanour was now quiet and inoffensive. (*ECA* 1: 90)

Thus, the discourse of epidermal difference, which seems simply the result of observation, is imbricated with an aesthetic discourse, which is in turn part of the pseudoscientific field of phrenology.

Fashionable in the first half of the nineteenth century, phrenology provided support for the belief that characteristics of skull shape signified particular qualities of temperament. Phrenology was based on the erroneous belief that the absence, or presence, of moral and intellectual characteristics causes particular physical features in the brain, which are reflected in the shape of the skull, and it was originally aimed at determining the psychology of the individual. However, racial scientists elided the difference between individuals and groups and it became usual to talk of the morals and abilities of races with reference to their cranial identity. Though never universally accepted by the scientific establishment, phrenology intersected with the scientifically respectable use of craniometry as a way of measuring intelligence.[17]

At least some explorers were converts. The convicts for Mitchell's journey into tropical Australia were selected, on his own admission, on the basis of a 'careful examination of the phrenological developments and police history of each' (*EITA* 418). Sturt's journal reflects the doubts surrounding phrenology, but also shows how the less controversial theory – that cranial shape indicates intelligence – could overcome this doubt. That the appearance of the Aborigines, he writes:

> is against them, cannot be doubted. If there is any truth in phrenology, they must have their share of brutal passions. The whole appearance of the cranium indeed, would lead to the conclusion that they possess few of the intellectual faculties; but, in a savage state, these are seldom called forth. (*ECA* 2: 277, cf Stokes 1:89)

Just as blackness was a sign of savagery, a particular shape of skull signified the absence of laudable moral characteristics and a low intelligence. But Sturt maintains an uneasy balance between constructing characteristics as innate and as environmentally determined; for him, the Aborigines possess some intellectual abilities but these are not exercised in their present state. It is such thinking that provides a rationale for the removal of the Aborigines from their environment to a place where they are subject to the 'civilising' mission of the white society.

Mitchell's Expedition into ... Tropical Australia brings together the issues of land ownership and physiognomy with an illustration of the

Aborigine, Bultje (see plate 10). Mitchell notes his 'singularly Socratic face' – continuing the positive association of Hellenic descriptions – but then argues that Bultje's 'settled disposition' is particularly worthy. He notes that meeting with Bultje after ten years 'in the same valley in a domesticated state, if it did not establish any claim to the soil, at least proved his strong attachment to it' (*EITA* 18). Mitchell may avoid the obvious here – why occupation does not establish a claim to the soil – but he does show an acute awareness of the mediatory difficulties of a figure such as Bultje, who communicates with both sides of a conflict. Mitchell congratulates him on his Socratic intellect, evident in his countenance, and on his survival, but skates over the moral and legal implications of this conflict.

Aborigines as devils

Bultje is seen as exceptional; for the most part Aborigines are portrayed as evil, and agents of the devil. Descriptions which fall into the categories of 'good' or 'evil' are usually strategic reactions to the particular moment rather than attempts to construct a stable description of a racial characteristic, as Todorov has pointed out.[18] Yet, the construction of the Aborigine as inherently evil is remarkably constant in the explorers' descriptions. The Aborigines are simply reflections of European fears and fantasies, and Mitchell's obsession with portraying them as devils, and the self-congratulatory wit that is evident in these descriptions, reveals this process of othering and its narcissistic base. Mitchell refers to Milton's *Paradise Lost* and Shakespeare's *Macbeth* to characterise Aborigines as devilish and diabolical:

> ... their hideous crouching postures, measured gestures, and low jumps, all to the tune of a wild song, with the fiendish glare of their countenances, at all times black, but now all eyes and teeth, seemed a fitter spectacle for Pandemonium, than the light of the bounteous sun. Thus these savages slowly retired along the river bank, all the while dancing in a circle like the witches in Macbeth ... (*3Ex* 1: 247–48)

This description is accompanied by an illustration crudely portraying an enraged and unindividualised group, framed by trees and explorers. On the left is Mitchell, in a rather extraordinary pose, firing a pistol (see plate 11).

The Aborigines are more likely to be constructed as devils if they are in any numbers: Stokes writes of the 'demoniacal aspect' (Stokes 2: 15) of a group, and Giles speaks of an antagonistic gathering as a 'multitude of howling demons' (Giles 2: 7). Mitchell's penchant for quoting Milton

Plate 10   *Bultje*, drawing by Mitchell. From Thomas Mitchell, *Expedition into ...*
Tropical Australia (p.17). Mitchell Library, State Library of New South Wales.

Plate 11   *Dance at the Report of a Pistol*, engraved by G. Foggo and G. Barnard after Mitchell's drawing. From Thomas Mitchell, *Three Expeditions into . . . Eastern Australia* (vol. 1, pl.14). Mitchell Library, State Library of New South Wales.

occasionally opens a space for the Aborigines to actually seem threatening, whereas, in the case of the Giles description it is the futility of the 'howling' which is emphasised. Mitchell (in *EITA* 109) describes how:

'the sound of gruff voices that rang from it strongly reminded me of Milton's description of Satan's army,
>   Their rising all at once, was as the sound
>   Of thunder heard remote.

Although again constructed through literary paradigms of devilishness, Mitchell's description actually presents Aborigines who are not 'managed' – as they often are in the accounts of these encounters. Instead, they are allowed to come over, in this description, as being potentially dangerous.

In other encounters, Mitchell's acute vision and his telescopic technology allow him to individualise the otherwise homogeneous mass and survey one particular Aborigine. 'Taking my telescope', Mitchell writes, 'I recognized the identical big savage of yesterday' (*EITA* 165). Mitchell's superior optics allow him to 'recognize', or 'know again' the Aborigine of the previous day. This knowledge Mitchell has is not simply superficial; it is a knowing of the Aborigine's deepest motivations, which are necessarily evil. The recognition of the Aborigine is accompanied in the text by a picture in which the Aborigine is portrayed in a way that seems remarkably similar to William Blake's picture of Nebuchadnezzar (see plate 12).[19]

The recognition that occurs seems to be one that takes place through paradigmatic ordering. Mitchell recognises the Aborigine not simply because he saw him the day before but because the Aborigine fits into a European type – that of the lost, wretched individual in the wilderness who has been forsaken by God. Mitchell's description of the Aborigine comes to seem like a set piece, an excuse for Mitchell to display both his learning and wit, and at the same time denigrate the Aborigines. He notes (*EITA* 165) that:

> Hamlet might here have exclaimed –
> 'What a piece of work is man!
> .... how infinite in faculties!
> In form and action how like a *quadruped*!
> In apprehension, how like a *devil*!'

Mitchell also intuits the evil nature of Aborigines from their facial features, combining Orientalist, biblical and anti-Semitic remarks. He describes one face as possessing 'features decidedly Jewish, having a thin aquiline nose, and a very piercing eye, as intent on mischief, as if it had belonged to Satan himself' (*3Ex* 1: 270). The 'piercing eye' is an interesting description; it intimates that this Aborigine is not a passive object of observation but is capable of a return investigative gaze which unsettles the explorer.

Mitchell is not alone in constructing the Aborigine as a devil, although others do so more guardedly. There is a remarkable description by Sturt which constructs the Aborigine as a devilish figure but does so in peculiarly vague terms. The Aborigine has set fire to a tree to catch an 'opossum':

> The effect of the scene in so lonely a forest, was very fine. The roaring of the fire in the tree, the fearless attitude of the savage, and the associations which his colour and appearance, enveloped as he was in smoke, called up, were singular, and still dwell on my recollection. (*2Ex* 2: 33)

In this passage the machinery of the categorisation of the Aborigine is partially revealed. The 'associations' with evil are exactly that – associations. Mostly, their associative status is repressed and colour, appearance and behaviour are compressed into signifiers which immediately mean savagery and evil. Most importantly, the scene is celebrated for its visual effect. Once again, the Aborigine is a prop in a scene consumed with

Plate 12   *Crawling Aborigine*, engraved by S. Williams after Mitchell's drawing.
From Thomas Mitchell, *Expedition into ... Tropical Australia* (p.165). Mitchell
Library, State Library of New South Wales.

pleasure by the explorer, and the Aborigine is valuable only in that he
performs the twin function of fulfilling the scene, and allowing that
scene's allegorical significance to be applied to him. But, as I will argue,
it is extremely difficult for the Aborigine to escape these paradigmatic
portrayals, without falling into other and equally limiting constructions.

Seeing into minds: assumptions about Aboriginal motivations

A common ethnographical practice by explorers was the establishment
of causal connections based on an intuiting of Aboriginal motivations –
such ascribed motivations usually being reached through the same
stereotypical categories that informed the 'pure' description. Returning
to an Aboriginal camp, Charles Sturt finds untouched a knife that he had
left as a gift, although the Aborigines had subsequently been in the
camp. The possibility that the Aborigines were simply not interested in
the gift is not considered. Sturt says that the knife was not accepted
because of the superstitious nature of the natives, and that 'there can be
no doubt but they took it for an evil spirit' (*ECA* 1: 253). On another
occasion an elderly Aborigine who was mauled by one of Sturt's dogs is
brought into the explorer's camp to recover. Sturt is quite surprised by
his apparent composure and remarks that his 'whole demeanour was

that of a calm and courageous man, who finding himself placed in unusual jeopardy, had determined not to be betrayed into the slightest display of fear or timidity' (*ECA* 1: 315). This description, it may be argued, merely compares the behaviour of the man to something Sturt is familiar with; but it also attempts to offer a plausible psychological explanation of what is observed. The group decision to ignore the gift of the knife can be neatly slotted into the psychology of the stereotypically superstitious native; the explanation of the individual's motivation is obviously Eurocentric.

There is one episode in his *Narrative of an Expedition into Central Australia* in which Sturt conspicuously fails to offer a motivational explanation. He observes that 'the natives, whose broad and well beaten paths leading from angle to angle of the creek we had crossed on our approach to it, had fired the grass, and it was now springing up in the bed of the most beautiful green' (*ECA* 2: 28–29). Although the causal connection between the firing and the new growth is clear, Sturt does not seek to construct the connection in terms of Aboriginal intention or cultural practice. He was not aware that the Aboriginal practice of firing the land destroyed the old and nutritionless grass, and that the resulting new growth of green grass encouraged the return of herbivores used as a food source by the Aborigines. When Sturt does explain the firing practices, in *Two Expeditions into . . . Southern Australia*, it is in terms of the 'mischievous' actions of the Aborigines directed against him (*2Ex* 1: 111, 113). But the growth of new grasses could hardly be explained as an action directed towards him and so Sturt is left in the unusual position of being without an explanation.

The interaction between the explorer and the Aborigine, as represented in the text, is largely determined by the explorer's view of the Aborigines' intentions: the deployment of the civilised/savage opposition ensures that the indigenes' motivations remain firmly in the field of the 'savage'. One of the chief markers of the savage is 'treachery'. In the space of a few pages Mitchell speaks in terms fairly typical of the explorers of 'barbarians . . . attacking treacherously' and of the 'midnight treachery of the aborigines' (*3Ex* 2: 103, 109). Once identified as a savage, the Aborigine cannot escape being seen as treacherous, for treachery is a biological characteristic. Sturt believes that 'treachery and cunning are inherent in the breast of every savage' (*ECA* 2: 275), and experience simply reflects this understanding. Aborigines whom Oxley contacts, for instance, are denied a heterogeneity of opinions but are instead all considered to be of the one treacherous mind. A party of friendly Aborigines camp with Oxley, receive haircuts and shaves to reduce the savageness of their appearance and then take their leave. The next day Oxley's men are 'treacherously' attacked by a small group of natives he recognises as being part of the previous day's gathering. Some time after they retreat he is approached by some men carrying 'fish as a peace offering to us' (Oxley 349). Oxley refuses to consider that there may be dissension amongst the Aborigines themselves as to how to react to the incursion of the explorers. Instead, they are homogenised into a general and treacherous mass, who can be dealt with only by the application of force. Oxley writes of the peace offering that 'I had determined if they had approached nearer to have made an example of them' (Oxley 350).

Occasionally, the trope of the treacherous native will break down. Indeed, one common construction – the native as an impetuous savage bereft of forethought – contradicts the notion of sullen Aborigines planning a swift reversal of loyalties. Grey argues that the 'peculiar characteristic of this savage race, appears to be that they in all cases act upon first impulses and impressions' (1: 157). Grey's point of view illustrates the strength of this preconception, as he had just been subject to an attack that was recognised in the text to be premeditated (1: 149). These two constructions of the Aborigine coexist uneasily: the indigene as thoughtless victim of animal impulse, and the indigene who plans the explorer's downfall. Indeed, flirting with unorthodoxy as usual, Grey's text undermines the very term 'treacherous'. He complains that because of the thickness of the vegetation surrounding his position, it was impossible to 'occupy it effectually against treacherous (or rather, bold and skilful) enemies' (2: 32). Even if the qualification is relegated to parenthetical status, and the use of 'treacherous' remains, the text bifurcates at this point, offering an ironic comment upon itself and the terms utilised. The contingency of all terms is revealed by this remark; they are 'treacherous' simply because the describer is on the wrong end of the spear. The alternative, the 'bold and skilful' savage, is just as much a paradigmatic description, borrowed from the catalogue of Rousseau-esque noble savagery tropes. But, even if Grey has failed to escape from stock characterisations, he has at least brought their sureness of use into question. Grey's alternative formulation also opens the obvious but usually unasked question of what loyalty the Aborigines owe the explorers in the first place. The assumption which underwrites the explorers' description of the treachery of the Aborigines, that the indigene's allegiance is theirs to command, is disturbed in other places by Grey, who characterises the attacks on Europeans as 'natural' rather than treacherous (1: 349).

The construction of the indigene as treacherous is useful, in that it relieves the European explorer of the burden of pursuing a peaceful diplomacy. If, as Stuart says, the Aborigines 'are not to be trusted: they will pretend the greatest friendship one moment and spear you the next' (374), then there is little reason to interact with them on any basis other than that of power. Sturt constructs one meeting almost purely in terms of a power relationship and realises that the balance of power does not necessarily reside with the exploring party: 'we were therefore wholly within their power, although happily for us perhaps, they were not aware of it'. But the balance of power is usually seen to favour the explorers: Sturt writes that, because of the Aborigines' lack of understanding of their advantage, he 'might certainly have commanded whatever they had' (*ECA* 2: 76).

The peaceful consequences of some of the explorations are seen to result from the display of power and there is little recognition that transgression of tribal boundaries and use of precious resources inevitably cause conflict. Sturt says that his horses and bullocks drink at least one thousand gallons of water a day – often taken from limited sources on which the Aborigines are dependent. When he reminds the reader of treachery inhabiting the breast of every native, Sturt neatly avoids discussion of the Aborigine's actions as a specific, strategic response to his presence, instead framing them in terms of innate and biological urges. Another function of the 'treacherous' construction is the role it plays in the denial of the limitations of knowledge. Meaning is directly open to the explorers by empirical observation and simple deduction. For example, Aborigines interested in Mitchell's hat have 'obviously' devious motives.

> While sitting in the dust with them, conformably to their custom, often have they examined my cap, evidently with no other view than to ascertain, if it would resist the blow of a waddy. Then, they would feel the thickness of my dress, and whisper together, their eyes occasionally glancing at their spears and clubs. The expression of their countenances was . . . hideous. (*3Ex* 1: 303)

As Aborigines are fully mapped in terms of the position they hold within the civilised/savage framework, it is generally not possible to find their motivations mysterious. Mitchell might have given other motivations – for example, thoughtful natives examine the novelty of the hat while cautiously ensuring their means of defence were safe – but this would be to step outside of the dominant paradigm of civilised/savage.

Ultimately, the Aborigines are almost completely entrapped within these paradigmatic structures by the dominant discourse and, even when acting in a completely non-threatening manner, they are positioned as essentially treacherous. Stuart interprets as 'timidity' the Aborigines' unwillingness to contact him and this is a 'very bad feature – such are often treacherous' (458). Even when their actions are in perfect accord with the ethical stance of the explorers, the Aborigines are still depicted as treacherous and disingenuous. A blanket from Sturt's party is stolen and the young souvenir-hunter is punished by his tribe and forced to return it. But Sturt gives the Aborigines little credit for collective rectitude, instead professing 'I cannot help thinking, however, that if the theft had not been discovered, the young rogue would have been applauded for his dexterity' (*ECA* 2: 14).

The explorer's system of morals is usually seen as universally valid, and if an Aborigine is charged with a transgression of this code then his or her guilt is an a priori assumption. Sturt recounts a remarkable story concerning two escaped Irish convicts whose dogs are coveted by Aborigines. The convicts' reluctance to hand over their dogs leads to their death, though not before one of them cuts the dogs' throats. Sturt, who is in the general region where the incident took place, questions the Aborigines, who preserve 'the most sullen silence, neither acknowledging nor denying the fact' (*2Ex* 1: 114) that they killed and ate the two men. Whereas in other cases the Aborigines' ignorance of English, while lamentable, is understandable, here it is transformed into an unwillingness to confess their obvious guilt. This is in many ways a classic moment of racist inquisition, where the silent are considered guilty because of their silence. But the notable aspect in this case is the status of Sturt's story: it is unsourced, being produced simply as an unquestionable 'fact'. It is indeed difficult to see how the story could have originated, since the Aborigines were silent and the Irishmen were dinner. The cannibalism of the story explains its currency at least, but it is significant that the narratives of Europeans need no substantiation, while those of Aborigines can never have proof enough.[20] As I will discuss (in chapter 6), the untruthfulness of the Aborigines is a construction undermined by the practice of exploration, in which the explorers rely heavily on Aboriginal information. Aborigines' untrustworthiness can never be easily dismissed or trained out of them, however, for the simple reason that Europeans 'know' that it is innate. 'Like all savages', Stokes opines, 'they are treacherous, – for uncivilized man has no abstract respect for truth' (Stokes 1: 59).

Christians vs heathens

Allied closely to the civilised/savage structure, which equates ownership with civilisation, there exists a Christian/heathen opposition, which is constructed geographically by Mitchell. On returning from his search for the mythical river 'Kindur', Mitchell evinces a strong notion of crossing the border between the savage and civilised lands, between the Christian and the heathen:

> The ford of Wallanburra was now our only separation from the christian world. That once passed, we might joyfully bid adieu to pestilence and famine, the lurking savage, and every peril of 'flood and field'. Under the sense of perfect security once more, and relieved from the anxiety inseparable from such a charge, every object within the territory of civilized man, appeared to me tinged *couleur de rose*. (*3Ex* 1: 139)

The medieval idea of the small outpost of civilisation opposed to the wild and dangerous outside gained new valency in the colonial context, and is transformed here to the frontier situation, where the border is less marked than a castle moat. Nevertheless, crossing the imaginary border works for colonial self-identification and its binary logic of inside/ outside and us/not us. The racist construction of the Aborigine positions him or her, like the 'wilderness' in opposition to the European; the heathen, then, is not simply non-Christian but the very opposite of Christian. This means that superstition is a prime feature of the Aborigine. In confirming that the Aborigines are at the 'very bottom of the scale of humanity', Sturt notes that the poles he finds fixed in the river are designed 'to propitiate some deity' and that the Aborigines 'dread evil agency' (*2Ex* 1: 107). That they may not worship deities, good or evil, is not something that occurs to Sturt.

Othering the Aborigines

The final and key stage in these constructions of the Aborigine is hierarchisation. Noting that some Aboriginal customs are similar to those in the Bible, Mitchell writes that:

> the savage tribes of mankind, as they approach nearer to the condition of animals, seem to preserve a stronger resemblance to themselves and to each other. The uniform stability of their manners seems a natural consequence of the uncultivated state of their faculties. (*3Ex* 2: 347–48)

They exist in an undifferentiated mass, are on the lowest scale of development and in their similarity with the people of the Bible can be seen as essentially similar to Orientals. Again, we find the ambiguous position Aborigines are given in the self/other schema. They are not the same as Europeans, but cannot be completely different either. For, if the Aborigine was granted absolute otherness, the judgemental/scientific schema of the explorer would be rendered invalid. The object of investigation is ultimately returned to the empire of knowledge the explorers carry with them. The Aborigines become fellow creatures: a woman is, to Mitchell, a 'humiliating specimen' but one of 'our race'; the Aborigines are 'fellow men' (*3Ex* 1: 49, 108). The return to the status of humanity is hardly beneficial to the Aborigines since, as 'specimens', they are subject to the unsympathetic gaze of 'superior' intelligences.

The difference Aborigines are constructed within is familiar to the explorers, founded as it is within the archives of European fantasy, and previous contacts with indigenes, the accounts of which are similarly influenced by myth. Very occasionally, one may find an allowance of true alterity – that is, a difference which is not already known to the European, and is not immediately transparent to this European view. The *Hobart Town Courier* allowed that this true difference existed.

> Sir Joseph Banks and the other philosophers who first visited this island to make comments on its Aboriginal people, called them an inferior and degraded race merely through ignorance. The being who appeared a naked, rude, comfortless savage to them, had nevertheless intellectual powers perhaps commensurate with those of his learned visitors but which being directed in a different channel could not be discerned.[21]

The opacity of the Aborigine and of his experience is not usually expressed in journals of exploration. The instructions given to Sturt specifically indicate that he is to observe the 'genius' of the Aborigines (*2Ex* 1: 187) – assuming that this is in any way open to observation. Strzelecki strongly attacks the general view of the inferiority of the Aborigines, but adheres to the general belief of empiricism that the worth of the Aborigines could be established by vision alone. He reverses the value judgement but leaves the specular method intact.

> Few spectacles can be more gratifying to the philosophers than to behold him and his in their own as yet uninvaded haunts; and few can exhibit a more striking proof of the bountiful dispensation of the Creator, than the existence of one whose destiny the singular presumption of the whites, in their attachment to conventional customs and earthly riches, has stigmatised and denounced as 'savage, debased, unfortunate, miserable.' To any one, however, who shakes off the trammels of a conventional, local, and therefore narrow mode of thinking, – to any one who studies and surveys mankind in personal travels, and by personal observation, – it will appear evident that Providence has left as many roads to the threshold of contentment and happiness as there are races of mankind. (Strzelecki 342–43)

Vision alone is still produced here as an unerring means of gathering knowledge: the viewer must experience the 'spectacle' of Aborigines untainted by contact, another example of the production of vision and the viewer as non-invasive. One must also 'survey' mankind with a quantifying and judgemental vision, producing people as objects, like land, to be measured, compared, and generally produced as objects of knowledge awaiting insertion into a particular category. Although the vocabulary of the measuring vision remains, Strzelecki's text is an example of resistance to the judgement inherent in the ethnographic gaze. But, without offering a critique of the gaze itself, Strzelecki has not disengaged vision from the production of the Aborigine as a corpus of knowledge, recomposed of 'already known' information about the indigene; hence, the 'other roads' to happiness (itself an image of European progressivity) will simply be constituted by alternate tropes of the indigene, such as those of the 'noble savage' paradigm.

6

Contesting the Gaze of Ownership

'Nothing visible inhabited that dreary desert': ownership and alienation

The dawn of liberty breaks upon them

To dispel the smoke and fire of the Aborigine/devil comes the explorer as herald of the arrival of white society. The usual method of proclaiming possession of a *terra nullius*, Frost notes, is by leaving proof of presence such as cairns of stones and inscriptions. The preliminary right to land was established by a claim supported by governmental authorisation, accompanied by 'symbolic acts of sovereignty' including the raising of the flag and the firing of salutes.[1] Stuart's needless repetition of this ritual in the centre of the continent reveals an anxiety about the actual status or validity of the white claim – as if the claim needs to be endlessly repeated. Yet it also represents the explorer as the first wave of Christianity. Stuart builds:

> a large cone of stones, in the centre of which I placed a pole with the British flag nailed to it. Near the top of the cone I placed a small bottle, in which there is a slip of paper, with our signatures to it, stating by whom it was raised. We then gave three hearty cheers for the flag, the emblem of civil and religious liberty, and may it be a sign to the natives that the dawn of liberty, civilization, and Christianity is about to break upon them. (Stuart 165–66)

In the building of the cairn and the raising of the flag, the explorer is part of the transformation of the landscape the journal looks towards. The flag is emblematic of civil and religious liberty, but this liberty is available only within a strictly Christian civilisation. Stuart hopes that the flag will act as a sign to the natives; but, in drawing attention to the flag's

153

'emblematic' qualities, he inadvertently highlights its arbitrariness as sign. He cannot really expect the 'natives' to understand the sign; all he can do is will this communication into existence. If the flag is emblematic and has gained associations in a certain culture, then it can have no possible meaning for the Aborigines; as the relativity of the sign is uncovered, so too is the relativity of the associated categories of 'liberty, civilization, and Christianity'. These can only be forcibly emplaced on the Aboriginal culture and the violence implicit in the phrase 'break upon them' prefigures this.

Elsewhere, the journals construct the explorers as messiahs, descending into encampments of diseased natives who are seemingly destined for extinction. Sturt visits one tribe which:

> was almost the only one that evinced any eagerness to see us. The lame had managed to hobble along, and the blind were equally anxious to touch us. There were two or three old men stretched upon the bank, from whom the last sigh seemed about to depart; yet these poor creatures evinced an anxiety to see us, and to listen to a description of our appearance, although it seemed doubtful whether they would be alive twenty-four hours after we left them. (*2Ex* 2: 135)

As Christ-like figures, the explorers are not only inherently superior but must be the centre of attention. That the Aborigines may be uninterested in them and their activities is not countenanced; but when evidence to this effect accumulates, it can be construed as something else. Camps that are empty on the explorer's arrival are the result of Aboriginal fear or timidity; Aborigines acting as guides who leave the exploring party are 'disloyal' or 'treacherous'.

Why, then, do all these structuring devices come into play so strongly in the writings of explorers? One answer is that the texts are generically contained to speak within a certain discourse of indigeneity, where the natives are always morally and intellectually inferior. This process of othering produces the knowledge necessary for exploration results, and safely and comfortably contains threatening difference within a taming discourse.

Exploration literature as a genre undergoes considerable change from the journals of Christopher Columbus to those of Ernest Giles. The journals become widely read, create generic expectations of their own, are increasingly penetrated by scientific concepts, and are vehicles for the expression of changing philosophical opinions. In the midst of this change the discursive construction of the indigene remains remarkably constant. Columbus's journal, like those of most Australian explorers, is obsessed with the nakedness, colour and technological poverty of the 'Indians' he sees. They are similarly treacherous, innocent, childlike, impulsive and repulsive.[2] The remarkable stability of the paradigms drawn from in descriptions of the indigenes cannot be explained simply in terms of their usefulness (admittedly great) in the generation of knowledge. Instead, they have a more immediate and interested use: the alienation of the land from the inhabitants.

Land rights and stereotypes

To see the treatment of Australia as a *terra nullius* as Alan Frost has done, as a regrettable but understandable mistake, is to simplify the mechanics of the dispossession of the Aborigines to a technical flaw in international law.[3] Henry Reynolds has shown how the actual status of Aboriginal rights to the land remained contested throughout the nineteenth century and into the twentieth century.[4] The construction of the Aborigine as lacking an agriculture encouraged the treatyless dispossession of the indigene, which happened nowhere but in Australia. Other discursive structures articulate with this, however, to guarantee the Aborigine's containment within a set of overlapping and reinforcing stereotypes which make dispossession, not merely a right according to international law, but also a natural process and divine duty.

In Australia, there are four main constructions of the indigene or the land which justify dispossession. First, there is the presentation of the indigene as the savage; this, as I have suggested above, disqualifies the indigene from consideration as a possible owner of land. Second, then, is the convenient concept that the Aborigines had no notion or practice of ownership: the country was a *terra nullius*, unowned, because the inhabitants individually did not understand ownership, and because they lacked a recognisable system of government or a sovereign from whom titular authority to land could devolve.[5] Third, and perhaps surprisingly, the country was seen as generally uninhabited and therefore unowned. Fourth, the fact that the Aborigines did not employ recognisable agricultural practices was taken as evidence that the land was inefficiently used and therefore justifiably appropriated by those who could make 'better' use of it. As simple as these structures are, they had to negotiate with contemporary international law. The confusion surrounding the actual legal status of the Aborigine and the land enabled the rapid expansion of colonisation, and the material appropriation of land, while legal debate took place. While, ultimately, the material desires of the encroaching colonists would hardly have been stemmed by legal niceties, it is necessary to set out briefly where the land and its inhabitants stood in relation to the law that was applied to them.

The legal construction of the land as *terra nullius* was a central enabling device for dispossessing the Aborigines of the land. Alan Frost has shown that the ways of acquiring land that was not already possessed by a European competitor power were:

– by persuading the indigenous inhabitants to submit themselves to its
overlordship; – by purchasing from those inhabitants the rights to settle part
or parts of it; – by unilateral possession, on the basis of first discovery and
effective occupation.[6]

In the Australian context there was no official attempt to persuade the
Aborigines to submit themselves to British 'overlordship', and attempts
to purchase settlement areas were exceptions to the general rule. The
adoption of the third option, unilateral possession, and the associated
treatment of Australia as a *terra nullius* was very much an exception in
international practice (a treaty acknowledging prior possession is
promised but little progress is currently being made towards it). For a
land to be treated as *terra nullius* it either had to be uninhabited or the
natives had to be considered propertyless. Land as property primarily
meant agricultural land to the European mind. That land must be *used*
had been urged by the ultimate authority – 'be fruitful, and replenish the
earth and subdue it' (Gen. 28) – and supported by the eighteenth
century property theory of John Locke: 'he that in Obedience to this
Command of God, subdued, tilled and sowed any part of it, thereby
annexed to it something that was his *Property*, which another had no Title
to, nor could without injury take from him'.[7]

Eminent eighteenth century jurists did not always agree with Locke,
however. Both Christian Wolff's *Law of Nations* and J. G. Heineccius's *A
Methodological System of International Law* held that nomadic practice
constituted occupation, and that no permanent cultivation was necessary
for a person or group to claim an area of land as property.[8] Henry
Reynolds points out that Emerich de Vattel, the authority often referred
to in questions of eighteenth century international law, generally agrees
with this, but contradictorily holds that the earth must be subdued,
ultimately arguing that settlers may alienate sections of land to their use,
restricting natives within certain bounds, but have no right to appropriate the whole of the land.[9] This is a solution, as will be subsequently
shown, which many explorers favour.

Since explorers were representatives of landholder-dominated colonial governments, and often of landholders directly, their liberality of
views regarding native rights to the land is somewhat surprising. It is not
difficult to find admissions that the Aborigines have had their land
unfairly taken away from them without recompense. Rather than being a
particularly liberated group, however, the explorers largely reflect the
contemporary discursive chaos which left the whole question of land and
land rights a confused field. Stokes espouses the conservative view that
saw the appropriation of land in the context of the biblically ordained
struggle against nature. 'There is always a feeling of pride and pleasure',
Stokes writes, 'engendered by the thought that we are in any way

instrumental to the extension of man's influence over the world which
has been given him to subdue' (Stokes 2: 2). Elsewhere, Stokes speaks of
the Aborigines as the 'present rightful owners' (1: 127), a description
which at least admits ownership even if it also intimates a future change.

Occasionally, Stokes mentions Aboriginal ownership positively, but
only in the context of European superiority and the necessity of
'managing' the Aborigines. He argues that others should treat the
Aborigines with the kindness that he has shown, not simply because they
are 'fairly entitled' to this 'from men so far their superiors in knowledge
and power, and who were moreover intruders upon their soil' (1: 379),
but also because this method when applied produces tractable indigenes.
The result – unfettered incursion into the land – he recommends as
being 'equally satisfactory elsewhere' (1: 379). Stokes creates the most
important contradiction in his explication of native title in his discussion
of the plight of the Tasmanian Aborigines. Noting that they were
persuaded to remove from Tasmania to a sealers' island by G. A.
Robinson, Stokes complains that the sealers were obliged to vacate as
they 'could not show title to the land they cultivated except that of
original occupancy – a title which I think should be respected, as it is the
only true basis of the right of property' (2: 467). Why Stokes chooses to
concentrate on the misfortune of the sealers is rather a mystery. Obviously, by his own logic, the Aborigines' original occupancy in Tasmania
is as valid a claim to land as the sealers' and more valid than that of the
Tasmanian settlers.

Part of the generic encouragement for the construction of land as
waiting for European inhabitation is that it makes the journal and the
journey more significant for the colony rather than being just a satiation
of curiosity. The journal's information can then be portrayed as immediately and materially useful. The rapid increase of the British
population is seen by Mitchell as justification for the idea that lands are
prepared for European inhabitance. Mitchell argues that:

> curiosity alone may attract us into the mysterious regions still unknown but a
> still deeper interest attaches to those regions, now that the rapid increase of
> the most industrious and, may we add most deserving people on earth,
> suggests that the land there has been reserved by the Almighty for their use
> (*EITA* Preface v).

Although this is prefatorial hyperbole, it nevertheless embodies the
imperial note of triumph and divine justification that is more usually
associated with explorers than is Stokes's confusion over land status. But
Mitchell allows that Aborigines have rights to the land, or at least to its
products, though the admission seems to be tainted with an incredulity
that they considered that it was their property. In communications with

them, he notes, 'they pointed to the earth and the water, giving us to understand in every way they could, that we were welcome to the water, which they probably considered their own' (*3Ex* 1: 232). In certain cases the explorers welcome Aboriginal possession, but only of land that is of no use for Europeans. Giles, for example, writes that the arid region through which he is travelling 'is occasionally visited by its native owners, to whom I do not begrudge the possession of it' (Giles 1: 68). This is to ignore that under British law the Aborigines had been dispossessed of their land, and that even if left alone they had no legal title to it. This is also forgotten by Sturt who speaks of the Aborigines as 'tenants' (*ECA* 2: 87) of the land – a word which can mean ownership by title, or merely occupation by lease; Sturt does not specify.

The explorer is often represented in the journals as the vanguard of European settlement. Grey's journal includes a struggle between the explorers and the Aborigines for the power of surveillance, and the analogy that Grey draws illustrates the unconsciously proprietorial view that the explorers themselves have to the land. The Aborigines have the advantage in height and are assumed to be watching Grey's camp. Grey looks back:

> with the help of my telescope I once distinguished their dusky forms moving about in the bush. A large flight of cockatoos, which lay between us and them, were kept in a constant state of screaming anxiety from the movement of one or the other party, and at last found their position so unpleasant, that they evacuated it, and flew off to some more quiet roosting place. Their departure, however, was a serious loss to us, as they played somewhat the same part that the geese once did in the Capitol; for whenever our sable neighbours made the slightest movement, the watchful sentinels of the cockatoos instantly detected it, and by stretching out their crests, screaming . . . gave us a faithful intimation of every motion. (Grey 1: 184)

The remarkable element of this description, of course, is that Grey is the settled Roman, and that the Aborigines are the invaders of his land. It would have been quite possible to reverse this formulation, since Grey's men also are described as disturbing the birds, thus revealing their presence. Instead, the Aborigines are the aggressors and trespassers upon the explorer's land, a position they implicitly occupy in most of the descriptions of attacks on exploration parties and their camps.

Explorers on Aboriginal ownership

Separate from debates over whether the Aborigines' occupation of the land constituted legal ownership, was the view that they had no concept of land ownership at all. Eyre combats this view in his summary of the conditions of the Aborigines, writing that it has 'generally been imagined, but with great injustice, as well as incorrectness, that the natives have no idea of property in land, or proprietary rights connected with it' (2: 296). He quotes a letter from the *Australian Register*, 1 August 1840, which holds that Aborigines have no proprietorial rights.

> It would be difficult to define what conceivable property rights were ever enjoyed by the miserable savages of South Australia, who never cultivated an inch of the soil, and whose ideas of the value of its direct produce never extended beyond obtaining a sufficiency of pieces of white chalk and red ochre wherewith to bedaub their bodies for their filthy corroberies. (quoted in Eyre 2: 296–97)

The self-serving construction of the Aborigine as propertyless is refuted by Eyre. Interestingly, the authority he refers to is not his own experience, or the experience of another explorer, but that of John Dunmore Lang. Eschewing the empiricism that explorers ostensibly employ, Eyre quotes Grey, who in turn quotes Lang, who answers the question of whether Aborigines have the concept of property 'most decidedly in the affirmative' (Grey 2: 233).

Lang's analysis of Aboriginal ownership works on the principle that, while Aboriginal cultivation is non-existent, tribes and individuals within these tribes consider portions of the land as their own for hunting purposes. Thus, Lang argues, 'the difference between the Aboriginal and the European ideas of property in the soil is more imaginary than real'. Intrusion upon these lands results in violence and is a frequent cause of 'Aboriginal, as it is of European wars; man, in his natural state, being very much alike in all conditions – jealous of his rights, and exceedingly pugnacious' (Grey 2: 234). At least Grey and Eyre, through their quoting Lang, support the idea that Aborigines understood the concept of ownership and that, by extension, they have some right to the land; but they do so only by denying an otherness to Aboriginal ownership systems. To be valid, Aboriginal ownership must be recognisable in European terms. Thus, the process of othering returns to the debate; the Aborigines are different, but ultimately just like us. It is difficult to deny that this was the only political strategy open to defenders of the Aborigines such as Grey and Eyre, but it demonstrates that othering governs all formulations of Aborigines and their management, whether progressive or not.

Despite the contentions of a few, in practice the treatment of Australia as a *terra nullius* depended upon the construction of the Aborigine as nomadic, living off the incidental produce of the land. There were other indices of the capacity for property – permanent housing, a governmental hierarchy, a system of trade – but agriculture stood as a primary marker. The opposition between the cultivating Europeans and the 'uncultivated' indigenes runs deeply through the descriptions of the

Aboriginal way of life. The 'Anglo Saxon race [is] already rooted' (*EITA* 2) in Australia, Mitchell writes; the colonial enterprise itself, constructed as an agricultural process, is thus opposed to the wandering and rootless natives.

Aboriginal firing practices

From off the coast James Cook saw the fires of the Aborigines but could not guess that these had an agricultural purpose – though it was not an agriculture that Europeans recognise. Instead, Cook saw Australia as being in a 'pure state of Nature',[10] thus positioning it as unused and therefore ownerless land. Cook is the first of many explorers who constructed the landscape as untouched when in fact it had been transformed by Aboriginal firing. The open grasslands that are the products of firing are admired by Mitchell for being similar to a 'nobleman's park on a gigantic scale' (*3Ex* 2: 212) at the same time as he comments on the lack of population.

These effects produced by the firing mean that the landscape is of visual value to the explorer. The only good that Oxley can see in burning is that it produces difference in the landscape, which he can perceive. 'A few acres in patches had been burned', he writes, 'occasionally relieving the eye from the otherwise barren scrubby appearance of the country' (Oxley 151). The reward that burning off vegetation gives to the European eye is emphasised by Mitchell, who in effect admits that rather than the explorer, it is the Aborigines and their firing practices which 'open up' the country. Firing prepared the country for white inhabitance; thus, much of the labour which usually attends colonisation was not necessary. If it was not for firing, Mitchell argues:

> the Australian woods had probably contained as thick a jungle as those of New Zealand or America, instead of the open forests in which the white men now find grass for their cattle, to the exclusion of the kangaroo ... the omission of the annual periodical burning by natives ... has already produced in the open forest lands near to Sydney, thick forests of young trees, where formerly, a man might gallop without impediment, and see whole miles before him. (*EITA* 412–13)

The visual and transportational penetration of the land has been enabled by Aborigines; moreover, firing has transformed the land into a ready-made farm to the explorers' instrumentalist gaze. The results of firing are often praised; the practice, however, is usually damned.

Explorers assume that Aboriginal grass fires are directed against them. This was undoubtedly an accurate inference at times, but Sturt, for example, draws on the 'already known' catalogue of Aboriginal behaviour to explain firing. Sturt writes that 'we knew that the natives never made such extensive conflagration, unless they had some mischievous object in view' (*2Ex* 1: 111). Subsequently, Sturt admits that firing may be used to cause a general exodus of animals, some of which would be caught and used for food, but portrays this as a desperate measure by people who had eaten all the available food, fish and mussels with 'characteristic improvidence' (*2Ex* 1: 113).

The journal which really explains the process of firing as a land-management practice is that of Ludwig Leichhardt. After stating several times that burning grass results in fresh regrowth areas, the journal makes the connection.

> The natives seemed to have burned the grass systematically along every watercourse, and round every water-hole, in order to have them surrounded with young grass as soon as the rain sets in ... it is no doubt connected with the systematic management of their runs, to attract game to particular spots, in the same way that stockholders burn parts of theirs in proper seasons; at least those who are not influenced by the erroneous notion, that burning the grass injures the richness and density of the *natural* turf. (Leichhardt 354–55)

The idea that the land was uncultivated gives way to a textual construction of firing as a practice similar to some strategies of European land-management. But this does not mean that the land is cultivated, merely that it is managed. Cultivation was defined in terms of recognised agricultural practices, but, for the purposes of deciding its relationship to ownership, it was considered simply as 'labour' added to the land. If this concept is considered, then explorers' descriptions supported the notion that Aborigines added value to the land through their labour. Grey accepts the difference between the stereotypes of the lazy indigene simply living off the incidental produce of the land and the actual work which needed to be invested. He writes that 'more had been done to secure a provision from the ground by hard manual labour than I could have believed it in the power of uncivilised man to accomplish' (2: 12). Mitchell takes up the point of firing as a laborious improvement of the land, connecting with it the usurpation of property by Europeans.

> The extensive burning by the natives, a work of considerable labour, and performed in dry warm weather, left tracks in the open forest, which had become green as an emerald with the young crop of grass ... how natural must be the aversion of the natives to the intrusion of another race of men with cattle: people who recognize no right in the aborigines to either the grass they have thus worked from infancy, nor to the kangaroos they have hunted with their fathers. (*EITA* 306)

Despite the vague mention of 'people' who fail to recognise the property rights of Aborigines, the removal of the indigene from the land is constructed as an 'Aboriginal tragedy'. This falls into the paradigmatic class of descriptions which lament the passing of the race, grieve at the injustice involved, but which ultimately avoid concrete criticisms of the political processes which encourage the wholesale appropriation of land.

Explorers are restrained in what they say. Mitchell, in particular, as surveyor-general, is inescapably connected with the mechanics of land alienation, and can hardly be expected to attack either his department, the larger bureaucratic establishment, or colonialism itself. Yet, at one point Mitchell comes remarkably close to a denial of two of the justifications of colonial expansion – that it will bring the benefits of Christianity and civilisation to the indigenes.

> The only kindness we could do for them, would be to let them and their wide range of territory alone; to act otherwise and profess good will is but hypocrisy. (*EITA* 66)

This is a remarkable suggestion for a surveyor-general, and perhaps the most constructive advice about European–Aborigine relationships in any of the journals. But the context in which the denial of the benefits of European contact occurs shows that Mitchell is not as enlightened as the quote suggests. He has previously noted the excellent condition of the Aborigines' health, and in particular the admirable quality of their teeth.

> Such health and exemption from disease; such intensity of existence, in short, must be far beyond the enjoyments of civilized men, with all that art can do for them; and the proof of this is to be found in the failure of all attempts to persuade these free denizens of uncultivated earth to forsake it for the tilled ground. They prefer the land unbroken and free from the earliest curse pronounced against the first banished and first created man ... we cannot occupy land without producing a change, fully as great to the aborigines, as that which took place on man's fall and expulsion from Eden. (*EITA* 65–66)

The presentation of Aborigines as pre-lapsarian figures is to return them to savages living off the fruit of the land, without the need for labour. Preserved from ill-health and the burden of labour, with a romanticised, indeed Wordsworthian, 'intensity of existence', the Aborigine as noble savage seems a figure to be envied. But the analogy of their existence with pre-lapsarian humanity inserts them into a particular narrative: they are destined, inevitably, and against their will, to a similar exile, as their already foreshadowed future is sealed. And as the events have already taken place, and can only be repeated in Australia, the European, although a cause of the fall, is also a bystander, watching the inevitable unfolding of the narrative from the vantage point of an imaginary experience. There is, associated with this, an evolutionary schema which presents Aborigines as doomed. This schema will be returned to subsequently, but first it is necessary to examine the most effective or, perhaps, ambitious trope to be applied to an indigenous population – that is, their non-existence.

Aboriginal population

In support of the idea that Australia was unpopulated, Mitchell quotes William Eden Auckland's *The History of New Holland*, in which it is considered that the number of inhabitants across the continent is 'small, and that the interior parts of the country are uninhabited' (*3Ex* 2: 351). Mitchell's limited exploration of the country allows him to opine that he sees 'no reason to entertain a contrary opinion', but he omits to mention that *The History of New Holland* was published in 1787, before any significant European exploration of the continent, apart from the coast, had taken place. Again, this is a case of the pre-existence of Australia as a *tabula rasa*, a blank page devoid of troublesome inhabitants – inhabitants who, though they might not present recognised legal documentation, would constitute some claim to ownership if seen in sufficient numbers. Auckland already 'knows' that the inland is uninhabited. It is rewarding to refer to his *History* to see how he knows.

> From shore to shore there is an immense tract of country wholly unexplored; but there is a great reason to believe that this immense tract is either wholly desolate, or at least still more thinly inhabited than the places which have been visited. It is impossible that the inland country should subsist inhabitants at all seasons without cultivation ... It is certain not a foot of ground was seen on the whole country in a state of cultivation; and therefore, it may reasonably be concluded, that where the sea does not contribute to feed the inhabitants, the country is not inhabited.[11]

Cultivation and habitation are intricately linked, a nexus Mitchell knew to be fatuous when he disingenuously produced Auckland as an authoritative source.

Auckland's evidence is the observations of earlier travellers such as Cook and Dampier. Apart from the dubious logic in drawing conclusions about inland populations from coastal observations, the use of observations themselves is a doubtful practice. There is the logic operating in *The History of New Holland* that if the indigenes cannot be seen, they do not exist. The reliance on specular analysis is particularly interesting. Sight is the principal method of information gathering, and that which is not tractable to this information formation is simply rendered non-existent. 'So few natives were seen in the interior', writes Oxley, 'that those extensive regions can scarcely be described as inhabited' (Oxley 211). Auckland's own evidence is that Cook never saw more than thirty

Aborigines at any one time; Dampier considered forty a great number.[12]
Many descriptions of arid areas also emphasise the unpopulated nature
of the country – as far as can be seen.

> We were then in one of the most gloomy regions that man ever traversed. The
> stillness of death reigned around us, no living creature was to be heard;
> nothing visible inhabited that dreary desert but the ant ... (*ECA* 1: 277–78)

A number of times, however, explorers by accident happen across
Aborigines who are only a few metres away, incidents which undermine
the implicit claim in the above description that sight can be a method of
population estimate – even if Sturt does specify that 'nothing visible'
inhabits the desert. To say that Aborigines are often invisible, however,
would be to confer a particular power on them, or at least to allow that
they could escape the power of European surveillance.

The descriptions which conclude that the country is uninhabited
because inhabitants are not seen, do not fit elegantly with the frequent
observations that the Aborigines are 'timid' and wish to avoid observation. But the central arrogance remains – the assumption that the
explorer's vision is all-encompassing, and that it can operate as a kind of
crude census-taker. It serves the same function as the other 'always
already known' categories of the savage. The country is pre-ordained as
empty by Auckland (and by cartographic representations), and
subsequent observations are constituted by this paradigm, not because it
is in some sense binding, generically or otherwise, but because its utility
remains. The discovery of an empty and promising land provides a
justification for the explorer on a number of grounds: the explorer's
decision to travel in a particular direction is vindicated, his heroic stature
as colonial vanguard can be emphasised, and the description provides a
moment of celebration in the journal.

> Here was an almost boundless extent of the richest surface in a latitude
> corresponding to that of China, yet still uncultivated and unoccupied by man.
> A great reserve, provided by nature for the extension of his race, where
> economy, art, and industry might suffice to people it with a peaceful, happy,
> and contented population. (*EITA* 292–93)

The joy of finding an area empty is that the mechanics of dispossession
are disguised at the very beginning of the process, and no further
justification for the usurpation of the land, such as agricultural improvement or civilising the heathen inhabitants, need be entered into.

The land is not invariably seen as vacant. Stokes remarks that the
northern coast 'seems pretty thickly populated' (1: 93). And if the land
is heavily populated, that is not necessarily good for the Aborigines. Grey

kills one Aborigine, and portrays this as a matter of regret – as do most explorers, at the murder of indigenes. Grey goes beyond stoic regret, however, saying that he is personally affected by the matter and that, while grieving, a sailor, Ruston, enters his tent to comfort him. Ruston reasons that the shooting of the Aborigine should not be a matter of true regret as 'they're very thick and plentiful up the country' (1: 159). This is a fairly rare moment, when a member of the party other than the leader gains a voice, even if his speech is reported by Grey and produced only as an 'amusing' anecdote. It demonstrates the variety of views regarding the Aborigines within the exploring party, and how some view the Aborigines as little better than wild game.

The lack of visibility of the Aborigines and their means of subsistence finally decide they must not exist, or at least that their population must be minimal. That they have means of gathering food beyond the knowledge of the European is unacceptable, at least to the early explorers. The greatest ignorance about the Aborigines is often accompanied by the greatest arrogance. However, so great was the desire to avoid admissions of ignorance, sure pronouncements on the uninhabited state of the continent were freely made. Attempts to explain the seemingly small populations resulted in ludicrous arguments, such as Oxley's belief that Aborigines ate poorly and that decent food – kangaroo, for instance – was only caught by 'accident'.

> The population of this country must be extremely small: as the natives derive their chief support from opposums, squirrels, and rats, which are known to frequent barren scrubs and hollow trees ... it must be mere accident that enables the natives to kill either a kangaroo or an emu ... (Oxley 196–97)

Oxley's absurd denigration of Aboriginal bush-knowledge is generally not repeated in the journals of later explorers; nevertheless, it is part of the representation of the country as unpopulated and under-used, which continued to be popular.

Explorers as petty thieves

Whatever the views of the individual explorer, exploration generally gave little respect to property rights of Aborigines. If there are numerous incidents involving Aborigines and the disappearance of the explorers' tools or food, then there are also cases of explorers' theft of Aboriginal materials. Occasionally, this is a matter of the explorers' survival, such as when they take food or water; or it can be a transportational necessity, such as when Oxley takes a native's dug-out, which suddenly becomes 'our little canoe' (Oxley 131). The gathering of knowledge requires this theft because of the material conditions of the expedition. But knowledge accumulation in the journals is necessarily acquisitive, the scientific gathering of data being also a material appropriation of artifacts. This can be in the form of an exchange rather than outright theft, such as Warburton's taking of a boomerang and leaving a blanket – an action which intimates the future organised distribution of blankets to Aborigines who have no further use for boomerangs. But more often the theft is a disruption of Aboriginal life and a denial of Aboriginal ownership and sensitivities.

The classic moment of the invasive investigation is the opening of burial sites. Stokes acknowledges the 'peculiar opinions about the especial sanctity' of burial grounds, a sanctity he admits 'we certainly were not altogether justified in disregarding' (1: 116). Perhaps there is a display of conscience here because the sanctity had a European parallel. Nevertheless, the bones in the grave are removed and sent to the Royal College of Surgeons in London to be catalogued, measured and judged by comparison as representing a particular evolutionary level, and finally to be displayed. The skeleton adds to the scientific system of knowledge because a place is already reserved for it; it will fall into a pre-existing category, or the system of categorisation will be extended to digest its difference. Moreover, inevitably it will produce evidence of the phrenological or evolutionary backwardness of the Aborigines, since skeletons from indigenes of the colonies invariably show the same thing. With his usual twisted whimsy, Giles wishes that he could preserve and return to England the bodies as well as the skeletons.

> When I patted him, he grinned like any other monkey. None of them were handsome; the old man was so monkey-like – he would have charmed the heart of Professor Darwin. I thought I had found the missing link, and I had thoughts of preserving him in methylated spirits, only I had not a bottle large enough. (Giles 2: 326–27)

The explorer himself is a link in a chain that maintains the flow of scientifically 'important' artifacts from colonial possessions to London, where they can be analysed, hierarchised and placed safely within a known category. The importance of Darwin is that he provides this hierarchy into which the Aborigine can be inserted.

However, not all 'artifacts' (and Giles certainly treats the Aborigine in this case as equivalent to an inert artifact, or at least an animal specimen) are equally tractable to insertion within European science. Warburton finds 'thin, flat stones ... marked with unintelligible scrawls' secreted in a hole, from which he 'ferrets' them out. 'No clue', he writes, 'could be gained as to what they meant or why they were deposited there ...

unfortunately these interesting objects had to be thrown away before the termination of the journey' (Warburton 182). The contingencies of the expedition result in the disposal of the stones, but the information is really lost because they are not easily categorised, and remain an uncomfortable puzzle. Warburton does not sketch them, but having appropriated too much is forced to discard them, and thus the disruption of the Aborigines' system of meaning does not even result in a false sense of accumulation of anthropological knowledge.

Vision and destruction

The historical narrative in which the relationship between the colonist and indigene is constructed by the European is remarkably stable, whether it is governed by the myth of the Fall or by an employment of evolutionary science. The Aborigine must, as a race, decrease and be superseded by the colonists – even the Aborigine knows this.

Edmund Kennedy, in Mitchell's party, finds a young Aborigine and an older women he presumes is her mother. The young woman, seeing the explorer, bares her neck and signals for him to chop her head off. Mitchell is silent on what this might imply about the reputation of whites among some Aborigines and concentrates his description on the old woman, who, he understands, is hurling abuse at Kennedy. Mitchell can construct her only in the stereotypical description of the ugly Aborigine. Even though Mitchell is met with a rather severe return gaze, this does not unsettle the explorer. He might have construed her gaze as the scrutiny of an independent subject, who is subjecting him to the same judgemental examination his own gaze does to her. Instead, her gaze is subsumed in the general description of her as a mad harridan. Rather than understanding the woman's fierce looks as indicative of her own thought processes, which were inaccessible to him, Mitchell somewhat suddenly interpolates a symbolic meaning into them: her 'fiendish' eyes were 'flashing fire, as if prophetic of the advent of another race, and the certain failure of her own' (*EITA* 356–57). Her anger at his intrusion is self-servingly transformed into a sign of inevitable decline. The gap between fiery eyes and Mitchell's meaning makes evident the mechanics of this reading. The woman's gaze is not penetrative, but simply a mirror of Mitchell's own desires and drive toward self-justification (see plate 13).

The visual also plays a role in the conventional, contemplative lament to the Aborigine. As Grey explores areas relatively untouched by Europeans, he actually anticipates the Aborigines' alienation from their land. A return to a previously mentioned description is needed to highlight the economy of visual delight which is invoked; only the

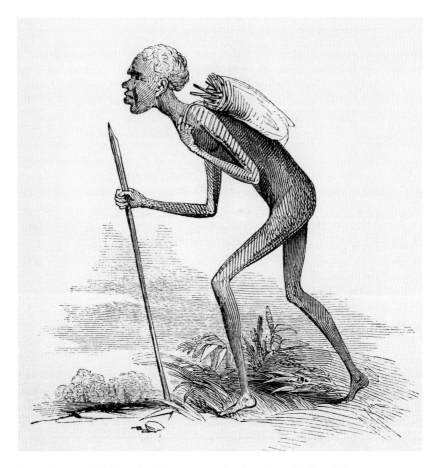

Plate 13 *An Old Aboriginal Woman*; drawing by Mitchell. From Thomas Mitchell, *Expedition into ... Tropical Australia* (p.357). Mitchell Library, State Library of New South Wales.

European, with his aesthetic education, can appreciate the beauty of the land.

> I sat in the fading light, looking at the beautiful scenery around me, which now for the first time gladdened the eyes of Europeans; and I wondered that so fair a land should only be the abode of savage men; and then I thought ... of their anomalous position in so fertile a country, – and wondered how long these things were to be. (Grey 1: 207)

If Grey's elegy does not actually advocate the appropriation of the Aborigines' land, then it certainly does not protest against the possibility.

The close association between visual and economic wealth is seen here. The Aborigines are savages who cannot (it is intimated) appreciate the aesthetic niceties of the land, and this failure of aesthetic sight is also a failure to produce wealth from the earth. Moreover, their position is 'anomalous', a description which places them in the category of all the other antipodean quirks of nature – perversities to be corrected by the European presence.

Mitchell's *Three Expeditions into . . . Eastern Australia* has one illustration which is iconic of this discourse of succession. *Tombs of a Tribe* (see plate 14) is that generically required 'Monarch of all I survey' moment in the exploration journal. The panoramic view afforded by the hill allows investigation with the telescope. Yet, in this illustration the explorer is not a lone figure overlooking the country; he is juxtaposed with the graves of Aborigines who, Mitchell supposes, have been swept away by the smallpox he has observed in the surrounding tribes.

Mitchell's description is an instructive example of the use of the 'melancholic picturesque':

> On this hill, were three large tombs of the natives . . . on each of them were piled numerous withered branches and limbs of trees, no inappropriate emblem of mortality . . . There were no trees on this hill, save one quite dead, which seemed to point, with its hoary arms, like a spectre to the tombs. A

Plate 14   *Tombs of a Tribe*, engraved by G. Barnard after Mitchell's drawing. From Thomas Mitchell, *Three Expeditions into . . . Eastern Australia* (vol. 1, pl.16). Mitchell Library, State Library of New South Wales.

> melancholy waste, where a level country and boundless woods, extended beyond the reach of vision, was in perfect harmony with the dreary foreground of the scene. (*3Ex* 1: 262)

What is left undiscussed, of course, is the source of the smallpox that has taken the lives of the natives. The employment of a picturesque vocabulary directs attention away from the political to the aesthetic, and, like so many of Mitchell's descriptions in particular, the composition becomes more important than the real.

Some descriptions of the Aborigines allow that they have an aesthetic appreciation of the land, and that they resent appropriation of the land because of this aesthetic attachment as well as because it offers them subsistence. It is necessary to quote Giles at some length on this matter to see how sight and destiny are mixed.

> No creatures of the human race could view these scenes with apathy or dislike, nor could any sentient beings part with such a patrimony at any price but that of their blood. But the great Designer of the universe, in the long past periods of creation, permitted a fiat to be recorded, that the beings whom it was His pleasure in the first instance to place amidst these lovely scenes, must eventually be swept from the face of the earth by others more intellectual, more dearly beloved and gifted than they. Progressive improvement is undoubtedly the order of creation, and we perhaps in our turn may be as ruthlessly driven from the earth by another race of yet unknown beings, of an order infinitely higher, infinitely more beloved than we. (Giles 1: 183–84)

The picturesque 'lovely scenes' are aesthetically appreciated by the indigenes, but in Giles's analysis they are really the background to an epic narrative set within a cosmic time-frame.

The imperial narrative's purpose, of course, is to disguise the volition of the colonial enterprise; the individual decisions and desires of the colonists and the colonial governments are reduced by this cosmic determinism to pre-written actions carried out without choice. Giles's explanation transforms a political series of actions to a divinely inspired drama. With this justification in mind he can then dispense with the hypocritical pleas for the Europeans to 'smooth the pillow' for the declining Aborigines. This vicious, racial Darwinism reveals the violence of the imperial project: the indigenes are to be 'swept from the face of the earth' by the Europeans. The de-politicisation of the attempted destruction of the Aborigines is achieved by a shrewd removal of the process from the historic to the cosmic: the Europeans in the distant future may also be 'ruthlessly driven from the earth' as the Aborigines have been. This 'if it happened to you it can happen to me' logic defuses the active political and moral policies being pursued. But perhaps it is also an early case of the fear of decline or invasion of the British Empire.

It was such fears that were evident in *War of the Worlds* by H. G. Wells, who was inspired by the attempted extermination of Tasmanian Aborigines: his Martians are more 'intellectual and gifted', if not 'beloved'. Giles, however, offers himself up as a focus for criticism from those unconvinced by such determinist logic while simultaneously defending himself as the innocent instrument of fate:

> On me, perchance, the eternal obloquy of the execution of God's doom may rest, for being the first to lead the way, with prying eye and trespassing foot, into regions so fair and so remote; but being guiltless alike in act or intention to shed the blood of any human creature, I must accept it without a sigh. (Giles 1: 183–84)

Giles's construction of himself as God's tool is not convincing; but it is interesting that the eye is presented as an intrusive vehicle of knowledge gathering, and one which inevitably leads to the disruption of native ways of life. The 'regions ... fair and remote' are those of an innocent fairy land, their aesthetic value permitting the central melancholy, but stoically accepted 'truth' of the narrative – that the Aborigines are doomed to leave their beautiful, sheltered and unexploited land. Hence, nostalgia is generated for an imagined land and uncorrupted way of life. This nostalgia places Aborigines firmly within the 'past' (as imagined), denies them a place in the present or future, and disguises the real political processes that have caused the destruction of the Aboriginal way of life.

Strzelecki notes that inquiries into the causes of the decrease of Aboriginal populations too often delivered the verdict 'Died by the visitation of God' (Strzelecki 345). Not all explorers accepted the notion that Aboriginal extirpation was divinely intended. Stokes allows that Aboriginal extinction is inevitable and that 'all we can do is to soothe their declining years, to provide that they shall advance gently, surrounded by all the comforts of civilisation, and by all the consolations of religion, to their inevitable doom' (Stokes 2: 470). Like most of the stereotypical formulations anticipating the end of the Aborigines, these recommendations of Stokes eschew any admission that it was the 'comforts' of civilisation that caused the Aborigines' population to decline in the first place. But Stokes disagrees with the belief that the decline of the indigenes is divinely directed.

> Most men seem willing to content themselves with the belief that the event is in accordance with some mysterious dispensation of Providence ... for my own part I am not willing to believe, that in this conflict of races, there is an absence of moral responsibility on the part of the whites; I must deny that it is in obedience to some all-powerful law, the inevitable operation of which exempts us from blame. (Stokes 463–64)

Stokes may be said to be representative of the way many explorers construct Aborigines in their relationship with the Europeans. There is confession of some complicity, but an assumption that the Aborigines in any case are irretrievably doomed. Overall, the attitudes to Aboriginal rights to land are far more complex in journals of exploration than one might expect.

Pastoralism and co-existence

The explorers understood that the pastoral development of the land was harmful to the Aboriginal way of life. In his *Narrative of an Expedition into Central Australia* Charles Sturt acknowledges that the advancing European occupation of the Murray region has a number of deleterious effects upon the Aborigines.

> The more ground our flocks and herds occupy, the more circumscribed become the haunts of the savage. Not only is this the inevitable consequence, but he sees the intruder running down his game with dogs of unequalled strength and swiftness, and deplores the destruction of his means of subsistence. The cattle tread down the herbs which at one season of the year constituted his food. The gun, with its sharp report, drives wild fowl from the creeks, and the unhappy aborigine is driven to despair. He has no country on which to fall back. The next tribe will not permit him to occupy their territory. In such a state what is he to do? (*ECA* 2: 213)

This may be a sympathetic appraisal of the Aborigines' situation but the discussion in which it takes place is riven with contradiction. Sturt offers a justification for Aboriginal resistance, and deals with white violence by constructing two types of settlers. One class is composed of men of 'bold and unscrupulous dispositions, used to crime' (*ECA* 2: 214), who openly provoke violence and hostility. Sturt argues that these men certainly deserve governmentally administered punishment, but says that too often the punishment devolves upon the stockholder, who may well be innocent of all mistreatment. The other class of settlers consists of those who have gone to 'take up stations' in the interior and have 'the honest intention of keeping on good terms with the natives, and who in accordance with such resolution have treated them with hospitality and consideration' (214) but, on being recognised as ordinary mortals by the Aborigines, have been subject to attack. In such cases 'resistance becomes a matter of personal defence' for which 'the [white] parties can hardly be brought to account' (214).

In effect, Sturt is saying that the violence actuated by the establishment of landholdings is justified, whereas certain types of aggression not immediately connected with settling are not. Sturt remarks on the mutually satisfactory 'tranquility' which 'everywhere prevails' and also of the 'whole line' of the Murray being occupied by stations. Yet here, and in his *Two Expeditions into . . . Southern Australia*, he showed how crucial the river was to the Aborigines. The 'tranquility' results from the establishment of Edward Eyre as the Protector of the Aborigines. In Sturt's journal Eyre operates as a *deus ex machina* to the problem of racial violence, and his arrival is 'equally beneficial to the settlers and the Aborigines'.

Paternalism for the poor children of nature

Sturt's celebration of the establishment of a paternalistic relationship with the Aborigines, activating the adult/child stereotype, is reminiscent of the explorers' stock descriptions of Aborigines as children. Grey speaks of the 'children of the desert' (1: 189), Stokes of the 'untutored children of the wilderness' (1: 124) and the Protector himself, Edward Eyre, calls the Aborigines 'children of the wild' (1: 93, 107) It is interesting that two of these descriptions are generated when the Aborigines are invisible to the explorers after Grey and Stokes both find that the Aborigines they wish to describe have disappeared. Perhaps to subsequently construct the Aborigines as children compensates for their threatening intractability to the explorers' sight. Occasionally, the text seems to attempt to deconstruct the stereotype of the childish indigene. Eyre attacks the idea of native as child, writing ironically that:

> I believe were Europeans placed under the same circumstances, equally wronged, and equally shut out from redress, they would not exhibit half the moderation or forbearance that these poor untutored children of impulse have invariably shown. (2: 156)

But Eyre can still write that cheerfulness 'appears usually to be the characteristic of Nature's children' (2: 212).

Sturt compares the Aborigines and the Murray with the Egyptians and the Nile; the periodic flooding of the Murray replenishes 'the poor children of the desert' (*ECA* 1: 9) with fish and fowl. Without this periodic rejuvenation:

> the first navigators of the Murray would not have heard a human voice along its banks; but so it is, that in the wide field of nature, we see the hand of an overruling Providence, evidences of care and protection from some unseen quarter, which strikes the mind with overwhelming conviction. (1: 10)

According to this construction of the Aborigines' relationship with the land, the settler society is surely usurping the divine intentionality inherent in the Aborigines' natural state. The protectorate literally takes the place of God. The explorers justify this in terms of the progressive Christian civilisation. This nevertheless sits uneasily with a notion of the original Aboriginal way of life as divinely intended, except that it can always be justified by the idea of a divinely guided history, wherein the Aborigines are given limited tenure until the arrival of the Europeans.

The actual dispossession of Aborigines is seen as almost cause for sentimental regret by Mitchell and Sturt. Sturt utilises the common notion of a barrier surrounding the desert, which acts as a natural protective device for the Aborigines.

> A veil hung over Central Australia that could neither be pierced or raised. Girt round about by deserts, it almost appeared as if Nature had intentionally closed it upon civilized man, that she might have one domain on the earth's wide field over which the savage might roam in freedom. (*ECA* 2: 2)

Almost, but not quite. The concept of the 'noble savage' still had some currency amongst the explorers, but they were also offering a heroic conquest of the desert, rending the veil by exploration and constraining the Aborigine to the role of a 'protected' people. Mitchell describes the Aborigine in Rousseauesque terms. Aborigines enjoyed 'contentment and happiness, within the precincts of their native woods. Their enjoyment seemed derived so directly from nature, that it almost excited a feeling of regret, that civilized men, enervated by luxury and all its concomitant diseases, should ever disturb the haunts of these rude but happy beings' (*3Ex* 1: 171). The protection of the Aborigines assuages the guilt, and gives them a place within the progressivist historical narrative, in which, Mitchell believes, the process of settlement is embedded. He rapturously praises the aesthetic improvement produced by 'British enterprise and industry' (*3Ex* 1: 160) and predicts future expansion into areas 'as yet unpeopled, save by the wandering aborigines, who may then, as at Bathurst now, enjoy that security and protection, to which they have so just a claim' (*3Ex* 1: 160). As Sturt puts it, their 'fancied right' (*ECA* 2: 213) to possession of the land disappears, but their right to 'security and protection' remains.

The paternalism that Eyre's protectorate practised was foreshadowed by earlier explorers. Mitchell had previously taken an Aboriginal girl, Ballandella, into his care after she had her leg broken by one of the drays. Mitchell writes that Ballandella is already acculturated to European ways by her acquaintance with the exploration party to such an extent that her 'mother at length despaired of being ever able to initiate her thoroughly into the mysteries of killing and eating snakes, lizards, rats, and similar food' (*3Ex* 2: 266). This self-serving description of the 'irreversibility' of Ballandella's cultural alteration justifies Mitchell's taking her to Sydney. So, too, does his report of the mother's opinion that, as she could see how 'much more her sex was respected by civilized men than savages', Ballandella would be better served by staying with the explorers. The true nature of Mitchell's stewardship can be seen by his analysis of the usefulness of the Aborigines in the same volume. He concludes his discussion of the ability of the Aborigine to 'progress' under European supervision by stating that 'my experiment with the little native girl, Ballandella, will be useful, I trust, in developing hereafter, the mental energies of the Australian aborigines' (*3Ex* 2: 352). In the *Journal of an Expedition into Tropical Australia* Ballandella again appears as a useful experimental subject, this time in the field of animal husbandry.

> It has long been a favourite project with me, to educate an aboriginal native, as a husband for Ballandella, and that their children should form, at least, one civilized family of the native race, upon which the influence of education and religious principles might be fairly tried. This has never yet been done, although the experiment is of much interest. (*EITA* 416)

The experimentation requires, at first, the forceful separation of the subject from her tribe and home, and then her mating, for the knowledge-reward of the explorer.

The knowledge gained about the Aborigines is not through a detached observation, but by invasive and even violent measures. And the knowledge itself is not acquired for the satiation of curiosity but for its use-value. An understanding of their 'circumstances and habits' (Eyre 2: 481) is important only insofar as it enables the effective management of the Aborigine: one can best dominate if one understands the social mechanics of the dominated and exploits this knowledge. Thus, under the heading 'Suggestions for the Improvement of the Aborigines', Eyre argues that the most important strategy of the colonist is to 'gain such an influence or Authority over the Aborigines as may be sufficient to allow us to induce them to adopt, or submit to any regulations that we make for their improvement, and that to effect this, the means must be suited to their circumstances and habits' (Eyre 2: 480–81). The knowledge is gained under conditions of domination – 'my wishes became their law' (2: 149), says Eyre – and reproduced so that Eyre's practices may be continued elsewhere.

Proper knowledge allows effective management, and this opens the possibility of the indigene being used as labourer to further colonial aims. Stokes notes that the indigenes 'individually appear peaceable, inoffensive, and well-disposed, and, under proper management, make

very good servants'; one man in particular shows natural talent as a
waiter (1: 58). More often than not, however, Aborigines resist interpellation into an economics of labour and reward. King recounts
Dampier's difficulty in finding good help on the west Australian coast.
(Dampier writes):

> We put [clothes] on them, thinking that this finery would have brought them
> to work heartily for us ... [we] put a barrel on each of their shoulders for
> them to carry to the canoe. But all the signs we could make were to no
> purpose, for they stood like statues, without motion, but grinned like so many
> monkeys, staring one upon another; for the poor creatures seem not
> accustomed to carry burthens ... so we were forced to carry our water
> ourselves, and they very fairly put the clothes off again ... I did not perceive
> that they have any great liking to them at first, neither did they seem to admire
> any thing we had. (Dampier, quoted in King 2: 101)

The explorer's failure to call the Aborigines into existence as labourers is
a failure of self-identification. The Aborigines are supposed to be conditioned to a helpful subservience to the master and his wishes and the
explorer defines his position by the Aboriginal reaction to his commands. The inability of the explorer to recreate the European divisions
of class and labour emerges as a threat to self-definition. The proposed
separation of explorer–employer and Aborigine–labourer collapses to a
point where the explorer himself has to undertake the work. That the
Aborigines do not work is not a refusal to labour; more disturbingly to
Dampier, is an incomprehension of what constitutes labour. A straight-
forward refusal to work would leave the concepts of labour and its
appropriate divisions across class intact, but the Aborigines' reaction
identifies their culture as one where labour itself seems not to exist. That
they do not covet the goods of the explorer is a double disappointment,
as it removes the leverage necessary to encourage their labour.

The process of exploration depended heavily on the advice and effort
of Aborigines. The journal of John and Alexander Forrest includes
newspaper reports of the various receptions given to the brothers, and
of the general recognition given to Aboriginal service. The Reverend
J. G. Wright, it is reported, proposing the health of Alexander Forrest,
was 'glad to see that the original holders of the land ... had been
employed in the work of exploration and opening up the country'
(Forrest 273). During the actual exploration itself there is the expectation that the Aborigines who accompany the explorers are virtually
indentured labourers. This expectation is applied even to those who are
not members of the original company but have voluntarily joined along
the way, such as three Aborigines who met with Forrest's party and

directed them. Their departure is portrayed in the journal as a betrayal, Forrest writing that 'the three natives ran away this morning, or at least left us without asking leave' (170). What loyalty is owed to the explorer is not explained; but, as we have seen, Aborigines are 'naturally' treacherous, so the question of loyalty never needs to be raised.

The promise of white protection for the Aborigines acts as a lubricant for the articulation of two constructions which would otherwise conflict. The Aborigines are placed within a strict biological hierarchy, immovably positioned within a great chain of being. As inherently inferior to the white settlers, they are 'naturally' displaced by a 'superior' culture. But they are also seen as undeveloped or 'uncultivated', and thus may be educated, civilised and generally improved. The idea of white protection offers the contradiction of changing a naturally structured and un-changeable order. At the same time, however, it promises an infinitely prolonged mission of education, in the course of which indigenes may be removed from their way of life and 'civilized' but not to the extent of ever threatening the ineradicable superiority of the white culture.

Mitchell's journal advances a strongly progressivist notion of history. The Bible is seen as the 'early history of mankind' and Aboriginal practices are compared to those of the biblical ancients (*3Ex* 1: 246 & 2: 81, 105, 153–54, 343–44, 346). Occasionally, the behaviour of the Aborigines is called upon to illustrate Holy Writ (*3Ex* 2: 347). Pre-Darwinian evolution places the Aborigine as roughly equivalent in development to the ancient people the Bible describes, and also opens the way for a white educative mission. Mitchell, as I have mentioned, wonders what might be 'the effect of education upon one of that race' if they could be separated from the Aboriginal culture (*3Ex* 2: 163); Sturt encourages the separation of children from their parents (*ECA* 2: 284). The possibility of development that the explorers advance does not always sit well with the hierarchical construction of the Aborigines. Sturt embodies the tension succinctly when he says that 'they are a people, at present, at the very bottom of the scale of humanity' (*3Ex* 2: 107). 'At present' offers the hope of improvement carried out under white care, but the civilising mission will mean removal of the Aborigines from their culture and their land. This vicious urge towards monoculturism is expressed, perhaps surprisingly, in Grey's journal, which otherwise embodies tendencies towards sympathy with the indigenes.

> With the wizard wand of commerce, he touches a lone and trackless forest, and at his bidding, cities arise, and the hum and dust of trade collect – away are swept ancient races; antique laws and customs moulder into oblivion … the Gospel is preached amongst ignorant and savage men … the tongue of England alone is heard … (Grey 2: 200–01)

Not only does 'improvement' necessitate removing Aborigines from their culture and land, it is also a linguistic refashioning, where English is triumphant, and even obligatory.

However, this regularisation of the indigenes via language is resisted. Mitchell's *Expedition into ... Tropical Australia* notes two females, neither of whom had any covering, 'but the younger wore, by way of ornament, a page of last year's Nautical Almanac, suspended by a cord from her neck' (*EITA* 358). The transformation of the authoritative book to a garment, the decontextualisation of the text, is an Aboriginal appropriation of a European artifact. The explorers had appropriated stones, spears, and rituals for insertion into ethnographical systems of meaning, thus altering their meaning from cultural work or practice to an object of knowledge – a 'native artifact'. Here, in just the same way, the page has been taken into another system of meaning, and its inherent 'authority' as knowledge undermined. The discursive contestation that the Aborigines offer in the journals is the subject of the next section.

'Look at them Sir! Look at them!'

Resistances to colonial discourses of Aboriginality

An examination of the exploration texts' stereotyping of the Aborigine offers no obvious point of resistance. One may deny the truth of the stereotypes; however, this rejection is not a textual practice but a social response. As Homi Bhabha has pointed out, to 'judge the stereotyped image on the basis of a prior political normativity is to dismiss it, not to displace it'.[13] Bhabha develops space for resistance by denying Said's suggestion that colonial power and discourse are always possessed by the coloniser, instead claiming that there is an inherent ambivalence in colonial texts. Working from the Derridean concept of *différance*, where all signifying elements refer necessarily to other, and absent, signs, Bhabha locates the construction of binary opposites as an operation of the repression of ambivalence within the seemingly unitary sign. This point for resistance he finds is not purely a post-structuralist textual aporia, a point from where all texts may be said to offer deconstructive interpretations of themselves; rather, it is thoroughly grounded in the political dynamics of the colonising moment.

In 'Signs Taken for Wonders', Bhabha charts how hybridisation of the Bible actually creates a readership which interrogates the text according to a specific cultural agenda which undermines the supposed alignment between God and Britain, and the Book and Authority.[14] There was no large-scale plan to reproduce colonial institutions in Australia under indigenous control, as there was in India; so Bhabha's notions of hybridisation and the deconstructive practice of 'mimicry' must be adapted. The Aborigines do not reveal the ambiguity of colonial authority through their culturally specific adaptations of texts, but through their responses to the practice of exploration itself. They constantly refuse to be interpellated as the helpful and subservient native guide, nor do they inevitably fall into the opposite category of the implacable savage.

The Aboriginal resistance to exploration takes place through control of local knowledge, and the invariably agonistic interchange of that information with the explorer. Rather than simply being sources of information, Aborigines are textually constructed as truth-tellers, liars, prevaricators, storytellers and advisors. But the boundaries of these categories shift so rapidly that stereotypical trapping becomes impossible, and the uncertainty with which the information is evaluated deconstructs the explorers' claim to have made the indigene knowable. Bhabha's account of hybridity and mimicry is useful because the Aborigines accompanying the exploration party reproduce, alter and often interrogate exploration practices, thus demonstrating the cultural specificity and limitations of these practices, as well as the flaws in their claim to superiority. Undoubtedly, violent action against the explorers is a form of Aboriginal resistance, but it is a kind which is easily categoris-able as a result of the inherent bloodthirstiness of the savage. What is less violent but more disturbing is the way that European rules of recognition are revealed and displaced by native ones.

Exchanging language

The episodes where the explorer and Aborigine communicate are par-ticularly interesting in their capacity for destabilisation. These en-counters may seem to offer an opportunity for an Aboriginal voice to emerge, testing and perhaps even deconstructing the presuppositions at the foundations of exploratory discourse. Optimistic as such a reading might be, it is usually misleading; the explorer rarely relinquishes direct control of the text, but constructs the dialogues in purely European terms. When the dialogue does threaten to evade the explorer's control, the threat of violence will often appear. An illustration of this can be found in Giles's *Australia Twice Traversed*, where the author is receiving what he concludes is a severe criticism from an Aborigine who:

> poured out the vials of his wrath upon us, as he probably thought to some purpose. I was not linguist enough to translate all that he said; but I am sure my free interpretation of the gist of his remarks is correct, for he undoubtedly stigmatised us as a vile and useless set of lazy, crawling, white-faced wretches,

> who came sitting on hideous brutes of hippogryphs, being too lazy to walk like
> black men, and took upon ourselves to occupy any country or waters we might
> chance to find ... depriving him and his friends of their natural, lawful food
> ... It appeared to me that his harangue required punctuation, so I showed
> him the rifle again, whereupon he incontinently indulged in a full stop. (Giles
> 1: 250–51)

The speech act of the Aborigine promises to reduce Giles into a term
within the indigene's discourse; Giles may become a 'thing' to the
Aborigine just as the Aborigine is an object to him. Rather than allow the
Aborigine to possess a subjectivity of his own, which would potentially
position the explorer himself as something to be evaluated and judged,
the discourse is neutralised, by being interpreted by Giles. His 'free
interpretation' annuls the threatening unknownness of the speech,
reducing it to a set of discrete complaints which represent the European
view of the Aboriginal mind. The speech, then, is simply an opportunity
for projection onto the Aborigine of the European expectation of
indigenous grievances. Some of these, such as the complaint of the
whites being too lazy to walk, are the result of the Aborigines' small-
minded provincialism; others, such as the charge of theft of land, are
more significant. Despite this effective neutralising of the speech act's
meaning, the harangue itself continues, and Giles emerges as the
linguistic regulator who supplies 'punctuation' for the indigene's unruly
language. The Aborigine is reduced to silence. This state is the most
useful one from the explorer's point of view, as he is no longer being
discursively challenged. The explorer's subjectivity is now secure, as is his
identity: by the violence of the gun he is returned as the speaking being
whose monologic pronouncements are unchallenged.

The initial difficulty in any cross-cultural communication, of course, is
linguistic. After noting that Aboriginal words appropriated into English
often mean 'what do you mean' or 'I do not understand' in the original
dialect, Stokes elucidates the importance of correct translation in
explorer–Aborigine communication. Talking about knowing Aboriginal
words, Stokes writes that 'the satisfaction is mutual – there is at once a
sympathetic link between you – you no longer appear as thorough
strangers to each other, and this slight knowledge of their dialect may
often be the means of making useful acquaintances' (Stokes 2: 25). The
importance of translation is that it allows the use of the Aborigine;
communication between the explorer and Aborigine in the journals is
often for pragmatic ends, which benefit the explorer. But this very
dependence opens up a space in the journals, where the Aborigines no
longer exist as subservient creatures, intellectually and morally back-
ward, but are far superior, and are recognised to be so, by the Europeans.
Stokes again stresses the utility of communicating with the indigenes

when he writes that, from the Aborigines 'we must always calculate on learning much that is useful and valuable, with regard to productions of the country; a knowledge that would otherwise consume much time to acquire' (1: 400). Gosse virtually admits that Aboriginal help saved his life (19).

When Sturt questions the Aborigines of the Murray river about the sea 'by pointing to the sky, and by other signs' (*2Ex* 2: 139) and they fail to answer him satisfactorily, their mental capabilities are again denigrated: they are a 'stupid people' who 'could not, or would not, give any information on the subject' (139). Sturt's universalist assumptions about sign language are what is immediately at fault, but the Aborigines' supposed reluctance or inability to give any information could well result, not from 'stupidity', but from there being a legitimate limit to their geographical knowledge. It also, however, opens the possibility that their failure to answer is a strategic withholding of information, and this possibility underlines the reliance of the explorers on the Aborigines and undermines the explorers' claims to inherent superiority. Sturt's condemnation of the Aborigines' stupidity is, in any case, a remarkable piece of intellectual hypocrisy since he had been involved previously in a communication wherein the Aborigines were willing to give him directions but he could not understand them.

> The natives, in attempting to answer my interrogatories, only perplexed me more and more. They evidently wished to explain something, by placing a number of sticks across each other as a kind of diagram of the country. It was, however, impossible to arrive at their meaning ... there was something more that they were anxious to explain, which I could not comprehend. The poor fellows seemed quite disappointed ... (*2Ex* 2: 101)

Other failures of communication are also made the fault of the Aborigines. Sturt complains that they 'evinced a strange perversity, or obstinacy rather, in repeating words, although it was evident that they knew they were meant as questions' (*2Ex* 1: 106). How the Aborigines 'knew' that they were meant as questions is unclear – perhaps Sturt expected the rising inflexion to be a universal signal of an interrogative.

Failing to harness Aboriginal skills

The dependency of the explorer on linguistic intermediaries loosens their control over the dialogues with the Aborigines. In a reverse of the racist construction of foreigners as people who can understand English if they really want to, Sturt and most other explorers believe that an Aboriginal translator can understand dialects of 'Aboriginal'. This linguistic homogenisation means that the Aboriginal translator has an advantage over his explorer master, as Sturt realises. Sturt's party 'surprises' six indigenes, and his translator talks to them: 'My boy understood them well; but the young savage had the cunning to hide the information they gave him, or, for aught I know, to ask questions that best suited his own purposes, and therefore we gained little intelligence from them' (*2Ex* 2: 43).

The power that is with the Aborigines in these meetings is emphasised even when there is attempted coercion on the part of the explorer. Warburton, having observed Aboriginal wells, initiates the practice of digging for water in the desert. Digging is the 'key of the country'; a metaphor that not only positions the land as locked, but locked from Europeans until they adopt Aboriginal methods. Warburton finds that, unlike the operation of a key, well-digging needs a particular skill and knowledge which he does not possess, and admits that out of forty-nine attempts at finding water only one was successful (180). Unable to find water of their own, such explorers in the desert frequently relied upon Aboriginal wells. In such a landscape, however, there is no visual sign that a well exists: sight, the central method of knowledge-gathering is rendered useless by the flatness of the land. Explorers then have to rely upon Aboriginal knowledge. Warburton was especially enamoured of capturing Aborigines and forcing them to show him where the native wells were, a strategy he constructs as a moment for celebration.

> We had captured a young native woman; this was considered a great triumph of art, as the blacks all avoided us as though we were plague-stricken. We kept her a close prisoner, intending that she should point out native wells to us. (Warburton 206)

The explorers, of course, *were* plague-stricken to the Aborigines, but Warburton's actions explain why the indigenes chose to keep out of his way. The need of explorers for interpreters of the land is an implicit empowering of the Aborigines in the process of exploration. But the paradigmatic constructions of Aborigines return to ensure that this power is only an illusionary one. Thus, they are not really more skilled than the European, but, being closer to the animals, their instinctive faculties are relatively more developed. So, the editor of Warburton's journal notes about the ability of the Aborigines to find water that 'it is curious to speculate on the instinct that enables the degraded inhabitants of this wilderness to find the few spots where the precious element is obtainable' (Warburton 179–80). The European may rank the Aborigine in comparison to himself, but hierarchisation can always backfire. The editor is forced to admit the Aborigine has the advantage over the European 'in this respect'; it is the advantage of instinct, however, rather than of culture or learning.

Warburton's capturing of Aborigines is at once a demonstration of power, and an admission of ignorance and, thus, a lack of power. Warburton secures another indigene after the first one escapes.

> Not far, however, from the camp a howling, hideous old hag was captured, and, warned by the former escape, we secured this old witch by tying her thumbs behind her back, and haltering her by the neck to a tree. (Warburton 208)

The dehumanising rhetoric Warburton employs may be a strategy to ward off complaints that perhaps this treatment was a little harsh. But it provides him with something of an excuse for what happens – the woman's malignity being an innate property rather than a response to his treatment of her.

> We let the old witch go. She was the most alarming specimen of a woman I ever saw; she had been of no use to us, and her sex alone saved her from punishment, for under pretense of leading us to some native wells, she took us backwards and forwards over heavy sandhills, exhausting the camels as well as my small stock of patience. The well we found was in the opposite direction to the one she was taking us to. (Warburton 208)

Warburton's recourse to forced servitude results in his looking rather foolish. The attempt to portray the woman as a fiend is not successful, especially in the context of his treatment of her. Instead, the strategic superiority of the Aborigine is displayed. The presentation of the woman as witch, allows the remarkable absence of the intuition of Aboriginal motivations here: since witches are known to be inherently malign, their thoughts do not need explication. This strategy allows avoidance of discussion of the woman's actions as revenge for how she had been treated. Such a discussion would have raised questions concerning the justice of the cruel treatment of indigenes; more importantly, it would have conferred upon the woman a subjectivity of her own as a thinking human being capable of reducing the explorer to her terms, and judging him according to her system of value. A similar situation arises when the Aborigines respond to the consumption of water by Stuart's horses. Surprised by how much water horses use, they 'would go no further with us, nor show us any more, and, in a short time after, left us' (Stuart 87). Again, there is the refusal to treat the Aborigines as a group making strategic decisions. It also avoids an analysis of their cessation of help as a response to the explorer's political presence as a consumer of scarce resources.

Warburton's practice of capturing Aborigines can hardly be said to be a mode of mutual communication. The Aborigine is forced into communication; even if she is the victor in strategic terms, she cannot be said to be the controller of the interchange. There are several occasions when the presumed communicative mastery of the explorer gives way to the Aborigine's control. Forrest records one occasion when 'one native told us not to sleep here, but to go away and not return, or the natives would kill and eat us, after which he turned away as if he did not wish to have any more words with us' (39). Here, the Aborigine not only controls the course of the discussion but also its cessation. There is some general awareness amongst explorers that complex speech protocols govern Aboriginal interlocutions, and that their attempts to communicate violate these codes. The silence of an Aborigine is at times a demonstration of the strength of these codes, as well as of the fact that dialogues are interdependent and cannot be forced unilaterally. An Aborigine's silence, however, is more often constructed as the result of timidity and fear than as an alterior mode of social interaction.

Uncertain truths

The most destabilising moment of communication for the explorer comes when he is trying to decide the use-value of the information given to him. The stereotype of the native as a naturally accomplished liar interferes with the easy acceptance of the information as valid. Leichhardt presents himself as a keen student of Aboriginal wiles, and argues that one may sift the truth from deceit simply by a careful examination of the Aborigine. Since it is important for the information to be collected by specular means, the dependence on Aboriginal knowledge threatens the dominant exercise of sight as information gatherer. Leichhardt's theory of close examination of the interlocutor guarantees sight's return to primacy. Frequent intercourse with the Aborigines, says Leichhardt: 'had taught me to distinguish between the smooth tongue of deceit, with which they try to ensnare their victim, and the open expression of kind and friendly feelings, or those of confidence and respect'. Leichhardt writes that he remembers:

> several instances of the most cold-blooded smooth-tongued treachery ... but I am sure that a careful observer is more than a match for these simple children of nature, and that he can easily read the bad intention in their unsteady, greedy, glistening eyes. (Leichhardt 506–07)

The return gaze of the Aborigine does not allow him a subjectivity; rather, it is a sheet that may be read to reveal his innermost intentions. In this way the gaze of the Aborigine is both transparent and a *tabula rasa*: it is a window of the soul, but also a site (sight) of projection, which displays everything the explorer already knows about the untrustworthiness of the indigene. Leichhardt does not valorise veracity so highly as to be averse to lying himself. He notes that the 'natives consider our animals to be large dogs, and had frequently asked whether they would bite (which I affirmed, of course); so that they themselves furnished us with protection' (340). Leichhardt admits the strategic use of untruths to his own communicative practice, but once the Aborigines are perceived by him to do the same they are treacherous and liars by habit. There is a deeper problem with the explorers' search for accuracy in the statements of Aborigines, however, besides the interfering stereotype of Aborigine as liar.

The knowledge that the Aborigines transmit is often encapsulated in narrative form, but Aboriginal storytelling does not seem to valorise 'facts' above the social value of the story. When explorers attempt to use these narratives, then, their interpretations are never entirely successful and the information gained is of questionable worth. The difficulty of finding veracious ethnographic information from informants who do not obey the same rules of mimetic reporting is realised to be a serious hindrance. Leichhardt attempts to find out why Aborigines break the wings of emus after capture and he is told it is to prevent their escape. Expressing puzzlement at this, he is told by his Aboriginal companion, Brown, that 'Blackfellow knows better than white fellow', and Brown then recites a narrative of how this procedure came into being. The fact that narrative is used to transmit knowledge confuses Leichhardt – although, ironically, an exploration journal itself uses a similar mode. Leichhardt eventually does not gain any usable information from Brown's narrative but can only conclude that the story was 'very probably one of Brown's yarns, made up for the occasion' (360–01). The uncertainty that Aboriginal narratives engender gives them a power that either recognisable veracity or untruth would not. Promising useful information, containing suggestive but ultimately incomplete and puzzling explanations, they force the explorer into the role of an inadequate interpreter, and reveal that there is a world of alternative signification and information transmission that is only partially open to Europeans. The closure of this threatening alterity can only be by valorising a particular kind of mimetic truth, and criticising its absence in Aboriginal discourse.

The suggestion that the Aborigines have no concept of truth is frequently found in the journals. On hearing that the Aborigines of a particular area have cried 'very much' when learning of his supposed death, Forrest reflects that Aboriginal stories are usually the products of exaggeration (Forrest 64) and criticises the value of the information given him (69, 70). Leichhardt's observation that Brown made up the story for the occasion also opens the possibility that the information is given as a social lubricant. Stokes inquires of Aborigines on the western coast about an inland source of water and finds that the answer, if interpreted as an accurate representation of the actuality, means that the Aborigines must have a much larger geographical knowledge than usually suspected.

> Their notions of distance are, to say the least, exceedingly rude; with them every thing is 'far away, far away.' The size of this water the natives describe by saying, that if a boy commenced walking around it, by the time he finished his task he would have become an old man! After all may not this be the great Australian Bight ... (Stokes 1: 51–52)

In attempting to find the 'reality' behind the story, Stokes eschews questions about the narrative being produced as a reaction to his presence. In most interlocution the question of the explorer's effect on the dialogue is forgotten; the possibility that the Aborigines are using narrative as a passive weapon against the explorer's intrusion is not considered.

The problem with how to treat Aboriginal narrative was that it could never be completely dismissed as a source of geographical information. It was clear that much Aboriginal information was encoded as narrative – sometimes a general social story or occasionally a private narrative. Giles marvels at how 'Jimmy' navigates through an area he has not visited since childhood without devices for fixing position, but he himself provides the answer to how the Aborigine was able to find his way. He writes that:

> in the course of a mile or so he would stop at a tree, and tell us that when a little boy he got a 'possum out of a hole which existed in it. At another place he said his mother was bitten by a wild dog, which she was digging out of a hole in the ground. (Giles 2: 101)

Giles nevertheless ignores the possibility that it is the narrative preservation of knowledge which allows the Aborigine to range over land and recognise it. The Aborigine's narrative-as-information – representing, as it does, an alterior system of knowledge preservation – operates as a disruption of the general logocentricity of the explorer's journal. Aboriginal narratives are frequently counter-discursively present in the journals, not only undermining the explorers' general claim to superior knowledge but revealing their ignorance of Aboriginal methods. Giles laughs at a young Aborigine's story about a giant serpent, but wonders how certain geographical elements of the story are known to the teller: 'Another thing was rather strange, and that was, how these coast natives should know there was any mountains to the north of them. I knew it,

because I had been there and found them ...' (Giles 2: 77). The
superiority of European empiricism, the will to see and therefore know
an object, is not demonstrated; instead, alterior possibilities are shown to
exist in the form of narrative. Giles's puzzlement shifts the balance of
power in the exchange; the containment of the Aboriginal narrative as a
ludicrous fantasy fails and provides space for the story to be construed as
opaque, mysterious, and yet ultimately valuable as information. The
Aboriginal narrative's resistance to being reduced to knowable object or
practice renders it a counter-discourse. It becomes a critique of European knowledge-gathering and retention, but one that, because of the
information it contains, cannot be dismissed out of hand.

Disruptive dialogues

The resistance of the Aborigine to interpellation as the simple native
informant is present in many dialogic encounters. As I have shown,
requests by explorers for information are not universally met with the
meek replies of the grateful native, but rather with counter-questions,
silence or linguistic confusion. The Aboriginal habit of mimicry was most
disturbing to the explorers' attempts to initiate dialogue that would be
helpful to them. Attempts to construct the natives in text and practice as
tractable to the linguistic desires of the Europeans fail utterly in the face
of this mirror stance. Gregory adopts the Western Australian 'York
dialect' to communicate with inland Aborigines in the belief that some
Aboriginal language is better than none. This homogenising of
Aboriginal language is met with a disruptive response that destroys any
possibility of an exchange useful to the explorers. Gregory writes that 'as
they seemed to prefer mimicking our attempts to speak the York dialect
to using their own, we could not obtain much information' (23).

Other dialogic episodes are framed in such a way as to prevent the
disruptiveness of the native speech. In Grey's *Journals* of his Western
Australian expeditions there is a long dialogue between Grey and the
Aborigine, Imbat, on the value of exploration. The text attempts to
frame the otherness of an Aboriginal system of values, by constructing
these values as homely, and ultimately the product of ignorance. The
importance Imbat places on being fat is another curiosity of the native
way of life, and the native himself can understand nothing of the
European desire to travel and conquer. Grey, 'worn out from fatigue ...
petulant and ill-tempered' (2: 92), is questioned by Imbat.

'What for do you who have plenty to eat, and much money, walk so far away in
the bush?' I felt amazingly annoyed at this question, and therefore did not
answer him. 'You are thin,' said he, 'your shanks are long, your belly is small

– you had plenty to eat at home, why did you not stop there?' I was vexed at his personalities, besides which it is impossible to make a native understand our love of travel – I therefore replied – 'Imbat, you comprehend nothing – you know nothing.' – 'I know nothing!' answered he; 'I know how to keep myself fat; the young women look at me and say, Imbat is very handsome, he is fat – they will look at you and say, He not good – long legs – what do you know? where is your fat? what for do you know so much, if you can't keep fat? I know how to stay at home, and not to walk too far in the bush – where is your fat?' 'You know how to talk; – long tongue;' was my reply; upon which Imbat, forgetting his anger, burst into a roar of laughter, and saying, 'and I know how to make you fat,' – began stuffing me with frogs, barde, and by-yu nuts. (Grey 2: 93)

Grey's description, typically, is unusual. Here, the explorer is decidedly on the losing end of the argument, and the wisdom of the Aborigine is displayed. But the Aborigine's discourse wins over Grey's only because it is parochial; the reader can see that the Aborigine's reasoning has clear cultural limits, and that, in the end, it is the explorer's wisdom and understanding which must be acknowledged. On one level, then, the possible threat of the Aboriginal discourse is neutralised. Imbat's association of fat and knowledge, and Grey's reaction to his questioning, however, allow space for the dialogue to emerge as a counter-discourse deconstructing the explorer's rationale. Grey's geographical knowledge may be greater than Imbat's, yet the indigene is able to construct Grey as ignorant of the everyday knowledge of the Aborigine, which is necessary for comfortable inhabitance of the country. Grey's reaction to Imbat's questioning – he was 'amazingly annoyed' – reveals the Aborigine's query to be an effective undermining of the basic precepts of exploration. Grey's reply can only be an abusive attempt to silence his interrogator by a charge of ignorance, which immediately collapses.

  Not all of the Aboriginal counter-discourses are found in the form of a combative dialogue. Leichhardt encounters a different form of mimicry when an Aboriginal appropriation of music, rather than language, is used to question the rationale of exploration.

Brown had, either by accident, or influenced by an unconscious feeling of melancholy, fallen into the habit of almost constantly whistling and humming the soldier's death march, which had such a singularly depressing effect on my feelings, I was frequently constrained to request him to change his tune. (Leichhardt 439)

What is most notable about this description (besides Brown's sense of humour) is Leichhardt's refusal to acknowledge that the whistling could have been in any sense deliberate. It is either accidental or unconscious, but it cannot be an intentional appropriation of a European code adopted and used as an interventionary discourse.

Mimicry and Aboriginal surveillance

Mimicry by the Aborigines is proof of their surveillance of the exploration parties. Early encounters with the Aborigines led to the characterisation of their sight as poor: the *History of New Holland* says that they had such bad eyes that they could not see others until they were very near.[15] Later explorers, however, admitted the power of Aboriginal sight. Mitchell argues for the superiority of the visual as well as judgemental abilities of the Aborigines, writing that 'they have been described as the lowest in the scale of humanity, yet I found those who accompanied me superior in penetration and judgement to the white men who accompanied my party' (*EITA* 412).

Aboriginal sight can also be turned towards the explorers themselves, of course. Yuranigh, an Aborigine who accompanied Mitchell, 'well knew the character of all the white men of the party. Nothing escaped his penetrating eye and quick ear.' (*EITA* 414). Sight as a 'penetration' of the land is, as we have seen, a trope explorers use for their own powers of sight, but here its subject is the exploration party, and the perspicacity is the Aborigine's. Sight is constructed as a violent invasion of what is seen, and the admission that the Aborigine has this power to visually invade the party accords Yuranigh a subjectivity and power rarely given to any indigene. Indeed, the threat that mimicry possesses in parodying the actions of the explorers is raised and dealt with a number of times in the journals. Mitchell writes of an Aborigine who amused 'the men occasionally – by enacting their leader, taking angles, drawing from nature, &c.' (*3Ex* 2: 277). The containment of this parody comes through the ethnographic observations of the Aborigine as keen observer and excellent mimic, and of the construction of the explorer as hearty enough to take the mimicking in good humour and to report it in his journal. But parodic mimicking reduces Mitchell into a term in the Aborigine's discourse; he becomes a figure who has been observed and judged an appropriate object of ridicule.

Even if the Aborigine's parody of the practice of exploration is construed as a result of her ignorance of its importance, the explorer is not a mysterious figure whom the Aborigines possess no means of signifying, rather he becomes a term within a system. Stuart vigorously attempts to guard himself against just such a fate, describing a similar situation.

> He imitated every movement we made, and burlesqued them to a very high degree, causing great laughter to his companions and us. He seems to be the buffoon of the tribe. The other natives delighted in making sport of him, by ridiculing the shortness of his stature and laughing at him behind his back. (Stuart 434)

The imperative in this description, of course, is to reduce the imitator to the status of 'buffoon' and thereby reduce the significance of his actions. The mimicry, as was the case with Mitchell, is a result of close observation. The great powers of sight explorers credited the Aborigines with are thus turned against the explorers in what is, in effect, a display of power: mimicry is the best possible method of indicating that the explorers are subject to Aboriginal surveillance.

The threat that the perspicacity of the Aborigine represents is dealt with via the two vectors of othering. First, the keen sight of the indigene is presented as another instinctive attribute of the savage, like direction-finding or hunting skills. Second, it resembles the sight of the explorer as prescribed in his instructions (for example, Sturt *2Ex* 2: 187), absorbing a multitude of detail. Stokes describes the observing gaze of Miago, writing that 'he watched everything, aye, every bush, with the most scrutinizing gaze: his head appeared to turn upon a pivot, so constantly was it in motion, with all that restless watchfulness for which the savage is ever remarkable' (Stokes 1: 78). The explorer's gaze is ultimately different from that of the 'savage', because he records the information gathered by sight, adding to a growing catalogue of knowledge, whereas the Aboriginal gaze is understood as only immediately useful. But Aboriginal sight emerges as a challenge even to the practices and tools of exploration; significantly, though, this occurs in the work of Lancelot Threlkeld, travelling missionary, rather than in the journal of an explorer. 'The local maps', Threlkeld writes:

> which are obtained directly or indirectly from the Colonial Surveyors, have very few natural boundaries laid down, for the guidance of a stranger; and the compass, is a very uncertain benefit, when standing on the margin of an extensive morass, or when fixed in the dilemma of a thicket. But the blacks, with a perspicacity of vision which appears almost preternatural, track footsteps over bare rocks, and in the darkest or most infrequent parts of the forest.[16]

The Aboriginal vision matches, and indeed is superior to, the cartographic technology of the Europeans. The perspicacity of the Aborigines is not compared with mapping in the exploration journals; rather, there, a fierce competition takes place between Aboriginal and European visual power.

The resistance of the Aborigines to the surveillance of the explorers is disguised by the invocation of the stereotype of the 'timid' native. Exploration instructions specifically demand that close observation of the indigene be undertaken, and timidity provides an excuse for the explorer's failure to achieve this. King apologises for the fact that he has seen no Aborigines, admitting that 'it is probable that they were not

ignorant of our presence, but from timidity intentionally avoided us'
(28). The construction of the indigene as inherently timid is useful for
the explorer, serving the double function of disguising Aboriginal
resistance to the explorer's intrusive gaze, and also providing an excuse
for his failure to collect ethnographic information. It is also interesting as
a case of the crude state of ethnography in the journals. The widespread
Aboriginal custom of averting the gaze from recently met people is read
as timidity; but Aboriginal timidity was a widespread trope used outside
exploration journals.

George Morgan's prize-winning poem 'Settlers in Australia' utilised
the desire of the indigene to be hidden from view, with the
characterisation of the return gaze as weak, to provide material for a
general condemnation of the Aborigine.

> And who is he who from the settler's gate
> Now timorous shrinks and now returns to wait;
> Whose narrow brow and vacant eye declare
> How faint the gleam of mind reflected there;
> Wild are his ways, unlike the ways of men,
> Child of the woods, Australia's denizen.[17]

Retiring from the explorer's, or in this case, the settler's sight is interpreted as a sign of weakness of intelligence. Morgan is also concerned
with neutralising the threat of the return gaze. Here, instead of signifying
an independent understanding and even judgement, Aboriginal sight is
'vacant'; the transparency of the eye allows the explorer to 'see' into the
indigenous mind. The Aboriginal gaze, then, is reduced in Morgan's
poem to another particle of ethnographic knowledge, which participates
in the self-serving and self-confirmatory reasoning of the European. A
certain physiognomy signifies inferiority; the Aborigines possess this
physiognomy, therefore they must be inferior. The triumph of Morgan's
poem – and similar constructions of the 'weakness' of Aboriginal sight
and, therefore, mental powers – is its prevention of a space for Aboriginal
subjectivity – a space in which the explorer may exist as an object of
observation and judgement.

When the explorers are inescapably caught within Aboriginal sight,
they must construct themselves as having a profound effect on the
viewers. Occasionally this can be somewhat difficult as, in contrast to the
eager visual investigations of the explorer, the Aborigines often survey
the Europeans with considerable indifference. Nevertheless, this lack of
interest is construed as merely superficial; as Stokes argues, 'notwith-
standing the apathetic indifference with which they regarded us, [we]
must have appeared a prodigy' (1: 81). Ultimately, it is important to move
themselves beyond the range of the Aborigine's understanding: the

explorers cannot be subsumed into an Aboriginal system of knowledge without becoming less than a sovereign subject; therefore, they are 'incomprehensible' to the natives. Grey, like Stokes, assumes that their appearance must profoundly affect the Aborigines, writing that 'it must have awakened strange feelings in the breast of these two savages, who could never before have seen civilised man, thus to have sat spectators and overlookers of the every action of such incomprehensible beings as we must have appeared' (1: 93). The charge that the Aborigines cannot comprehend the significance of the explorers or their actions is one defence against being subsumed as an object of knowledge into an alien system.

The explorers' emphasis, however, on themselves as spectacle to the Aborigine forces them into an allowance that they will be reproduced narratively. This again threatens them with becoming an object of knowledge, but there are effective controls to indigenous narrative. Savage legends are already known to be errant, superstitious and parochial by the European. Known, they are an element within a European system of knowledge and, therefore, less threatening than unknown ways of reproducing information. The explorers seen by Aborigines are placed within the normal fantastic myths of the savage. Stokes is certain that observation of his party will result in new legends (1: 81), and Grey writes that the relation of the story of their appearance 'could not have been, to them, a whit less marvellous than the tales of the grey-headed Irish peasant, when he recounts the freaks of the fairies, "whose midnight revels by the forest side or fountain" he has watched intently from some shrub-clad hill' (1: 93). The comparison of the Aborigine with someone from England's first colony is significant in itself, but the most interesting strategy is producing Aboriginal narrative as something already 'known', in the same way that the story of the fairies is. Grey does not compare them in any simple way. The comparison circles, rather, on the respective marvellousness of the tales; yet, crucially, the very act of comparison is a claim that Aboriginal narrative can be known, and indeed is known, in the same way as Irish fairy stories have been absorbed into a sphere of ethnographic knowledge. Irish fairy stories, of course, are a form that calls for a particularly condescending understanding, and Aboriginal narrative is here constructed in the same way.

Fighting for visual power

The confluence within the Aborigine of native sharp-sightedness and an ability to avoid the surveillance of the European shifts the balance of visual power towards the indigene. For the explorer to 'discover', he must rip away the veil of the country and peer into its unshielded face.

But the Aborigines can avoid this sort of discovery. Oxley writes that 'it is probable that they may see us without discovering themselves, as it is much more likely for us to pass unobserved the little family of wandering natives, than that our party ... should escape their sight, quickened as it is by constant exercise in procuring their daily food' (163).

The Aborigines have the ability to survey the explorers without the gaze being returned. What might be innocent curiosity is construed as a reconnaissance before an attack; because of this, the exploration parties are subjected to pressure by all Aboriginal surveillances. After revealing how dependent he is on native information, Eyre describes how his party is watched by the Aborigines at an inopportune moment. Eyre was trying to bury some stocks that he hoped would be left alone by the indigenes, but they watch, and will not depart. 'For eight long hours had those natives sat opposite to us watching' (1: 210), writes Eyre, revealing how disabling Aboriginal surveillance could be to the ordinary exercises of an expedition. Thus, the natives' return gaze emerges in the journals as a site of resistance; sight itself becomes a site of discursive contestation between the imperial and resistant indigenous gazes.

Mitchell's *Expedition into . . . Tropical Australia* contains an illustration of this competition for sight. The description is Edmund Kennedy's rather than Mitchell's, being a section of a report included in the journal:

> I had not gone far before the cooys from the tents made me aware that the natives were by this time in sight. I therefore returned, and the first object which caught my eye was the bait – a gin, dancing before some admiring spectators; and behind her was a fine, lusty native advancing by great strides, as he considered the graceful movements of his gin were gaining as fast upon the hearts of the white men. (*EITA* 358)

This is accompanied with an illustration, which far from showing a striding 'lusty' native, positions him with arms folded observing the proceedings (see plate 15).

It might be possible to pass this picture off as evidence of Mitchell's declining taste in humour, but it is probably more productive to understand it in terms of the refraction of various gazes. Most obviously, the gaze of the smirking men, whose bodily stances suggest judgement, is sexually interested, as legs akimbo the woman dances before them. Her head position indicates she is looking back at them, but the nature of this gaze is uncertain. Removed from this immediate scene is the male Aborigine, who seems to be an observer that the explorers do not themselves observe. This may be understood as a case of Aboriginal visual power, an illustration of Aboriginal ability to see without being seen. But of course, this depiction is only possible through the superior view of Kennedy, from whose view the illustration is taken, and into which view

Plate 15 *An Aboriginal Dance,* engraved by R. Carrick after Mitchell's drawing. From Thomas Mitchell, *Expedition into ... Tropical Australia* (pl.7). Mitchell Library, State Library of New South Wales.

the reader is inserted. Aboriginal powers of observation may be depicted, but representation is inevitably predicated on the European's ultimate superiority of vision.

In chapter 3 I have described how looking from an eminence is constructed as a position of power and possession while at the same time being a cartographical necessity. Ethnographic surveillance has no such requirement for height. Yet, the adversarial nature of the explorer–Aborigine interaction creates height as a strategic and military advantage, and this concept of a 'commanding' position is found in Eyre's description of a competitive encounter between his party and a group of Aborigines, which is worth recounting at length.

> Our camp had been on the low ground, near the water, in the midst of many hills, all of which commanded our position. There were now a great many well armed natives around us, and though they were very kind and friendly, I did not like the idea of their occupying the acclivities immediately above us ... I therefore had everything removed to the hill next above them, and was a good deal amused by the result of this manoeuvre, for they seemed equally uneasy as we had been at the heights above them being occupied. In a very short time they had also broke up camp, and took possession of the next hill beyond us ... I determined [to] take up our position on the highest hill we could find. This was a very scrubby one, but by a vigorous application of the axes for an hour or two, we completely cleared its summit; and then taking up the drays,

tent, baggage &c. we occupied the best and most commanding station in the neighborhood. (Eyre 1: 226–27)

The language of military arrogation of land is difficult to miss: the two parties 'occupy' and take 'possession' of the land, and positions are also 'taken'. The real estate scramble is not for its own sake, or to obtain 'innocent' scenic views, but to carry out surveillance on the other group. If politics may be defined as who does what to whom, then this kind of surveillance is an exercise of political power, though the important question here is who gets to watch whom. The explorer's final conquest and possession of the highest hill is only an advantage when it is transformed into a treeless summit – an activity which displays the interdependence of power and surveillance. The technological feat of deforestation is an exercise of physical power that enables surveillance, a power in itself. The final victory of the explorers should not disguise the fact that the passage contains the resistance of the Aborigines to this exercise of power. The Europeans' surveillance is met with a response which demonstrates that the power in the text does not solely reside with the colonising force.

7

The Bosom of Unknown Lands

Western discourses have a history of constructing the object of scientific investigation as female. As Teresa de Lauretis argues in *Technologies of Gender*, the discursive formation of scientific study and mythological quest operate in a similar way.

> As he crosses the boundary and penetrates the other space, the mythical subject is constructed as human being and male; he is the active principle of culture, the establisher of distinction, the creator of difference. Female is what is not susceptible to transformation, to life or death; she (it) is an element of plot – space, a topos, a resistance matrix and matter.[1]

Exploration is gendered as a practice. It is structured in terms of an active male penetrating the inert yet resistant female land. I have suggested that the scopic regimes of exploration have a strongly Cartesian orientation, and that this is a part of the way exploration journals authorise their claim to truth. This Cartesian viewpoint is also exclusively male, expressed as a male domination of the continent through the persistent metaphor of land as female. The best known example of this is the already quoted description (see chapter 6) by Sturt, in *Expedition into Central Australia*, of Nature's protected domain: 'A veil hung over Central Australia that could neither be pierced or raised. Girt round about by deserts, it almost appeared as if Nature had intentionally closed it ...' (*ECA*: 2:2). The veiled, mysterious and alluring continent tempts a specifically male viewer to lift the veil and reveal the hidden. Occasionally 'she' is coquettish and playful, ultimately relenting to the explorers' overtures: 'It almost appeared as if nature had resisted us in order to try our perseverance, and that she had yielded in pity to our efforts' (*2Ex* 2:162).

Annette Kolodny in *The Lay of the Land* and Kay Schaffer in *Women and the Bush* have noted the prevalence of the trope of land as woman in early descriptions of (respectively) the American and Australian continents. Although Kolodny has identified the potentially emasculating appearance of the New World (9), *The Lay of the Land* does not seek to show how the metaphor of land as a woman is part of the phallocentric discourse of early colonial descriptions.[2] This chapter will examine some of the repercussions of constructing the land as female; it will suggest that in some ways this personification establishes many more anxieties than it resolves.

In *Three Essays on Sexuality* Freud associates scopophilia (the pleasure in looking) with the objectifying gaze which takes other people (or, in the explorers' case, land as well as people) as objects. In particular, he was interested in seeing how voyeurism in young children was a kind of scopophilia, where the young child investigated other people's genital status, curious about the presence or absence of the penis. At the very heart of Freud's thesis resides a visual event, the primal scene, the recognition and disavowal of the mother's lack of a penis. The male gaze's creation of the female always carries with it a replay of the primal scene, the recognition of the lack of a penis and the threat of castration it represents. Patriarchal social structures and phallocentric discourses construct the woman as a biological 'other', devoid of that which signifies masculinity, strength and rationality. Indeed, Freud's own theory constructs woman as lacking, and, essentially, as a victim of castration. This sight of this 'castration' causes an inherent anxiety in the male, who may fear it is his destiny.

Laura Mulvey's pioneering article on the male gaze, 'Visual Pleasure and Narrative Cinema', argues that voyeurism offers one way of escape from this castration anxiety. This escape is through preoccupation with the re-enactment of the original trauma (investigating the woman, demystifying her mystery), counterbalanced by the devaluation, punishment or saving of the guilty object.[3] This describes exactly the relationship of the explorer to the new land. On the one hand, it is a puzzle – a mysterious woman from whom the veil needs to be ripped and who is to be ruthlessly interrogated visually. On the other hand, new continents are also produced as places to be saved from the dark ignorance of the original inhabitants, or from the moral evil of slavery – the European rationale for the nineteenth century division of Africa and one of the reasons for conquest provided in Henry Morton Stanley's voyeuristic description noted in chapter 1.

The production of an area of Australia by the explorer John Lort Stokes shows how the gaze employed is a peculiarly masculine one,

visually interrogating a recumbent feminised land. The sexual nature of
the description hardly needs to be noted.

> To ascend a hill and say you are the first civilized man that has ever trod on
> this spot; to gaze around from its summit and behold a prospect over which
> no European eye has ever before wandered; to descry new mountains; to dart
> your eager glance down unexplored valleys, and unvisited glens; to trace the
> course of rivers whose waters no white man's boat has ever cleaved, and which
> tempt you onwards into the bosom of unknown lands:– these are the charms
> of an explorer's life. (Stokes 2: 50)

Mulvey notes that the sadistic investigation and assertion of control over
the woman is particularly appropriate for the creation of narrative.[4]
Indeed, it is this sadism, a battle of will and strength, victory/defeat
which forms the basis of the narrative of an exploration journal.

Mulvey also notes that there is another response to the castration
threat the view of a woman incites. This second response, which Mulvey
calls fetishistic scopophilia, is the complete disavowal of castration by the
substitution of a fetish object or turning the represented figure into a
fetish so that it becomes reassuring rather than dangerous.[5]

I will re-read Sturt's description of Sydney in light of Mulvey's theories.
Sturt utilises the usual stereotypes of the opposition between city and
bush, denying the potentially castrating absences of the wilderness/
woman by fetishising the substitutive western constructions.

> A single glance was sufficient to tell me that the hills upon the southern shore
> of the port, the outlines of which were broken by houses and spires, must once
> have been covered with the same dense and gloomy wood which abounded
> everywhere else. The contrast was indeed very great – the improvement
> singularly striking ... success has been complete: it is the very triumph of
> human skill and industry over Nature herself. The cornfield and the orchard
> have supplanted the wild grass and the brush; a flourishing town stands over
> the ruins of the forest; the lowing of herds has succeeded the wild whoop of
> the savage; and the stillness of that once desert shore is now broken by the
> sound of the bugle and the busy hum of commerce. (2Ex 1: xv)

As I have discussed earlier (see chapter 3), the main trope within this
description is that of succession: what was there, the original wilderness,
has been replaced by new sights and sounds. The struggle is to tame a
wild, feminised nature which is an absence – the lack of business, of
creative noise, of permanent buildings. The manly activity of European
society is compared to this natural absence and it is significant that it is at
this point that nature is feminised. Phallocentric discourse positions man
as creator of meaning, and woman as the bearer of this meaning. In
metaphorising nature as woman, this process is made more visible; the

patriarchal symbolic order, erasing women as possible makers of meaning, produces them as silent images on which language projects fantasies of control. The land (woman) is blank and empty until controlled and inscribed by manly European culture. The absence that structures the description of the wilderness/woman has its castration threat removed by the fetishistic substitution of the phallic spires of civilisation.

The use of land as woman for a mark of otherness invites questions about the relationship between linguistic and scopic practices. This work has looked at the discursive construction of scopic regimes through particular inscriptions. Before using Lacan to launch a psychoanalytic interrogation of the text, I want to examine the relationship between voyeurism and phallocentric texts outside of the specific Lacanian schema.

Both voyeurism and phallocentrism operate through an economy of presence and lack. Christian Metz writes that the voyeur represents in space the fracture which forever separates him from the object: he represents his very dissatisfaction (which is precisely what he needs as a voyeur) and, thus, also his satisfaction, insofar as it is of a specifically voyeuristic type.[6] The Derridean project identifies a similar dynamic in Western logocentrism (or for our purposes, phallogocentrism). Deconstruction espies a constitutive discourse of lack imbricated in a philosophy of presence.[7] The desire for presence means that Western epistemes carry as part of their economy a destination of non-satisfaction.[8] To contain this non-satisfaction and the threat to logocentricity it represents, non-satisfaction (that is, absence) is given a specific discursive site, collectively known as otherness. The non-West performs this role for logocentrism; women for phallogocentrism. In the explorers' journals these two fields of otherness are joined: the other land is metaphorised through the other gender.

The voyeuristic occasions, like logocentricity, function in an economy of a desire for presence, which is based on the reality of absence. It will be remembered that Jonathan Culler argues that:

> the Cartesian cogito, in which self is immediately present to itself, is taken as the basic proof of existence, and things directly perceived are apodictically privileged. Notions of truth and reality are based on a longing for an unfallen world in which there would be no need for the mediating systems of language and perception, but everything would be itself with no gap between form and meaning.[9]

One might further argue then that this unfallen world is the prelinguistic moment when the mother/child dyad is undisturbed by the mirror phase and the development of the ego ideal. How can scopophilia, which my argument has associated with the Cartesian cogito, be linked to this desire for self to be immediately present to itself? In 'Instincts and their Vicissitudes', Freud redefines scopophilia as originally auto-erotic. The male look still has an object, but that object is the subject's own body.[10] This construction of the male look as fundamentally narcissistic can be explained through the Lacanian notion of the gaze.

Lacan's mirror phase describes this initial moment when the male's seeing his own image offers the illusion of completeness. The reciprocity between the subject looking, and what is looked at, creates the illusion that the seeing subject contemplates itself, and thus a perfect self-conciousness is possible.[11] It is this illusion of completeness that imperial descriptions allow of the other. Imperial discourse, indeed, looks in a mirror; everything it sees is a reflection of itself. For the other it constructs is merely a reflection of repressed desires and urges, the dark fantasies of the European archive projected upon the world. The symbolic order driving this essentially solipsistic construction of difference works to deny the castration threat difference implies. As an illustration of how this gaze operates, one need only recall the explorer's ravening eye in the passage quoted previously (chapter 1) from John Coetzee's *Dusklands*:

> I become a spherical reflecting eye ... Destroyer of the wilderness, I move through the land cutting a devouring path from horizon to horizon. There is nothing from which my eye turns, I am all that I see ... What is there that is not me? I am a transparent sac with a black core full of images ...[12]

Indeed, there is nothing that is not the explorer Jacobus Coetzee, and the repository of knowledges and stereotypes of which he is comprised. And the voyeurism of empire is such that nothing it sees is not empire; its objects of vision are its own fears, cruelties, and dreams projected.

That the gaze of exploration is ultimately narcissistic does not mean that it is untroubled and comfortably self-contained. Rather, the dynamic itself is disturbing in a number of ways. The fetishistic construction of the other does not completely disguise the fact that the land as female necessarily disturbs. The spires of civilisation can in Sydney provide a fetishistic response to this absence, but none such is to be found in the desert. There is no inland sea, no lost civilisation, nor can Ludwig Leichhardt be found. I would like to turn away for a moment from the journals themselves to look at the way late nineteenth-century culture coped with some of the anxieties of difference that exploration itself established.

Fictionalisations of exploration such as J. F. Hogan's *The Lost Explorer: An Australian Story* (1890), W. Carlton Dawe's *The Golden Lake*, or *The Marvellous History of a Journey Through the Great Lone Land of Australia* (1894), and Alexander MacDonald's *The Lost Explorers* (1906) compensate for the failure to find the sea, mountains, or lost explorer that was looked for in the interior.[13] That there must be (or should have been) *something* in the centre of the continent is the basis of these fantasies. As the narrator of MacDonald's *The Lost Explorers* says: 'Across their scintillating sands what wonderful haven may be hid? Surely it is not all desert, something must lie beyond the far horizon.'[14] In the novels there are secrets aplenty to be uncovered by the energetic male eye. Ludwig Leichhardt was lost but now he is found. Civilisations are not absent, as was thought, they are merely degenerate. In particular, there is the penile verticality so lacking in the exploration journals' description of horizontal land. All absences are filled.

Hogan's *The Lost Explorer* begins on the farm of Arthur Louvain, son of the famous missing explorer Leonard Louvain. His father has many parallels with the historical Leichhardt: he has travelled to Port Essington on a journey many thought beyond him, he is deeply scientific, and has disappeared, lost for over twenty years after attempting to cross Australia from East to West.

Louvain is sitting with a few friends one day when a flight of birds passes over the farm, which is somewhere north of Cooper's Creek. The birds are a reference to the flights of birds which Charles Sturt in *Expedition into Central Australia* adduced as evidence of an inland sea. The talented Aborigine 'Uralla' strikes down two swans heading north towards this inland water and tells the station owner, the narrator Arthur Louvain, that 'big water up there' (apparently sharing the European cartographic conceit that north is 'up'). Louvain and his friends decide to search for this water.[15]

What begins lightheartedly as a search for an 'Australian Niagara' reputedly flowing in the desert, quickly turns into a serious exploration in *The Lost Explorer*. Arthur discovers this 'big water', the Australian Niagara, but also finds a pseudo-Aborigine 'Wonga', who lies near death at the falls. On Wonga's arm there are inscribed two words – 'Leonard Louvain'.

The Golden Lake begins with a dinner party at which Archibald Martesque and Dick Hardwicke discuss a rumour of an Aborigine being found in the desert wearing a gold ankle-bracelet. 'Plenty o' that stuff', he is recorded as having said when asked about the gold.[16] At the recitation of this story the servant at the dinner trembles violently and drops all the glasses.

> No more was said at that moment, but, strange as it may seem, this apparently unimportant incident was but the beginning of a series of remarkable revelations which culminated in the undertaking of one of the most surprising journeys ever attempted by man.[17]

The servant never really recovers from this nervous attack, and reveals in a letter after his death that he knows of this oasis of gold, having escaped there as a convict with a friend and his friend's daughter twenty years ago. His friend died and he abandoned the little girl to live with the tribe of semi-civilised Aborigines who lived in this region. Archie and Dick decide to find this oasis, rescue the girl and make their fortunes. In a priceless piece of dialogue they speculate that the little girl abandoned in the wilderness may now be a grown woman.

'Though you must remember that some little girl, if alive, is now a woman of twenty-three or twenty-four, and may be married to a chief and the mother of a family of savages – horrid, black, dirty savages'.
'What a horrible idea, Dick'.
'It's not pleasant is it', he replied. 'But what is a girl to do?' [18]

At that moment a canoe being paddled by a woman hoves into view amidst a flurry of penile imagery. She is being pursued by a 'big savage', who is shaking his huge spear threateningly at her. She shields herself from its 'dreaded thrust', and he continues to 'flourish the dreadful spear'. Dick Hardwicke (and even his name is suspicious here), who has been 'fingering his rifle dexterously' while aiming at some black swans, turns his rifle on the 'native', who is killed. The woman, dressed in dark feathers and skins, approaches the explorers and lifts her feathered clothing a little to show that she is white. Underneath the covering of the anomalously black feathers of the swan normality is present. MacDonald's *The Lost Explorers* is another story of a recovered loss. James Mackay, an otherwise infallible character has misread the bones he found on his previous expedition. They were not the bones of his friend Richard Bentley and of his party as Mackay had thought. The friend Mackay thought dead, Richard Bentley, is found alive. One of the vectors of the loss/recovery dynamic in the stories, then, is centred on these lost characters who are found.

A second vector of loss/recovery involves the civilisation of the 'natives'. As I mentioned in chapter 6, one of the problems imperial discourses had with Aborigines is that empirical observations did not always allow the easy production of the social organisation of indigenes within pre-existent descriptions. I have argued that Aboriginal social order is described in a number of ways; to some explorers at least, Aborigines seemed to have little or no social hierarchy, no political structures, no 'king' or 'chief'. This 'lack' is a constructed one: Aboriginal social relations were simply invisible to investigators, who were looking for recognisable and familiar signs. The perceived lack of social formations emerges as a distinct threat to imperial ethnological discourse because it is shown to have limitations.

One of the achievements of the fictions of exploration is to provide a substitute for this lack. George Grey operates as a starting point for explanation of Aboriginal history in *The Lost Explorer*. On discovering paintings with 'truth to nature', Arthur Louvain quotes Grey in support of the idea that the Aborigines are a degenerate race – a history that explains their lack of a recognisable social order. These paintings by the 'lost race', Louvain speculates, may be the 'sole surviving remnant of the superior, semi-civilised native race that once inhabited the interior of the great southern continent'.[19] The present Aborigines, then, are degenerates. But even this is too good for the indigenes. Arthur Louvain finds that the inland city is not the product of his hypothesised race of civilised natives, but rather was built by a race of civilised and cultured white people 'who employed blacks as slaves or servants', and who have since disappeared.[20] After the apocalyptic ending of the novel, the few survivors of this city are once again employed by a white man – Arthur Louvain.[21]

The novels also return that organisation expected of indigenous people but apparently lacking in the Aborigines. Malua, the inland city in *The Lost Explorer* is controlled by an evil female chief Mocata, and her equally evil priest Mooroop. The lost race's society in *The Golden Lake* is also strictly hierarchical, being run by an evil chief Kalua and his equally evil priest.

It perhaps need only briefly be mentioned that these novels are replete with common stereotypical descriptions of Aborigines. They are regularly referred to as 'niggers', their intelligence denigrated, and their rituals taken as evidence of essential barbarism. One particular description of a corroboree is interesting for the castration anxiety which underlies it. The narrator of *The Golden Lake* writes that it was a 'shocking, sickening sight, enough to make us wonder if the same god made us all', a reaction more than reminiscent of that which Freud argues is initiated in the primal scene.[22] One response to this, as I have argued in reference to Sturt's journals, is to fetishise the corroboree, produce it as theatre to assuage its disturbing difference. Another response to the realisation of difference is the development of an exhibition complex. Freud argues this is a 'means of constantly insisting upon the integrity of the subject's own (male) genitals and it reiterates his infantile satisfaction at the absence of a penis in those of women'.[23] The exhibition of the phallic weaponry of the explorers plays a main role in their interaction with the gunless (feminine) natives – indeed, this is true of factual as well as fictional journals. The plot in *The Golden Lake*, for example, turns upon the explorers' display of their weaponry.

The lack of verticality is a feature of the desert as described in exploration journals and fictions of exploration. But the role of these fictions is to compensate for this. Thus, we almost inevitably have a giant

volcanic explosion providing the narrative climax. Indeed, the challenge
to masculinism in *The Lost Explorer*, the female chief Mocata, is killed by
ejaculate from the local volcano. This is not to say all verticality should
be read as male in the novels. Some verticality is the barrier to inspection,
the female 'veil' which must be surmounted. Taking crude Freudianism
to extremes (and why not), we come to a view of landscape penetration
as adolescent sexual fumbling.

> We clambered up as fast as we could, only to find ourselves confronted by that
> impregnable barrier of solid rock ... Perplexed and disheartened for this
> moment at the absence of any perceptible opening, we cast enquiring glances
> at Wonga, who wore an expression of smiling serenity that revived my confi-
> dence in his capacity to guide us aright. He divined our bewildered thoughts,
> and pushing one of the stunted trees aside, revealed to our astonished gaze a
> narrow irregular opening at the base of the rocky barrier.[24]

It is one of the points on which these novels as well as factual journals of
exploration deconstruct themselves: so often it is the Aborigine who
gives the explorer the 'key' to the locked country.

As I have argued, the construction of the land as a woman, and
specifically as a woman's body, allows the operation of the ensemble of
discourses of penetration, unveiling, and so on. And indeed in the novels
there are images of emasculation by the land: the masculine explorers
having been swallowed up, the 'hidden glens' becoming *vaginae dentatae*.

> But then, how was the mystery of the missing explorers to be explained? If
> they had not somehow succeeded in forcing their way into the desert ... what
> had become of them? ... But, as matters stood, they had disappeared as
> completely as if the ground had opened and swallowed them.[25]

The compensatory fetishistic mountains are a return to the phallic
mother, the mother who exists for the child before her or his knowledge
of castration. The horror of difference is assuaged – the woman/land is
ultimately the same as man. Barbara Creed has pointed out that there is
a frequent confusion of the phallic mother and the woman as castrator
and that the terms are quite separate in Freud's work, and should serve
separate functions in analysis of their appearance.[26] Creed argues that
'the former ultimately represents a comforting phantasy of sexual
sameness, and the latter a terrifying phantasy of sexual difference'.[27] But
the exploration fictions are then thrown into another difficulty.
Although comforting in its sameness, the phallic mother is also powerful
– a female with a gun, to use Creed's example. This potential power, the
very fetish that the stories set up to disguise the castration anxiety, must
be dealt with. The explosive end of the novels which feature a volcano as

the geographical fetish confirms the potential power of the phallus, while destroying the land's possession of that power. The volcano destroyed, the anomalous race of pseudo-civilised natives erased, the heroes of the novel may now enjoy a land which is female, supplicant, yet no longer threatening in its 'emptiness'.

8

Conclusion

'What is the climate of Guatemala?
Has steam navigation been introduced along the coasts of
    Peru and Chile?
What is the religion of the Arafuras?
            Thomas Mitchell *An Australian Geography: with*
    the shores of the Pacific and those of the Indian Ocean.
            Sydney: J. Moore, 1851. pp.79, 36, 45.

While exploration was still in its concluding phases concern was being
expressed at the declining readership of exploration journals. As Giles
complained, 'let me ask how many boys out of a hundred in Australia, or
England ... have ever read Sturt or Mitchell, Eyre, Leichhardt, Grey or
Stuart ... is it because these narratives are Australian and true that they
are not worthy of attention?'[1] Although the journals themselves may have
been taken up and read less often as the century drew to a close, a process of cultural incorporation was working upon the explorers. They
became icons of the new nation and intimately tied to how it imaged
itself.

During the depression years there was a flurry of monument construction in country towns in Australia. Many of these commemorated the
exploits of explorers who had passed through these districts. The celebrations surrounding the dedication of these monuments served to give
the communities a cohesive sense of history in the land. This was a
process of history making which became particularly necessary after the
events of the Second World War and its threat of apparently imminent
invasion of Australia raised questions about white society's hold on the
vast continent. The centenary of a large number of exploration journeys
occurred towards towards the end of the war, or just after it, and
substantial statues, such as the one of Charles Sturt in Adelaide, were
erected. Re-enactments were held: for example, there was the 1946
centenary celebration in Blackall, Queensland, in which 'Mitchell' and
his Aboriginal guide 'Yuranigh' paraded through the town on the back of
a truck.[2] In a time of disillusionment with the British Empire and a re-
alignment of relationships towards the United States these community
celebrations not only re-affirmed the legitimacy of occupation but

soothed concerns that Australia was moving away from its roots, which were understood as British. As originary figures, land explorers not only demarcated the beginning of Australian history; they also, with the exception of Strzelecki and Leichhardt, pointed to a particularly British beginning.

But the decolonising movements around the world, and a left-over feeling of dissatisfaction with Britain's lack of support for Australia in the Second World War, as well as Britain's subsequent entry into the European Community, resulted in more distant and strained ties. As I have already noted, Bill Peach argued in 1984 that there was a tendency to scoff at the achievements of explorers and to see them as wilful and self-interested buffoons. In part, this is perhaps the result of explorers' failure to be completely accepted as Australian heroes; their connection to Britain does not always allow their easy assimilation into nationalist pantheons. The ambivalent attitude of present Australians towards these figures can be seen in two (rather unsuccessful) films of 1985. *Burke and Wills* told the story of these two hapless explorers, who, after crossing the country from south to north, expired on the return journey. Though showing the human flaws of the characters, it was in many respects a fairly solemn effort. Less respectful was the parodic *Wills and Burke*, which presented the journey as the farcical misadventures of two inept amateurs. Produced in the same year, these films together represent the poles of Australian attitudes towards explorers.

Whereas adult representations of exploration have some degree of ambiguity, the materials used in schools have a tired fixity in older understandings. At the annual Royal National Exhibition in Queensland, amidst the displays of cakes, preserves and leatherwork, one may see exhibits of the schoolwork of young children. Invariably these will include posters delineating the paths taken by explorers, next to which will be a little icon of the relevant explorer. One might question whether this kind of learning is much more valuable than the segmented and discrete questions that Mitchell presents in *Australian Geography*, or those which in Arthur Mee's *The Children's Encyclopedia* construct the world as a collection of inert objects to be ingested. The nature of these representations of explorers has, it seems to me, remained unchanged, while the general view of colonial history has moved on. Two years after the 1992 schoolbook argument (referred to in chapter 1), a major debate broke out over proposed alterations to schoolbook representations of colonial history. The textbooks for Year Five students were to be reviewed for their obsession with explorers; most controversially, the term 'settlement' was to be replaced by 'invasion'. This last suggestion angered a generation of Australians who had been raised within the very representations the educationalists were attempting to alter. Lowering the emphasis on exploration and admitting that the country was 'invaded' was simply too much for many.

It is a pity that those who objected to the changes had not read exploration texts more thoroughly, for as I have indicated, the idea that the continent had indeed been invaded by Europeans was not uncommon in the journals themselves. The open admission that the country was invaded, that settlement meant war, is common in nineteenth century discourses, as Henry Reynolds has argued. Even journals of exploration, those texts most central to developing colonial mythology, show at least an intermittent moral awareness that what was being done required the destruction of another culture. But it was too much for the Queensland government, and Premier Wayne Goss intervened in the affairs of the Education Department to order a halt to the suggested school textbook changes.[3]

There is the suspicion, then, that nominally post-colonial countries like Australia have not sloughed off the legacies of various colonial ideologies. Moreover, one suspects that, despite some feelings of ambiguity towards explorers as originary figures, white Australians need them as an anchorage for a mythological justification of possession. Removing explorers or displacing the cartographic and iconic representations of their struggles from the curriculum is to threaten the legitimacy of anglo-Australian occupation. Many non-Aboriginal Australians want founding mythologies: male, heroic and representing the victory over a feminised nature. For, if these are removed, the horror of the void remains – a void beyond even the comforting void of the 'dead heart' European discourse has created of the desert.

This work has argued that colonial discourse 'operated not only as an instrumental construction of knowledge but also according to the ambivalent protocols of fantasy and desire'.[4] Indeed, I have suggested that knowledge generation proceeds through the fantastic and the imaginary of the European archive. The privileged position of vision's role in knowledge generation should not disguise the fact that sight, and the discursive construction of sight, are mediated through a long history of repression and projection. The gaze of empire is ultimately narcissistic, as whatever it views is already a product of this gaze. One might argue that the place of colonial history, and exploration in particular, in contemporary culture is caught within similar dynamics of fetish and disavowal.

Notes

Method of citation in notes

Full bibliographic details are contained in the bibliography, for material cited in the notes. Books are cited by title and author for first reference in each chapter; subsequent references in the chapter are by name (unless author has more than one title). To avoid an accumulation of notes, follow-up page references to works are given in the course of discussion on them in the main text.

1 Introduction

1. Arthur Mee (ed.), *The Children's Encyclopedia*, vol. IV, p.2446.
2. *Courier-Mail*, Brisbane, 24 April 1992.
3. *Courier-Mail*, Brisbane, 30 April 1992.
4. Edward Soja, *Postmodern Geographies: The Reassertion of Space in Critical Social Theory*, p.120.
5. Soja also emphasises that physical and ideational space in turn determine the social production of space, pp.120–21.
6. Soja, p.124.
7. John Coetzee, *Dusklands*, p.84.
8. Michel de Certeau, *On the Practice of Everyday Life*, p.36.
9. *ibid.*
10. Henry Morton Stanley, *Through the Dark Continent, or, The Sources of the Nile Around the Great Lakes of Equatorial Africa and Down the Livingstone River to the Atlantic Ocean*, vol. II, p.222.
11. Stanley, vol. II, pp.222–23.
12. Timothy Reiss, *The Discourse of Modernism*, p.42.
13. Jonathan Culler, *Structuralist Poetics: Structuralism, Linguistics and the Study of Literature*, p.132.
14. Bob Hodge and Vijay Mishra, *Dark Side of the Dream: Australian Literature and the Postcolonial Mind*, p.157.
15. Bill Peach, *The Explorers*, p.7.
16. *ibid.*

17. Paul Carter, *The Road to Botany Bay: An Essay in Spatial History*. For a useful summary of the critical reception of Carter, see George Seddon, 'On The Road to Botany Bay' *Westerly* 33(4) (1988), pp.15–26.
18. Paul Carter, *Road to Botany Bay*, p.xvi.
19. The titles of these works by Mitchell and Sturt will henceforth be given in the abbreviated forms found in square brackets here for citations and references.

2   Exploring Culture

1. *Blackwood's Edinburgh Magazine*, 'New South Wales' 44 (1838), pp.706–07.
2. Paul Carter, *Road to Botany Bay*, p.106.
3. Forrest's biographer F. K. Crowley records that Forrest was fascinated by Gregory, Oxley, Sturt, Eyre and other Western Australian explorers. See Francis Crowley *Forrest 1847–1918*, pp.20, 28.
4. Edgar Beale, *Sturt, The Chipped Idol: A Study of Charles Sturt, Explorer* p.35.
5. Beale p.49. This lack of individuation of the party is also a property of Warburton's journal. The camel drivers are introduced as Sahleh and Halleem, but are referred to in the text only as the 'Afghan[s]', e.g. pp.153, 154.
6. J. C. Beaglehole (ed.), *The Journals of Captain Cook on His Voyages of Discovery*, vol. I, p.399.
7. *Blackwood's Edinburgh Magazine*, 'Colonization' 64 (1848), p.71. Mitchell was also criticised in the *Blackwood* review of his earlier *Three Expeditions into the Interior of Eastern Australia*. When the journal expresses some sympathy for the plight of the Aborigines, the reviewer opines that 'we cannot help on observing this interesting passage, that here Major Mitchell indulges in a little sentimentality – the only instance of doubtful taste which we have observed in his volumes' ('New South Wales' 44 [1838], p.697).
8. Marie Boas Hall, *All Scientists Now: The Royal Society in the Nineteenth Century*, p.4.
9. S. F. Cannon, *Science in Culture: The Early Victorian Period*, pp.170–71.
10. See Boas Hall, ch. 6.
11. Clements R. Markham, *The Fifty Years' Work of the Royal Geographical Society*, p.7.
12. Boas Hall, p.210.
13. D. R. Stoddart. *On Geography and Its History*, pp.18–19.
14. Robert A. Stafford. *Scientist of Empire: Sir Roderick Murchison, Scientific Exploration and Victorian Imperialism*, p.10.
15. John Scott Keltie, 'Thirty Years' Work of the Royal Geographical Society', *Geographical Journal*, 49 (1917), p.350.
16. Ian Cameron, *To the Farthest Ends of the Earth: 150 Years of World Exploration by the Royal Geographical Society*, p.18.
17. Stoddart, p.60
18. Giles's career after his explorations finished shows how public elevation became an expected reward and how these expectations were occasionally disappointed. See Ray Ericksen, *Ernest Giles: Explorer and Traveller, 1835–1897*, pp.263–69.
19. Stafford, *Scientist of Empire*, p.216
20. 2 Sept 1834 Report and letter, Mitchell to Secretary of State Murray, quoted in William Foster, *Sir Thomas Livingston Mitchell and His World 1792–1855, Surveyor-General of New South Wales 1828–1855*, pp.151, 170.

21. Ray MacLeod, 'Of Medals and Men: A Reward System in Victorian Science 1826–1914', *Notes and Records of the Royal Society of London* 26 (1971), p.99.
22. Markham, p.67.
23. Cameron, Appendix II.
24. Markham, p.63.
25. Cameron, Appendix II.
26. *Times*, 2 Dec 1865, p.5. See Stafford, *Scientist of Empire*, p.31.
27. Cameron, Appendix II.
28. Markham, pp.61–62, 83.
29. Stoddart, p.63.
30. Markham, p.150–52.
31. Cameron, p.18. See also p.47.
32. Dora Howard, 'The English Activities on the North Coast of Australia in the First Half of the Nineteenth Century', *Proceedings of the Royal Geographical Society of Australia South Australian Branch* 33 (1931–32), pp.21–194.
33. *Historical Records of Australia* (1) vol. 16, p.562.
34. The allusions are to the discussion of this in chapter 1 and to Jonathan Culler, *Structuralist Poetics*, p.132, which was cited there.
35. *Blackwood's Edinburgh Magazine*, 'New South Wales' 44 (1838), p.697.
36. Robert Stafford, ' "The Long Arm of London": Sir Roderick Murchison and Imperial Science in Australia', in *Australian Science in the Making*, p.169.
37. Wendy Birman, *Gregory of Rainworth: A Man in His Time*, p.22.
38. Daniel Brock, *To the Desert With Sturt: A Diary of the 1844 Expedition*. See also Michael Langley, *Sturt of the Murray: Father of Australian Exploration*, p.254.
39. Alan Andrews, *Stapylton With Major Mitchell's Australia Felix Expedition 1836*, pp.38–39.
40. John Harris Browne, 'Journal of the Sturt Expedition 1844–1845', *South Australiana* 6.1 (1966), pp.23–54.
41. Beale, p.211.
42. Emile Benveniste. *Problems in General Linguistics*, pp.218, 224–226.
43. Andrew Hassam, ' "As I Write": Narrative Occasions and the Quest for Self-Presence in the Travel Diary', *Ariel* 21.4 (1990), p.36.
44. Gerard Genette, *Narrative Discourse: An Essay in Method*, p.217.
45. Foster analyses how rewriting for publication allows the interpolation of material. Mitchell followed the course suggested by George 'the Barber' Clarke, an escaped convict who claimed he had found a river called the 'Kindur'. In the published journal Mitchell writes the land 'had been exactly described by the bushranger, and the scene made me half believe his story.' (*3Ex* 1: 42) Foster points out that the original field journal displays an explorer who is fully convinced by Clarke's story (221).
46. M. G. Cooke, 'Modern Black Autobiography', *Romanticism: Vistas, Instances, Continuities*, p.259.
47. Genette, p.219.
48. Genette, p.219.

3   Picturesque Visions

1. Arthur Young, *A Six Months Tour Through the North of England*, pp.x, xi.
2. Arthur Young, *Travels in France and Italy During the Years 1787–88–89*, pp.3, 4.
3. William Gilpin, *Forest Scenery*, quoted in Christopher Hussey, *The Picturesque: Studies in a Point of View*, p.120.

4. Barron Field, *Geographical Memoirs of New South Wales*, pp.422–23.
5. William Gilpin, *Three Essays: On Picturesque Beauty, On Picturesque Travel, and On the Art of Sketching Landscapes*, p.26.
6. See Leichhardt, p.284, and Grey vol.1 p.52 and pp.59–60.
7. John Barrell, *The Idea of Landscape and the Sense of Place*, pp.14–20.
8. Carole Fabricant, 'The Aesthetics and Politics of Landscape in the C18th', in *Studies in Eighteenth-Century British Art and Aesthetics*, p.73.
9. William Gilpin, *Forest Scenery*, quoted in Malcolm Andrews, *The Search for the Picturesque: Landscape Aesthetics and Tourism in Britain, 1760–1800*, p.70.
10. For an analysis of the various landscape aesthetic controversies of the time, see Walter Hipple, *The Beautiful, The Sublime, and The Picturesque in Eighteenth-Century British Aesthetic Theory*, pp.83–98 and pp.185–278; Malcolm Andrews, *The Search for the Picturesque*, pp.56–66; Ann Bermingham, *Landscape and Ideology: The English Rustic Tradition, 1740–1860*, pp.63–73.
11. Uvedale Price, *Essays on the Picturesque as Compared with the Sublime and the Beautiful:, And On the Use of Studying Pictures for the Purpose of Improving Real Landscape*, p.37.
12. 'Notes on Foregoing Poem' section of *Three Essays*, p.29.
13. 'Notes on Foregoing Poem', p.28.
14. Carl Barbier, *William Gilpin: His Drawings, Teaching, and Theory of the Picturesque*, p.35.
15. Eric Shanes, *Turner's Picturesque Views in England and Wales 1825–1838*, p.25.
16. John Ruskin, *The Works*, vol. VI, p.340.
17. Bernard Smith, *European Vision and the South Pacific*, p.274.
18. Thomas Mitchell, sketches of Fall of Cobaw, Mitchell Library, DG V2B/24 and notes, PXn 713.
19. William Westall, *Drawings By William Westall, Landscape Artist Aboard HMS Investigator During the Circumnavigation of Australia by Matthew Flinders, R.N., in 1801–1803*, Pl.11.
20. Westall, Pl.18.
21. In fact, Mitchell had read Gilpin, as well as several other writers on landscape. See Paul Carter, *The Road to Botany Bay*, p.115.
22. William Gilpin, *Observations Relative Chiefly to Picturesque Beauty, made in the Year 1772, on Several Parts of England*, vol. I, p.36.
23. Bermingham, p.14.
24. Humphry Repton, *Observations on the Theory and Practice of Landscape Gardening*, p.34.
25. For a brief history of the ha-ha see S. A. Mansbach, 'An Earthwork of Surprise: The 18th-Century Ha-Ha', *Art Journal* 42 (1982) pp.217–21.
26. Repton, p.2.
27. The word 'clump' was a recognised member of the picturesque lexicon though, of course, not limited to it. See Repton pp.46–48 for a full discussion of the aesthetic strategies of 'clumping'.
28. I. S. MacLaren, 'Retaining Captaincy of the Soul: Response to Nature on the First Franklin Expedition', *Essays on Canadian Writing* 28 (1984), p.69.
29. For other descriptions of rock formations which resemble castles or cathedrals see: Grey, vol. I p.97; Giles, vol. I, p.90; Mitchell, *Expedition into . . . Tropical Australia*, p.203; King, pp.177, 301.
30. William Hoskins, *The Making of the English Landscape*, p.134.
31. Young, *Travels in France and Italy*, p.301.

32. Howard Tanner and Jane Begg, *The Great Gardens of Australia*, p.14.
33. Mitchell saw the Australian garden as an opportunity to recreate the tamed nature of Britain and produce a gentle nostalgia: 'but in the garden, to him who seeks a home in distant colonies, must ever be an object of peculiar interest; for there ... the recollection of early days, and of the country of his birth is awakened' (*3Ex* 2: 6–7).
34. Colonel Mundy, *Our Antipodes*, quoted in Tanner and Begg, p.14.
35. Fabricant, p.56.
36. Edmund Burke, *A Philosophical Enquiry into the Origin of Our Ideas of the Sublime and Beautiful*, p.57.
37. Thomas Percy, 'Observanda in the Tour into Scotland August 8 1773', quoted in Malcolm Andrews, p.76.
38. Richard Terdiman, 'Ideological Voyages: Concerning a Flaubertian Dis-Orient-ation', in Francis Barker et al. (eds) *Europe and Its Others*, p.28.
39. John White, *The Birth and Rebirth of Pictorial Space*, p.192.
40. Jose Rabasa, 'Allegories of the Atlas', in Francis Barker et al. (eds) *Europe and Its Others*, p.9.
41. Gilpin, *Observations Relative Chiefly to Picturesque Beauty*, pp.151–52, quoted Fabricant p.56.
42. William Cowper, *Poetical Works*, 'The Task' ll.288–90.
43. William Mason, quoted in Barbier p.137.
44. See Mary Louise Pratt, 'Scratches on the Face of the Country; or, What Mr Barrow Saw in the Land of the Bushmen', *Critical Inquiry* 12.1 (1985) p.124 for a discussion of the impulse towards self-effacement in the journals of explorers.
45. Ralph Hyde in *Panoramania!* notes that Robert Barker's early panorama, 'Grand Fleet at Spithead in 1791' depended on the audience having entered through a darkened tunnel so that the picture would seem to be lit by bright sunlight in contrast. See p.20.
46. The building in which Robert Barker's panorama was housed prevented viewers from approaching too close to the painting See Hyde p.20.
47. Hyde p.131. See Robert Altick, *The Shows of London* for a detailed discussion of moving panoramas (198–202) and, indeed, of the whole genre of panoramas.
48. William Bingley, *North Wales Delineated from Two Excursions Through All the Interesting Ports of That Beautiful and Romantic Country and Intended as a Guide to Future Tourists*, p.125. There are a number of descriptions of vistas being 'bird's-eye views' in the journals. See Stokes vol. I, p.84, Giles vol. I, pp.60, 70 and King p.50 for a representative sample. The explorers' use of this term is another example of their utilisation of art terminology, but one that has cartographical possibilities.
49. Svetlana Alpers, 'The Mapping Impulse in Dutch Art', in David Woodward (ed.) *Art and Cartography: Six Historical Essays*, p.89.
50. Barbara Stafford, *Voyage Into Substance: Art, Science, Nature and the Illustrated Travel Account, 1760–1840*, p.435.
51. Altick, p.464.
52. Samuel Edgerton, 'From Mental Matrix to Mappamundi to Christian Empire: The Heritage of Ptolemaic Cartography in the Renaissance', in David Woodward (ed.) *Art and Cartography: Six Historical Essays*, p.36.
53. Preface to Henry Hexham's edition of Ortelius's *Atlas* quoted in Jose Rabasa, 'Allegories', p.9.

54. Philip Corrigan, 'On Visualization as Power: "Innocent Stupidities": De-Picturing (human) Nature. On Hopeful Resistances and Possible Refusals: Celebrating Difference(s) – Again', in Gordon Fyfe and John Law (eds) *Picturing Power: Visual Depiction and Social Relations*, p.266.
55. Jose Rabasa, 'Allegories', p.9.

4   Maps and their Cultural Constructedness

1. J. B. Harley, 'Deconstructing the Map', *Cartographica*, 26.2 (1989), pp.1–2.
2. An example of this is Charles Beazley's, *The Dawn of Modern Geography*, vol. III, p.528.
3. Denis Wood and John Fels, 'Designs on Signs: Myth and Meaning in Maps', *Cartographica* 23.3 (1986), p.64.
4. For map reading as an acquired facility, see also Denis Wood, 'Cultured Symbols/Thoughts on the Cultural Contexts of Cartographic Symbols', *Cartographica* 21.4 (1984) pp.9–37.
5. J. B. Harley, 'Maps, Knowledge, and Power', in Denis Cosgrove and Stephen Daniels (eds), *The Iconography of Landscape: Essays on the Symbolic Representation, Design, and Use of Past Environments*, p.300.
6. Harley, 'Maps, Knowledge, and Power', p.278.
7. J. B. Harley and David Woodward (eds), *The History of Cartography: Volume I: Cartography in Prehistoric, Ancient, and Medieval Europe and the Mediterranean*, Pl.10.
8. Harley and Woodward (eds), *The History of Cartography*, Pl.11.
9. Harley and Woodward (eds), *The History of Cartography*, p.335.
10. Harley and Woodward (eds), *The History of Cartography*, p.507.
11. Brian Elliot, 'Antipodes: An Essay in Attitudes', *Australian Letters* 7 (1966), p.51.
12. Macrobius, *Commentary on the Dream of Scipio*, p.204.
13. Cicero, *The Academics*, p.81.
14. Lucretius, *De Rerum Natura*, Book I, ll.1061–1064 and ll.1072–1073.
15. Cosmas (Indicopleuestes) An Egyptian Monk, *The Christian Topography of Cosmas, An Egyptian Monk*. p.17.
16. Cosmas, p.17 n.1
17. Augustine, *The City of God Against the Pagans*, Book xvi.viii.
18. Ranulf Higden, *Polychronicon*, quoted in John Friedman, *The Monstrous Races in Medieval Art and Thought*, p.43.
19. Sydney Smith, *Works*, vol. II, p.254, quoted in Bernard Smith, *European Vision and the South Pacific*, p.226.
20. Marcus Clarke, quoted in Bernard Smith (ed.), *Documents on Art and Taste in Australia: The Colonial Period 1770–1914*, p.135.
21. Tomasso Campanella, *City of the Sun*, quoted in Paul Foss, 'Meridians of Apathy', *Art & Text*, 6, p.85.
22. Richard Brome, *The Antipodes*, I, iv, ll.90–92.
23. Brome, I, vi, l.127 and I, vi, l.142
24. Joseph Hall, *Another World and Yet the Same: Bishop Joseph Hall's Mundus Alter et Idem*, pp.56, 63.
25. Friedman, p.10.
26. J. C. Porter, *The Inconstant Savage: England and the North American Indian, 1500–1660*, p.48.

27. Geoffrey Atkinson, *The Extraordinary Voyage in French Literature*, I, p.16.
28. M. F. Péron, *A Voyage of Discovery to the Southern Hemsiphere Performed by Order of the Emperor Napoleon During the Years 1801, 1802, 1803, and 1804*, p.291
29. Quoted in Alfred Crosby, *Ecological Imperialisms: The Biological Expansion of Europe, 900–1900*, p.7.
30. Péron, p.291 and pp.307–08.
31. Richard White, *Inventing Australia: Images and Identity, 1688–1980*, p.9 and Geoffrey Serle, *From the Deserts the Prophets Come: The Creative Spirit in Australia 1788–1972*, p.5.
32. Baldwin Spencer quoted in Andrew Markus, *Governing Savages*, p.38.
33. Christopher Marlowe, *Tamburlaine the Great*, Part 1, IV, iv, ll.143–46.
34. Harley and Woodward (eds), *The History of Cartography*, Pl.12. The biblical evidence for there only being three continents was the foundation of Augustine's argument against the existence of the antipodes, and it was difficult to explain the native American population when that continent was discovered. See Porter, *The Inconstant Savage*, pp.92–98, for various explanations of the origin of the American people.
35. Harley and Woodward (eds), *The History of Cartography*, p.304.
36. Friedman, ill.19.
37. R. A. Skelton, *Looking at an Early Map*, ill.5.
38. Patricia Gilmartin, 'The Austral Continent on 16th Century Maps/An Iconological Interpretation', *Cartographica* 21.4 (1984), p.45.
39. Mercator quoted in Skelton, *Looking at an Early Map*, pp.193–94.
40. Alexander Dalrymple quoted in Skelton, *Looking at an Early Map*, p.229.
41. Ronald Tooley, *The Mapping of Australia*, Pl.12.
42. Jonathan Swift, *Jonathan Swift*, 'On Poetry: A Rapsody', ll.177–180.
43. Tooley, Pl.12.
44. Some general accounts are found in: R. A. Skelton, Explorer's Maps: *Chapters in the Cartographic Record of Geographical Study* and Glyndwr Williams and Alan Frost, *Terra Australis to Australia*. George Wood's *The Discovery of Australia* supports the traditional view of Dutch priority in discovery, and has been joined by J. P. Sigmond and L. H. Zunderbaan's *Dutch Discoveries of Australia: Shipwrecks, Treasures and Early Voyages Off the West Coast*, in arguing the Dutch claim. The case for Portuguese priority has been argued by George Collingridge in his seminal work, *The Discovery of Australia*, and by Kenneth McIntyre in *The Secret Discovery of Australia*.
45. Mark Akenside, *The Poetical Works*, Book I, ll.100–02.
46. George Berkeley, *The Works of George Berkeley, Bishop of Cloyne*, vol. V, pp.121, 120, 231.
47. Gayatri Spivak, 'The Rani of Sirmur', in Francis Barker et al. (eds), *Europe and Its Others*, p.133.
48. Eliza Berry, *Australian Explorers: From 1818 to 1876, In Rhyme*, ll.15–18.
49. Robinson notes that, while the concept of population had been understood for a long time, no population map of any sophistication had appeared before 1828. These maps in any case could record only non-nomadic populations. See Arthur Robinson, *Early Thematic Mapping in the History of Cartography*, p.113.
50. Catherine Martin, *An Australian Girl*, vol. II, p.269.
51. Paul Wenz quoted in Werner Friederich, *Australia in Western Imaginative Prose Writings 1600–1960: An Anthropology and a History of Literature*, p.202.

52. D. H. Lawrence, *Kangaroo*, p.365.
53. Rhys Jones, 'Ordering the Landscape', in Ian and Tasman Donaldson (eds), *Seeing the First Australians*, p.207.

5   Seeing the Aborigines put in their Place

1. Richard Terdiman, 'Ideological Voyages: Concerning a Flaubertian Dis-Orient-ation', in Francis Barker et al. (eds), *Europe and Its Others*, p.31. See also Paul Carter's insightful discussion of the theatricalisation of the corroboree in 'Making Contact: History and Performance', in *Living in a New Country: History, Travelling and Language*, pp.159–85.
2. Richard Terdiman, 'Ideological Voyages', p.32.
3. Edward Said, *Orientalism: Western Conceptions of the Orient*, p.58.
4. Said, p.59.
5. Mary Louise Pratt, 'Fieldwork in Common Places', in James Cillord and George Marcus (eds), *Writing Culture: The Poetics and Politics of Ethnography*, pp.35–43.
6. Johannes Fabian, *Time and the Other: How Anthropology Makes Its Object*, p.35.
7. Michel Foucault, *Discipline and Punish: The Birth of the Prison*, p.200.
8. Jose Rabasa, 'Allegories of the Atlas', in Barker et al. (eds), *Europe and Its Others*, p.1.
9. Jose Rabasa, 'Allegories of the Atlas', p.7.
10. Stephen Slemon, *Allegory and Empire: Counter-Discourse in Post-Colonial Writing*, p.118.
11. Richard Eden, The Decades of the Newe Worlde, quoted in J. C. Porter, *The Inconstant Savage: England and the North American Indian, 1500–1660*, p.28.
12. James Clifford, 'On Ethnographic Allegory', in Cillord and Marcus (eds), *Writing Culture: The Poetics and Politics of Ethnography*, p.100.
13. See Robert Dixon, *The Course of Empire*, pp.6–24 and Bernard Smith, *European Vision and the South Pacific*, *passim*, for discussions of precursors to illustrations of indigenes. See David Lawton, 'Naming the Interior', in Margaret Harris and Elizabeth Webby (eds), *Reconnoitres*, pp.17–19, for an examination of this illustration.
14. Stephen Greenblatt, 'Learning to Curse: Aspects of Linguistic Colonialism in the Sixteenth Century', in Fredi Chiappelli (ed.), *First Images of America: The Impact of the New World on the Old*, pp.574–75.
15. Abdul Jan Mohamed, 'The Economy of Manichean Allegory: The Function of Racial Difference in Colonialist Literature', *Critical Inquiry* 12.1 (1985), p.60 and *passim*.
16. Homi Bhabha, 'The Other Question: Stereotype, Discrimination and the Discourse of Colonialism', in *The Location of Culture*, p.75.
17. Douglas Lorimer, *Colour, Class, and the Victorians: English Attitudes to the Negro in the Mid-Nineteenth Century*, pp.136–37 and Nancy Stepan, *The Idea of Race in Science: Great Britain, 1800–1960*, pp.23–28, 45–46.
18. Tzvetan Todorov, *The Conquest of America: The Question of the Other*, p.30.
19. For a possible source in Cranach for Blake's Nebuchadnezzar, see Kenneth Clark, *Blake and Visionary Art*, p.16. For an early medieval image of the mad Nebuchadnezzar, see Francis Klingender, *Animals in Art and Thought to the End of the Middle Ages*, p.234.

20. See Peter Hulme, *Colonial Encounters*, pp.78–87, for an analysis of cannibalism as a trope within colonial discourse, and especially pp.84–86 for a description of its origin within a European mechanism of repression and projection.

21. *Hobart Town Courier*, quoted in Henry Reynolds, *Frontier: Aborigines, Settlers and Land*, p.101.

6   Contesting the Gaze of Ownership

1. Alan Frost, 'New South Wales as a *Terra Nullius*: The British Denial of Aboriginal Land Rights', *Historical Studies* 19.77 (1981), p.515.

2. Christopher Columbus, *The Voyages of Christopher Columbus*, pp.156–58 and *passim*.

3. Frost, 'New South Wales as a *Terra Nullius*', pp.522–23.

4. Reynolds, *Frontier*, pp.133–38.

5. Henry Reynolds, *Law of the Land*, pp.12–14.

6. Frost, 'New South Wales as a *Terra Nullius*', p.514.

7. John Locke, *Two Treatises of Government*, p.309.

8. Reynolds, *Law of the Land*, pp.17–18.

9. Reynolds, *Law of the Land*, p.18.

10. J. C. Beaglehole (ed.), *The Journals of Captain Cook on His Voyages of Discovery*, vol. I, p.397.

11. William Eden Auckland, *The History of New Holland From its First Discovery in 1616, to the Present Time*, pp.231–32.

12. Auckland, p.230.

13. Bhabha, 'The Other Question . . .', *Screen* 24.6 (1983), pp.18–19.

14. Homi Bhabha, 'Signs Taken for Wonders: Questions of Ambivalence and Authority Under a Tree Outside Delhi, May 1817', *Critical Inquiry* 12.1 (1985), p.161.

15. Auckland, p.235.

16. Lawrence Threlkeld, quoted in Henry Reynolds, *With the White People*, p.34.

17. George Morgan, 'Settlers in Australia', quoted in Ross Gibson, *The Diminishing Paradise*, p.149.

7   The Bosom of Unknown Lands

1. Lauretis, Teresa de, *Technologies of Gender: Essays on Theory, Film, and Fiction*, pp.43–44.

2. For more on the role of gender in exploration see Louis Montrose, 'The Work of Gender in the Discourse of Discovery', *Representations* 33 (1991), pp.1–41. Carole Merchant's *The Death of Nature* and Patricia Parker's *Literary Fat Ladies: Rhetoric, Gender, Property* (esp. pp.126–54) both insightfully analyse the interaction between discourses of gender and exploration. Clare Le Corbeillier's 'Miss America and Her Sisters: Personifications of the Four Parts of the World', *Metropolitan Museum of Art Bulletin* 2, 19 (1961), pp.209–23 is a useful collection of visual representations of 'other' continents personified as women.

3. Laura Mulvey, *Visual and Other Pleasures*, p.21.

4. Mulvey, p.22.

5. Mulvey, p.21.

6. Christian Metz, *Psychoanalysis and Cinema: The Imaginary Signifier*, p.60.

7. Homi Bhabha, 'Difference, Discrimination and the Discourse of Colonialism', in Francis Barker et al. (eds), *The Politics of Theory: Proceedings of the Essex Conference on the Sociology of Literature*, p.195

8. Mark Cousins, quoted in Homi Bhabha, 'Difference, Discrimination and the Discourse of Colonialism', p.195.

9. Jonathan Culler, *Structuralist Poetics*, p.132.

10. Sigmund Freud, *The Standard Edition of the Complete Psychological Works of Sigmund Freud*, xiv, p.140.

11. Jacques Lacan, *The Four Fundamental Concepts of Psycho-Analysis*, pp.71–75.

12. John Coetzee, *Dusklands*, p.84.

13. For a discussion of these books from a different point of view, see Robert Dixon, *Writing the Colonial Adventure: Race, Gender and Nation in Anglo-Australian Popular Fiction, 1875–1914*.

14. Alexander Macdonald, *The Lost Explorers: A Story of the Trackless Desert*, p.193.

15. James Hogan, *The Lost Explorer: An Australian Story*, p.10.

16. W. Carlton Dawe, *The Golden Lake, or the marvellous history of a journey through the great lone land of Australia*, p.12.

17. Dawe, p.12.

18. Dawe, p.154.

19. Hogan, p.139

20. Hogan, p.166.

21. Hogan, p.327.

22. Dawe, p.208

23. Freud, VII, p.157n.

24. Dawe, pp.65–66.

25. Hogan, pp.25–26.

26. Barbara Creed, *The Monstrous-Feminine*, pp.156–58.

27. Creed, p.158.

8   Conclusion

1. Ernest Giles, *Australia Twice Traversed*, pp.xxxvi–xxxvii. See also A. Martin's ('Dio') *Heroes of Notasia* (1888), in which the author states that 'the vast volumes will remain a sealed book to the rising generation in these Southern Lands, unless some attempt is made to popularise the narratives which are so full of romance yet truth', p.1.

2. May Dunn (ed.), *Queensland Geographical Journal*, Diamond Jubilee Issue 1885–1945, vol. 50 (36), p.15.

3. For a summary of the affair, see Ray Land (ed.), *Invasion and After: A Case Study in Curriculum Politics*.

4. Robert Young, *Colonial Desire*, p.161.

Bibliography

Primary Sources

Eyre, Edward John. *Journals of Expeditions of Discovery into Central Australia and Overland from Adelaide to King George's Sound, in the Years 1840–1.* 2 vols. London: T. & W. Boone, 1845.

Forrest, John. *Explorations in Australia: I. – Explorations in Search of Dr. Leichhardt and Party. II. – From Perth to Adelaide, Around the Great Australian Bight. III. – From Champion Bay, Across the Desert to the Telegraph and to Adelaide.* London: Sampson Low, 1875.

Giles, Ernest. *Australia Twice Traversed: The Romance of Exploration: Being a Narrative Compiled From the Journals of Five Exploring Expeditions Into and Through Central Australia and Western Australia, from 1872 to 1876.* 2 vols. London: Sampson Low, 1889.

Gosse, W. C. *W.C. Gosse's Explorations . . . Report and Diary of Mr. W.C. Gosse's Central and Western Exploring Expedition, 1873.* Adelaide: Government Printer, 1874.

Grant, James. *The Narrative of a Voyage of Discovery: Performed in Her Majesty's Vessel The Lady Nelson, of Sixty Tons Burthen, with Sliding Keels in the years 1800, 1801 and 1802, to New South Wales.* Adelaide: Libraries Board of South Australia, 1973.

Gregory, A. C. and F. T. Gregory. *Journals of Australian Explorations.* 2 vols. London: T. & W. Boone, 1841.

Gregory, A. C. 'Progress of the North Australian Expedition'. *Proceedings of the Royal Geographical Society* 1 (1855–56): 32–35.

Grey, George. *Journals of Two Expeditions of Discovery in North-west and Western Australia, during the years 1837, 38, and 39, under the Authority of Her Majesty's Government Describing Many Newly Discovered, Important, and Fertile Districts, with Observations on the Moral and Physical Condition of the Aboriginal Inhabitants.* 2 vols. London: T. & W. Boone, 1841.

King, Phillip Parker. *Narrative of a Survey of the Inter-Tropical and Western Coasts of Australia Performed Between the Years 1818 and 1822.* 2 vols. London: Murray, 1827.

Leichhardt, Ludwig. *Journal of an Overland Expedition in Australia, from Moreton Bay to Port Essington, a Distance of Upwards of 3000 Miles, During the Years 1844–45.* London: T. & W. Boone, 1847.

Mitchell, Thomas Livingston. *Three Expeditions into the Interior of Eastern Australia: with Descriptions of the Recently Explored Region of Australia Felix and of the Present Colony of New South Wales.* 2 vols. 2nd edn. London: T. & W. Boone, 1839 [abbreviated in text as *3Ex*].

———. *Journal of an Expedition into the Interior of Tropical Australia: in Search of a Route from Sydney to the Gulf of Carpentaria.* London: Longmans, 1848 [abbreviated in text as *EITA*].

Oxley, John. *Journals of Two Expeditions into the Interior of New South Wales, Undertaken by Order of the British Government in the Years 1817–18.* London: Murray, 1820.

Péron, M. F. *A Voyage of Discovery to the Southern Hemisphere Performed by Order of the Emperor Napoleon During the Years 1801, 1802, 1803, and 1804.* London: Phillips, 1809.

Stokes, John Lort. *Discoveries in Australia; with an Account of the Coasts and Rivers Explored and Surveyed During the Voyage of H.M.S. Beagle, in the years 1837–43.* London: T. & W. Boone, 1846.

Strzelecki, Paul Edmund. *Physical Description of New South Wales and Van Diemen's Land.* London: Longmans, 1845.

Stuart, John McDouall. *The Journals of John McDouall Stuart During the Years 1858, 1859, 1860, 1861, & 1862, When He Fixed the Centre of the Continent and Successfully Crossed It From Sea to Sea.* 2nd edn. London: Saunders, 1865.

Sturt, Charles. *Two Expeditions into the Interior of Southern Australia, during the years 1828, 1829, 1830, and 1831: with Observations on the Soil, Climate, and General Resources of the Colony of New South Wales.* 2 vols. London: Smith & Elder, 1833 [abbreviated in text as *2Ex*].

———. *Narrative of an Expedition into Central Australia, Performed under the Authority of Her Majesty's Government, During the Years 1844, 5 and 6 together with a Notice of the Province of South Australia, in 1847.* 2 vols. London: T. & W. Boone, 1849 [abbreviated in text as *ECA*].

Warburton, Peter Egerton. *Journey Across the Western Interior of Australia with an Introduction and Additions by Charles H. Eden.* Edited by H. W. Bates. London: Sampson Low, 1875.

Secondary Sources

Akenside, Mark. *Pleasures of the Imagination.* In *The Poetical Works.* London: Bell and Daldy, 1867.

Alpers, Svetlana. 'The Mapping Impulse in Dutch Art'. In David Woodward (ed.), *Art and Cartography: Six Historical Essays,* Chicago: Chicago University Press, 1987. pp.51–96.

Altick, Robert. *The Shows of London.* Cambridge: Harvard University Press, 1978.

Andrews, Alan E. J. *Stapylton With Major Mitchell's Australia Felix Expedition 1836.* Hobart: Blubber Head Press, 1986.

Andrews, Malcolm. *The Search for the Picturesque: Landscape Aesthetics and Tourism in Britain, 1760–1800.* Stanford: Stanford University Press, 1989.

Ashcroft, Bill; Griffiths, Gareth, and Tiffin, Helen. *The Empire Writes Back: Theory and Practice in Post-Colonial Literatures.* London: Routledge, 1989.

Atkinson, Geoffrey. *The Extraordinary Voyage in French Literature*. 2 vols. New York: Burt Franklin, nd (reprint 1922).

Auckland, William Eden. *The History of New Holland From its First Discovery in 1616, to the Present Time*. London: John Stockdale, 1787.

Augustine. *The City of God Against the Pagans*. 7 Vols. Translated by Eva Sanford and William Green. London: Heinemann, 1965.

Bagrow, Leo and R. A. Skelton. *The History of Cartography*. Cambridge: Harvard University Press, 1984.

Barbier, Carl Paul. *William Gilpin: His Drawings, Teaching, and Theory of the Picturesque*. Oxford: Clarendon, 1963.

Barkhan, Leonard. *Nature's Work of Art: The Human Body as Image of the World*. New Haven: Yale University Press, 1975.

Barrell, John. *The Idea of Landscape and the Sense of Place*. Cambridge: Cambridge University Press, 1972.

Beaglehole, J. C. (ed.). *The Endeavour Journal of Joseph Banks 1768–1771*. Sydney: Trustees of Public Library of NSW and Angus & Robertson, 1962.

———. *The Journals of Captain James Cook on His Voyages of Discovery*. Cambridge: Cambridge University Press, 1955–74.

Beale, Edgar. *Sturt, The Chipped Idol: A Study of Charles Sturt, Explorer*. Sydney: Sydney University Press, 1979.

———. *Kennedy, the Barcoo and Beyond*. Hobart: Blubber Head Press, 1983.

Beazley, Charles R. *The Dawn of Modern Geography*. 3 vols. London: Frowde, 1897–1906.

Benveniste, Emile. *Problems in General Linguistics*. Translated by Mary E. Meek. Florida: University of Miami Press, 1971.

Berkeley, George. *The Works of George Berkeley, Bishop of Cloyne*. Edited by A. A. Luce and T. E. Jessop. London: Thomas Nelson, 1948.

Berman, Morris. 'Hegemony and the Amateur Tradition in British Science'. *Journal of Social History* 1 (1975): 30–50.

Bermingham, Ann. *Landscape and Ideology: The English Rustic Tradition, 1740–1860*. London: Thames & Hudson, 1987.

———. 'Reading Constable'. *Art History* 10.1 (1987): 38–58.

Berry, Eliza. *Australian Explorers, From 1818 to 1876, In Rhyme*. Melbourne: Gordon & Gotch, 1892.

Bhabha, Homi K. *The Location of Culture*. London: Routledge, 1994.

———. 'Difference, Discrimination and the Discourse of Colonialism'. In Francis Barker et al. (eds), *The Politics of Theory: Proceedings of the Essex Conference on the Sociology of Literature, July 1982*. Colchester: University of Essex Press, 1983. pp.194–211.

———. 'The Other Question ...'. *Screen* 24.6 (1983): 18–36.

———. 'Representation and the Colonial Text: A Critical Exploration of Some Forms of Mimeticism'. In Frank Gloversmith (ed.), *The Theory of Reading*. Sussex: Harvester Press, 1984. pp.93–122.

———. 'Signs Taken For Wonders: Questions of Ambivalence and Authority Under a Tree Outside Delhi, May 1817'. *Critical Inquiry* 12.1. (1985): 144–65.

Bingley, William. *North Wales Delineated from Two Excursions Through All the Interesting Ports of That Beautiful and Romantic Country and Intended as a Guide to Future Tourists*. London: Longmans, 1814.

Birman, Wendy. *Gregory of Rainworth: A Man In His Time*. Nedlands: University of Western Australia Press, 1979.

Blackwood's Edinburgh Magazine. 'New South Wales' 44 (1838): 690–716. 'Colonization' 64 (1848): 66–76.

Bonyhady, Tim. *Images in Opposition: Australian Landscape Painting, 1801–1890.* Melbourne: Oxford University Press, 1985.

———. *Burke & Wills: From Melbourne to Myth.* Sydney: David Ell Press, 1991.

Brock, Daniel. *To the Desert With Sturt: A Diary of the 1844 Expedition.* Edited by Kenneth Peake-Jones. Adelaide: Royal Geographical Society of Australasia, South Australian Branch, 1975.

Brome, Richard. *The Antipodes.* London: Edward Arnold, 1967.

Browne, John Harris. 'Journal of the Sturt Expedition 1844–1845'. Edited by H. J. Finnis. *South Australiana* 6.1 (1966): 23–54.

Burford, Robert. *Description of a View of the Town of Sydney, New South Wales, the Harbour of Port Jackson and Surrounding Country; Now Exhibiting in the Panorama, Leicester Square.* London, 1829.

Burke, Edmund. *A Philosophical Enquiry into the Origins of Our Ideas of the Sublime and Beautiful.* Edited by J. T. Boulton. London: Routledge and Kegan Paul, 1958.

Campbell, Mary. *The Witness and the Other World: Exotic European Travel Writing 400–1600.* Ithaca: Cornell, 1988.

Cameron, Ian. *To the Farthest Ends of the Earth: 150 Years of World Exploration by the Royal Geographical Society.* New York: Dutton, 1980.

Cannon, S. F. *Science in Culture: The Early Victorian Period.* London: Dawson, 1978.

Carter, Paul. *The Road to Botany Bay: An Essay in Spatial History.* London & Boston: Faber & Faber, 1987.

———. *Living in a New Country: History, Travelling and Language.* London: Faber and Faber, 1992.

Certeau, Michel de. *On the Practice of Everyday Life.* Translated by Steven F. Rendall. Berkeley: University of California Press, 1984.

Cicero. *The Academics.* Translated by James S. Reid. London: Macmillan, 1885.

Clancy, Robert and Alan Richardson. *So Came They South.* Shakespeare Head Press, 1988,

Clark, Kenneth. *Blake and Visionary Art.* W. A. Cargill Memorial Lectures in Fine Art 2. Glasgow: University of Glasgow Press, 1973.

Clifford, James. 'On Ethnographic Allegory'. In Clifford, James and George E. Marcus (eds), *Writing Culture: The Poetics and Politics of Ethnography.* Berkeley: University of California Press, 1986. pp.98–121.

Coetzee, John M. *Dusklands.* Johannesburg: Raven Press, 1974.

Collingridge, George. *The Discovery of Australia: A Critical, Documentary and Historic Investigation Concerning the Priority of Discovery in Australasia by Europeans Before the Arrival of Lieut. James Cook, in the Endeavour in 1770.* Gladesville: Golden Press, 1983 (reprint).

Columbus, Christopher. *The Voyages of Christopher Columbus.* Translated by L. Cecil Jane. London: Argonaut Press, 1930.

Cook, Terry. 'George R. Parkin's British Empire Map of 1893'. *Cartographica* 21.4 (1984): 5–65.

Cooke, M. G. 'Modern Black Autobiography'. *Romanticism: Vistas, Instances, Continuities.* Ithaca: Cornell University Press, 1973. pp.255–280.

Corrigan, Philip. 'On Visualization as Power: 'Innocent Stupidities': De-Picturing (human) Nature. On Hopeful Resistances and Possible Refusals: Celebrating Difference(s) – Again'. In Gordon Fyfe and John Law (eds),

Picturing Power: Visual Depiction and Social Relations. Sociological Review Monograph 35. London: Routledge, 1988. pp.255–81.

Cosgrove, Denis and Stephen Daniels (eds), *The Iconography of Landscape: Essays on the Symbolic Representation, Design, and Use of Past Environments.* Melbourne: Cambridge University Press, 1988.

Cosmas (Indicopleuestes), An Egyptian Monk. *The Christian Topography of Cosmas, An Egyptian Monk.* Edited by J. W. McCrindle. New York: Burt Franklin, 1967.

Cowper, William. *Poetical Works.* Edited by H. S. Milford. 4th edn. London: Oxford University Press, 1934.

Creed, Barbara. *The Monstrous-Feminine: Film, Feminism and Psychoanalysis.* London: Routledge, 1993.

Crone, Gerald R. *Maps and Their Makers: An Introduction to the History of Cartography.* Hamden: Archon, 1978.

Crosby, Alfred. *Ecological Imperialisms: The Biological Expansion of Europe, 900–1900.* Cambridge: Cambridge University Press, 1986.

Crowley, Francis K. *Forrest 1847–1918.* St Lucia: University of Queensland Press, 1971.

Culler, Jonathan. *Structuralist Poetics: Structuralism, Linguistics and the Study of Literature.* London: Routledge and Kegan Paul, 1975.

Dawe, Carlton. *The Golden Lake, or, the marvellous history of a journey through the great lone land of Australia.* London: Marsden, 1894.

Dixon, Robert. *The Course of Empire: Neo-Classical Culture in New South Wales.* Melbourne: Oxford University Press, 1986.

———. *Writing the Colonial Adventure: Race, Gender and Nation in Anglo-Australian Popular Fiction, 1875–1914.* Melbourne: Cambridge University Press, 1995.

———. 'Scenic Tours in New South Wales: The Nineteenth Century Travel Essay'. *Southerly* 3 (1982): 324–36.

Dunn, May (ed.). *Queensland Geographical Journal.* Diamond Jubilee Issue 1885–1945, vol. 50 (36): 15.

Eaden, P. R. and Mares, F. H. (eds), *Mapped But Not Known: The Australian Landscape and the Imagination: Essays and Poetry Presented to Brian Elliot.* Adelaide: Wakefield Press, 1986.

Edgerton, Samuel Y. *The Renaissance Rediscovery of Linear Perspective.* New York: Basic Books, 1975.

———. 'From Mental Matrix to Mappamundi to Christian Empire: The Heritage of Ptolemaic Cartography in the Renassance'. In David Woodward (ed.), *Art and Cartography: Six Historical Essays.* Chicago: Chicago University Press, 1987. pp. 10–50.

Elliot, Brian. 'Antipodes: An Essay in Attitudes'. *Australian Letters* 7 (1966): 51–75.

Ericksen, Ray. *Ernest Giles: Explorer and Traveller, 1835–1897.* Melbourne: Heinemann, 1978.

Fabian, Johannes. *Time and the Other: How Anthropology Makes its Object.* New York: Columbia University Press, 1983.

———. 'Presence and Representation: The Other and Anthropological Writing'. *Critical Inquiry.* 16.4 (1990): 753–72.

Fabricant, Carole. 'The Aesthetics and Politics of Landscape in the C18th'. In Ralph Cohn (ed.), *Studies in Eighteenth-Century British Art and Aesthetics.* Berkeley: University of California Press, 1985. pp.49–81.

Favenc, Ernest. *The History of Australian Exploration from 1788 to 1888.* London: Griffith, 1888.

————. *The Secret of the Australian Desert*. London and Glasgow: Blackie, 1895.

Field, Barron. *Geographical Memoirs of New South Wales*. London: Murray, 1825.

Foss, Paul. 'Meridians of Apathy'. *Art & Text* 6 (1986): 74–88.

————. 'Theatrum Nondum Cognitorum'. In Peter Botsman, Chris Burns and Peter Hutchings (eds), *The Foreign Bodies Papers*. Local Consumption Publications Series 1, 1989.

Foster, William C. *Sir Thomas Livingston Mitchell and His World 1792–1855, Surveyor-General of New South Wales 1828–1855*. The Institution of Surveyors, 1985.

Foucault, Michel. *Discipline and Punish: The Birth of the Prison*. Translated by Alan Sheridan. New York: Vintage, 1979.

————. 'Of Other Spaces'. *Diacritics* 16 (1986): 22–27.

————. 'Space, Knowledge and Power'. *The Foucault Reader*. Edited by P. Rabinow. New York: Pantheon, 1984. pp.239–56

Freeman, T. W. 'The Royal Geographical Society and the Development of Geography'. In E. H. Brown (ed.), *Geography Yesterday and Tomorrow*. Oxford: Oxford University Press, 1980. pp.1–99.

Freud, Sigmund. *The Standard Edition of the Complete Psychological Works of Sigmund Freud*. Translated by James Strachey. London: Hogarth, 1953–74.

Friederich, Werner Paul. *Australia in Western Imaginative Prose Writings 1600–1960: An Anthropology and a History of Literature*. Chapel Hill North Carolina: University of North Carolina, 1967.

Friedman, John Block. *The Monstrous Races in Medieval Art and Thought*. Cambridge, Mass: Harvard University Press, 1981.

Frost, Alan. 'Botany Bay or Arcady: Nineteenth Century Images of Australia'. *World Literature Written in English* 11 (1972): 33–52.

————. 'What Created, What Perceived? Early Responses to New South Wales'. *Australian Literary Studies* 7 (1975): 185–205.

————. 'New South Wales as a *Terra Nullius*: The British Denial of Aboriginal Land Rights'. *Historical Studies* 19.77 (1981): 513–23.

————. 'On Finding 'Australia': Mirages, Mythic Images, Historical Circumstances'. *Australian Literary Studies* 12.4 (1986): 482–99.

Genette, Gerard. *Narrative Discourse: An Essay in Method*. Translated by Jane E. Lewin. Ithaca: Cornell University Press, 1980.

Gibson, Ross. *The Diminishing Paradise: Changing Literary Perceptions of Australia*. Sydney: Sirius, 1984.

Gilmartin, Patricia. 'The Austral Continent on 16th Century Maps/An Iconological Interpretation'. *Cartographica* 21.4 (1984): 38–52.

Gilpin, William. *Observations Relative Chiefly to Picturesque Beauty, made in the Year 1772, on Several Parts of England*. 2 vols. London: np, 1786.

————. *Three Essays: On Picturesque Beauty, On Picturesque Travel, and On the Art of Sketching Landscapes*. London: Blamire, 1792.

Goldie, Terry. *Fear and Temptation: The Image of the Indigene in Canadian, Australian and New Zealand Literatures*. Kingston: McGill University Press, 1989.

————. 'The Necessity of Nobility: Indigenous Peoples in Canadian and Australian Literature'. *Journal of Commonwealth Literature* 20 (1985): 131–47.

————. 'Emancipating the Equal Aborigine: J. B. O'Reilly and A. J. Vogan'. *SPAN* 20 (1985): 47–66.

Greenblatt, Stephen. 'Learning to Curse: Aspects of Linguistic Colonialism in the Sixteenth Century'. In Fredi Chiappelli (ed.), *First Images of America: The*

Impact of the New World on the Old. Berkeley: University of California Press, 1976. pp.561–80.

Hall, Joseph. *Another World and Yet the Same: Bishop Joseph Hall's Mundus Alter et Idem (1605).* Translated by and edited by John Millar Wands. New Haven: Yale University Press, 1981.

Hall, Marie Boas. *All Scientists Now: The Royal Society in the Nineteenth Century.* Cambridge: Cambridge University Press, 1984.

Hardy, John and Alan Frost. *Studies from Terra Australis to Australia.* Canberra: Australian Academy of the Humanities, 1989.

Harley, J. B. 'Meaning and Ambiguity in Tudor Cartography'. In Sarah Tyacke (ed.), *English Map-Making 1500–1650.* London: The British Library Board, 1983. pp.22–45.

———. 'Maps, Knowledge, and Power'. In Denis Cosgrove and Stephen Daniels (eds), *The Iconography of Landscape: Essays on the Symbolic Representation, Design, and Use of Past Environments.* Melbourne: Cambridge University Press, 1988.

———. 'Deconstructing the Map'. *Cartographica* 26.2 (1989): 1–20.

———. 'Historical Geography and the Cartographic Illusion'. *Journal of Historical Geography* 15.1 (1989): 80–91.

———. 'Cartography, Ethics and Social Theory'. *Cartographica* 27.2 (1990): 1–23.

Harley, J. B. and David Woodward (eds), *The History of Cartography: Volume 1: Cartography in Prehistoric, Ancient, and Medieval Europe and the Mediterranean.* Chicago: University of Chicago Press, 1987.

Hassam, Andrew. '"As I Write": Narrative Occasions and the Quest for Self-Presence in the Travel Diary'. *Ariel* 21.4 (1990): 33–47.

Healy, J. J. *Literature and the Aborigine in Australia 1770–1975.* New York: St Martin's, 1978.

Hipple, Walter John. *The Beautiful, The Sublime, and The Picturesque in Eighteenth-Century British Aesthetic Theory.* Carbondale: South Illinois University Press, 1957.

Historical Records of Australia. Sydney: Library Committee of the Commonwealth Parliament, 1914–25.

Hodge, Bob and Vijay Mishra. *Dark Side of the Dream: Australian Literature and the Postcolonial Mind.* Allen & Unwin, 1990.

Hogan, James F. *The Lost Explorer: An Australian Story.* Sydney: Edwards, Dunlop, 1890.

Hoskins, William. *The Making of the English Landscape.* London: Hodder & Stoughton, 1956.

Howard, Dora. 'The English Activities on the North Coast of Australia in the First Half of the Nineteenth Century'. *Proceedings of the Royal Geographical Society of Australia South Australian Branch* 33 (1931–32): 21–194.

Hulme, Peter. *Colonial Encounters: Europe and the Native Caribbean, 1492–1797.* London: Methuen, 1986.

Hussey, Christopher. *The Picturesque: Studies in a Point of View.* 2nd edn. London: Cass, 1967.

Hyde, Ralph. *Panoramania!: the Art and Entertainment of the 'All-Embracing' View.* London: Trefoil, 1988.

James, W. T. 'Nostalgia for Paradise: Terra Australis in the Seventeenth Century'. *Australia and the European Imagination: Papers from a Conference Held at the Humanities Research Centre, ANU, 1981.* Canberra: Humanities Research Centre, ANU, 1982.

Jan Mohamad, Abdul. 'The Economy of Manichean Allegory: The Function of Racial Difference in Colonialist Literature'. *Critical Inquiry* 12.1 (1985): 58–87.

Jones, Rhys. 'Ordering the Landscape'. In Ian and Tamsin Donaldson (eds), *Seeing the First Australians*. Sydney: Allen & Unwin, 1985. pp.181–209.

Keltie, John Scott. 'Thirty Years' Work of the Royal Geographical Society'. *Geographical Journal* 49 (1917): 350–70.

Klingender, Francis. *Animals in Art and Thought to the End of the Middle Ages.* Cambridge, Mass: MIT Press, 1971.

Kolodny, Annette. *The Lay of the Land: Metaphor as Experience and History in American Life and Letters.* Chapel Hill: University of North Carolina Press, 1975.

Lacan, Jacques. *The Four Fundamental Concepts of Psycho-Analysis.* Edited by Jacques Alain Miller. Translated by Alan Sheridan. Harmondsworth: Penguin, 1979.

Land, Ray (ed.). *Invasion and After: A Case Study in Curriculum Politics.* Brisbane: Queensland Studies Centre, 1994.

Langley, Michael. *Sturt of the Murray: Father of Australian Exploration.* London: Hale, 1969.

Lauretis, Teresa de. *Technologies of Gender: Essays on Theory, Film, and Fiction.* Bloomington: Indiana University Press, 1987.

Lawrence, David H. *Kangaroo.* Harmondsworth: Penguin, 1950.

Lawton, David. 'Naming the Interior: Major Mitchell's Fight for Place'. In Margaret Harris and Elizabeth Webby (eds), *Reconnoitres: Essays in Australian Literature in Honour of G.A. Wilkes.* Sydney: Sydney University Press, 1992.

Le Corbeillier, Clare. 'Miss America and Her Sisters: Personifications of the Four Parts of the World'. *Metropolitan Museum of Art Bulletin* 2. 19 (1961): 209–23.

Lejeune, Philippe. 'Autobiography in the Third Person'. *NLH* 9.1 (1977): 27–50.

Locke, John. *Two Treatises of Government.* Edited by Peter Laslett. Cambridge: Cambridge University Press, 1968.

Lorimer, Douglas A. *Colour, Class, and the Victorians: English Attitudes to the Negro in the Mid-Nineteenth Century.* Leicester: Leicester University Press, 1978.

Lucretius. *De Rerum Natura.* 2 vols. Edited by Cyril Bailey. Oxford: Clarendon, 1947.

McDonald, Alexander. *The Lost Explorers: A Story of the Trackless Desert.* London and Glasgow: Blackie, 1906.

McIntyre, Kenneth. *The Secret Discovery of Australia.* Medindie, SA: Souvenir Press, 1977.

Mackay, David. *In the Wake of Cook: Exploration, Science and Empire, 1780–1801.* Wellington: Victoria University Press, 1985.

McLaren, Ian F. *Australian Explorers By Sea, Land and Air, 1788–1988.* 9 vols. Parkville: University of Melbourne Library, 1988–.

MacLaren, I. S. 'Retaining Captaincy of the Soul: Response to Nature on the First Franklin Expedition'. *Essays on Canadian Writing* 28 (1984): 57–92.

———. 'The Aesthetic Map of the North, 1845–1859'. *Arctic* 38 (1985): 89–103.

———. 'The Aesthetic Mapping of Nature in the Second Franklin Expedition'. *Journal of Canadian Studies* 20 (1985): 39–57.

MacLeod, Ray. 'Of Medals and Men: A Reward System in Victorian Science 1826–1914'. *Notes and Records of the Royal Society of London* 26 (1971): 81–105.

Macrobius. *Commentary on the Dream of Scipio.* Translated by W. H. Stahl. New York: Columbia University Press, 1952.

Manganyi, N. Chabani. 'Making Strange: Race, Science and Ethnopsychiatric Discourse'. In Francis Barker et al. (eds), *Europe and Its Others*. Proceedings of the Essex Sociologies of Literature Conference 1984. Colchester: University of Essex Press, 1985. 1: 107–27.

Mansbach, S. A. 'An Earthwork of Surprise: The 18th-Century Ha-Ha'. *Art Journal* 42 (1982): 217–21.

Markham, Clements R. *The Fifty Years' Work of the Royal Geographical Society*. London: John Murray, 1881.

Markus, Andrew. *Governing Savages*. Sydney: Allen & Unwin, 1990.

Marlowe, Christopher. *Tamburlaine the Great*. Edited by J. S. Cunningham. Manchester: Manchester University Press, 1981.

Martin, A. ('Dio'). *Heroes of Notasia*. Mercury: Tasmania, 1888.

Martin, Catherine. *An Australian Girl*. 3 vols. London: Bentley, 1890.

Mee, Arthur (ed.). *The Children's Encyclopedia*. 10 vols. London: Educational Books, 1922–25.

Merchant, Carole. *The Death of Nature: Women, Ecology and the Scientific Revolution*. San Francisco: Harper & Row, 1980.

Metz, Christian. *Psychoanalysis and Cinema: The Imaginary Signifier*. Translated by Celia Britton et al. London: Macmillan, 1982.

Millar, Ann. *'I See No End to Travelling': Journals of Australian Explorers 1813–1876*. Sydney: Bay Books, 1985.

Miller, Christopher L. *Blank Darkness: Africanist Discourse in French*. Chicago: University of Chicago Press, 1985.

Mills, Sara. *Discourses of Difference: An Analysis of Women's Travel Writing and Colonialism*. London: Routledge, 1991.

Montrose, Louis. 'The Work of Gender in the Discourse of Discovery'. *Representations* 33 (1991): 1–41.

Moyal, A. M. (ed.). *Scientists in Nineteenth Century Australia: A Documentary History*. Melbourne: Cassell, 1975.

Muehrcke, Philip and Juliana. *Map Use: Reading, Analysis and Interpretation*. Madison: JP Publications, 1978.

Mulvaney, D. J. *Encounters in Place: Outsiders and Aboriginal Australians, 1606–1985*. St Lucia: University of Queensland Press, 1989.

Mulvey, Laura. *Visual and Other Pleasures*. London: Macmillan, 1989.

Parker, Patricia. *Literary Fat Ladies: Rhetoric, Gender, Property*. New York: Methuen, 1987.

Parry, Benita. 'Problems in Current Theories of Colonial Discourse'. *Oxford Literary Review* 9.1/2 (1987): 27–58.

Peach, Bill. *The Explorers*. Sydney: ABC, 1984.

Perry, Thomas. *The Discovery of Australia: Charts and Maps of the Navigators and Explorers*. Melbourne: Nelson, 1982.

Porter, J. C. *The Inconstant Savage: England and the North American Indian, 1500–1660*. London: Duckworth, 1979.

Pratt, Mary Louise. *Imperial Eyes: Travel Writing and Transculturation*. London: Routledge, 1992.

———. 'Scratches on the Face of the Country; or, What Mr Barrow Saw in the Land of the Bushmen'. *Critical Inquiry* 12.1 (1985): 119–43.

———. 'Fieldwork in Common Places'. In James Clifford and George E. Marcus (eds), *Writing Culture: The Poetics and Politics of Ethnography*. Berkeley: University of California Press, 1986. 27–50.

Price, Uvedale. *Essays on the Picturesque as Compared With the Sublime and the Beautiful; and On the Use of Studying Pictures for the Purpose of Improving Real Landscape.* facsimile edn. London: Gregg, 1971 [1810].

Proudfoot, Helen Baker. 'Botany Bay, Kew, and the Picturesque: Early Conceptions of the Australian Landscape'. *Journal of the Royal Australian Historical Society* 65.1 (1979): 30–45.

Rabasa, Jose. 'Allegories of the Atlas'. In Francis Barker et al. (eds), *Europe and Its Others.* Proceedings of the Essex Sociologies of Literature Conference 1984. Colchester: University of Essex Press, 1985. 2: 1–16.

———. 'Dialogue of Conquest: Mapping Spaces for Counter-Discourse'. *Cultural Critique* 6 (1987): 131–60.

Rainaud, Armand. *Le Continent Austral: Hypothèses et Découvertes.* Paris: Colin, 1893.

Rees, Ronald. 'Historical Links Between Cartography and Art'. *Geographical Review* 70 (1980): 60–78.

Reiss, Timothy J. *The Discourse of Modernism.* Ithaca: Cornell University Press, 1982.

Repton, Humphry. *Observations on the Theory and Practice of Landscape Gardening.* Oxford: Oxford University Press, 1980.

Reynolds, Henry. *Frontier: Aborigines, Settlers and Land.* Sydney: Allen & Unwin, 1987.

———. *Law of the Land.* Ringwood, Victoria: Penguin, 1987.

———. *Aboriginal Land Rights in Colonial Australia.* Canberra: National Library of Australia, 1988.

———. *With the White People.* Ringwood, Victoria: Penguin, 1990.

Robinson, Arthur H. *Early Thematic Mapping in the History of Cartography.* Chicago: Chicago University Press, 1982.

Robinson, Arthur H. and Barbara Barty Petchenik. *The Nature of Maps: Essays Towards Understanding Maps and Mapping.* Chicago: Chicago University Press, 1976.

Roderick, Colin. *Leichhardt: The Dauntless Explorer.* Sydney: Angus and Robertson, 1980.

Rosaldo, Renato. 'Imperialist Nostalgia'. *Representations* 26 (1989): 107–22.

Ross, Angus and David Woolley. *Jonathan Swift.* The Oxford Authors Series. Oxford: Oxford University Press, 1984.

Rudstrom, Robert A. 'Mapping, Postmodernism, Indigenous People and the Changing Direction of North American Cartography'. *Cartographica* 28.2 (1991): 1–12.

Ruskin, John. *The Works.* Edited by E. T. Cook and Alexander Wedderburn. London: Allen, 1903–12.

Said, Edward W. *Orientalism: Western Conceptions of the Orient.* London: Routledge & Kegan Paul, 1978.

Schaffer, Kay. *Women and the Bush: Forces of Desire in the Australian Cultural Tradition.* Cambridge: Cambridge University Press, 1988.

Schulz, Juergen. 'Jacopo de Barbari's View of Venice: Map Making, City Views, and Moralized Geography Before the Year 1500'. *Art Bulletin* 60 (1978): 425–74.

Seaton, Dorothy. 'Discourses of the Land in Australia and Western Canada: Dominance and Resistance'. (unpublished) MA thesis, University of Queensland, 1988.

————. 'Land and History: Inter-discursive Conflict in Voss'. *Australian and New Zealand Studies in Canada* 4 (1990): 1–14.

Seddon, George. 'On The Road to Botany Bay'. *Westerly* 33.4 (1988): 15–26.

Sellick, Robert. 'The Epic Confrontation: Australian Explorers and the Centre, 1813–1900: A Literary Study'. (unpublished) PhD dissertation. University of Adelaide, 1973.

————. 'The Explorer as Hero: Australia Exploration and the Literary Imagination'. *Proceedings of the Royal Geographical Society of Australia South Australian Branch* 78 (1977): 1–16.

————. 'From the Outside In: European Ideas of Exploration and the Australian Experience'. *Australia and the European Imagination: Papers from a Conference Held at the Humanities Research Centre, ANU, 1981.* Canberra: Humanities Research Centre, ANU, 1982.

Serle, Geoffrey. *From the Deserts the Prophets Come: The Creative Spirit in Australia 1788–1972.* Melbourne: Heinemann, 1973.

Shanes, Eric. *Turner's Picturesque Views in England and Wales 1825–1838.* London: Chatto and Windus, 1980.

Sigmond, J. P. and L. H. Zunderbaan. *Dutch Discoveries of Australia: Shipwrecks, Treasures and Early Voyages Off the West Coast.* Adelaide: Rigby, 1979.

Skelton, R.A. *Explorers' Maps: Chapters in the Cartographic Record of Geographical Discovery.* London: Routledge and Kegan Paul, 1958.

————. *Looking at an Early Map.* Lawrence, Kansas: University of Kansas Library, 1965.

Slemon, Stephen. 'Allegory and Empire: Counter-Discourse in Post-Colonial Writing'. (unpublished) PhD thesis, University of Queensland, 1988.

Smith, Bernard. *The Antipodean Manifesto: Essays on Art and History.* Melbourne: Oxford University Press, 1976.

————. *Place, Taste and Tradition: A Study of Australian Art Since 1788.* 2nd edn. Melbourne: Oxford University Press, 1979.

————. *European Vision and the South Pacific 1768–1850: A Study in the History of Art and Ideas.* 2nd edn. Sydney: Harper & Row, 1984.

———— ed. *Documents on Art and Taste in Australia: The Colonial Period 1770–1914.* Melbourne: Oxford University Press, 1975.

Soja, Edward J. *Postmodern Geographies: The Reassertion of Space in Critical Social Theory.* London: Verso, 1989.

Spivak, Gayatri. 'The Rani of Sirmur'. In Francis Barker et al. (eds), *Europe and Its Others.* Proceedings of the Essex Sociologies of Literature Conference 1984. Colchester: University of Essex Press, 1985. 1: 128–51.

Sprat, Thomas. *The History of the Royal Society of London.* Edited by Jackson I. Cope and Harold Whitmore Jones. London: Routledge and Kegan Paul, 1959.

Stafford, Barbara. *Voyage into Substance: Art, Science, Nature and the Illustrated Travel Account, 1760–1840.* Cambridge, Mass: MIT Press, 1984.

Stafford, Robert A. *Scientist of Empire: Sir Roderick Murchison, Scientific Exploration and Victorian Imperialism.* Cambridge: Cambridge University Press, 1989.

————. '"The Long Arm of London": Sir Roderick Murchison and Imperial Science in Australia'. In R. W. Home (ed.), *Australian Science in the Making.* Cambridge: Cambridge University Press, 1988.

Stanley, Henry Morton. *Through the Dark Continent, or, The Sources of the Nile Around the Great Lakes of Equatorial Africa and Down the Livingstone River to the Atlantic Ocean.* 2 Vols. London: Low, Marston, Searle & Rivingston, 1878.

Stepan, Nancy. *The Idea of Race in Science: Great Britain, 1800–1960*. London: Macmillan, 1982.

Stoddart, D. R. *On Geography and its History*. Oxford: Basil Blackwell, 1986.

Sturt, Napier G. *Life of Charles Sturt: Sometime Capt. 39th regt. and Australian Explorer*. London: Smith & Elder, 1899.

Swift, Jonathan. *Jonathan Swift*. Edited by Angus Ross and David Woolley. Oxford: Oxford University Press, 1984.

Tanner, Howard and Begg, Jane. *The Great Gardens of Australia*. South Melbourne: Macmillan, 1979.

Terdiman, Richard. *Discourse/Counter-Discourse The Theory and Practice of Symbolic Resistance in Nineteenth-Century France*. Ithaca: Cornell University Press, 1985.

———. 'Ideological Voyages: Concerning a Flaubertian Dis-Orient-ation'. In Francis Barker et al. (eds), *Europe and Its Others*. Proceedings of the Essex Sociologies of Literature Conference 1984. Colchester: University of Essex Press, 1985. 1: 28–40.

Thomas, Nicholas. *Colonialism's Culture: Anthropology, Travel and Government*. Princeton: Princeton University Press, 1994.

Thompson, Christina. 'Romance Australia: Love in Australian Literature of Exploration'. *Australian Literary Studies*, 13.2 (1987): 161–71.

Thompson, F. M. L. *Chartered Surveyors: The Growth of a Profession*. London: Routledge and Kegan Paul, 1968.

Thrower, Norman J. *Maps and Man: An Examination of Cartography in Relation to Culture and Civilization*. New Jersey: Prentice Hall, 1972.

Todorov, Tzvetan. *The Conquest of America: The Question of the Other*. Translated by Richard Howard. New York: Harper & Row, 1984.

Tooley, Ronald. *The Mapping of Australia*. London: Holland, 1979.

Walford, Thomas. *The Scientific Tourist Through England, Wales and Scotland: In Which the Traveller is Directed to the Pricipal Objects of Antiquity, Art, Science and the Picturesque*. 2 vols. London: Booth, 1818.

Webster, E. M. *Whirlwinds in the Plain: Ludwig Leichhardt – Friends, Foes and History*. Carlton: Melbourne University Press, 1980.

Westall, William. *Drawings by William Westall, Landscape Artist Aboard HMS Investigator During the Circumnavigation of Australia by Matthew Flinders, R.N., in 1801–1803*. Edited by T. M. Perry and Donald H. Simpson. London: Royal Commonwealth Society, 1962.

White, Hayden. *Metahistory: The Historical Imagination in Nineteenth-Century Europe*. Baltimore: Johns Hopkins University Press, 1973.

White, John. *The Birth and Rebirth of Pictorial Space*. London: Faber, 1957.

White, Richard. *Inventing Australia: Images and Identity, 1688–1980*. Sydney: Allen & Unwin, 1981.

Williams, Glyndwr. '"Far more happier than we Europeans": Reactions to the Australian Aborigines on Cook's Voyage'. *Historical Studies* 19 (1982): 499–512.

Williams, Glyndwr and Alan Frost. *Terra Australis to Australia*. Melbourne: Oxford University Press, 1988.

Wood, Denis. 'Cultured Symbols/Thoughts on the Cultural Contexts of Cartographic Symbols'. *Cartographica* 21.4 (1984): 9–37.

Wood, Denis and Fels, John. 'Designs on Signs: Myth and Meaning in Maps'. *Cartographica* 23.3 (1986): 54–103.

Wood, George A. *The Discovery of Australia*. London: Macmillan, 1922.

————. 'Ancient and Medieval Conceptions of Terra Australis'. *The Australian Historical Society Journal and Proceedings* 3.10 (1916): 455–65.

Woodward, David (ed.). *Five Centuries of Map Printing.* Chicago: Chicago University Press, 1975.

————. *Art and Cartography: Six Historical Essays.* Chicago: Chicago University Press, 1987.

Wright, John K. *The Geographical Lore in the Time of the Crusades: A Study in the History of Medieval Science and Tradition in Western Europe.* 2nd edn. New York: Dover, 1965.

Young, Arthur. *A Six Months Tour Through the North of England.* 4 vols. London: Strahan, 1770.

————. *Travels in France and Italy during the Years 1787–88–89.* Edited by Constantia Maxwell. Cambridge: Cambridge University Press, 1929.

Young, Robert J. C. *Colonial Desire: Hybridity in Theory, Culture and Race.* London: Routledge, 1995.

Youngs, Tim. '"My Footsteps on these Pages": The Inscription of Self and "Race" in H. M. Stanley's How I Found Livingstone'. *Prose Studies* 13.2 (1990): 230–49.

Index

Aboriginal characteristics
  cannibalism, 149
  as children, 173
  as devils, 11, 141–45
  intellect, 140, 151
  motivational, 145–46
  and phrenology, 139–41, 166
  skin colour, 137–39
  stereotyped, 137–38, 154–55, 178–79, 184
  treachery, 146–49, 176–77, 184
  see also Ballandella; Bultje; Imbat; Miago; picturesque, the; Yuranigh
Aborigines
  as anomalous, 111–12, 168–69
  and attachment to land, 140; see also land rights
  as blank slates, 134–35
  and class, 28–31
  compared to other cultures, 136, 150, 173, 177
  counter-discourse from, 188–90
  dialogue with, 12, 167, 180–81, 182, 185–89
  effacement of, 125–26
  and ethnography, 11, 134, 135, 178, 185, 191
  evolutionary ideas and, 162, 166, 170–71, 177
  firing practices of, 146, 160–61
  and hierarchies, 3, 137, 139, 150–51, 166, 177, 182, 202–03
  as noble savage, 29–30, 162, 174
  and paternalism, 174–75
  resistance of, 179–80, 183, 184, 187–89
  and sight, 12, 60–61, 128, 151–52, 163, 167, 184, 189, 191

and signs, 122
subsistence by, 163, 165
and surveillance, 89, 132–34, 163–64, 171, 189–90, 192–95
and theatre, 129, 130–32
and *The Children's Encyclopedia*, 2
violence towards, 164–65, 172–73, 182, 183
accuracy, 3–4, 8, 9–10, 49, 52, 54–56
Akenside, Thomas, 122
allegory, 134–35, 137–38
Alpers, Svetlana, 98
Andrews, Alan, 44
Andrews, Malcom, 9, 85
antipodes, 10, 105–06,
  and Aborigines, 111–12
  and the fourth part of the world, 113–15
  nature as perverse in, 106–11
Auckland, William Eden, 163
Augustine, Saint, 107

Ballandella, 174–75
Banks, Joseph, 32, 33
Barrell, John, 58
Barrow, John, 37
Beale, Edgar
  works by, 13, 27
Benveniste, Emil, 47
Berkeley, Bishop, 122–23
Bermingham, Ann, 9, 72
Berry, Eliza, 123
Bhabha, Homi, 11–12, 15, 138, 178–79
Bingley, William, 98
Blackwood's Edinburgh Magazine, 23, 30, 41, 75, 210 n.7
Bonyhady, Tim, 14
Bowen, Emmanuel, 116